SAT MATH SUCCESS
in 20 Minutes a Day

SAT MATH SUCCESS
in 20 Minutes a Day

LEARNINGEXPRESS®

NEW YORK

Cataloging-in-Publication Data is on file with the Library of Congress.

ISBN 978-1-61103-064-8

Printed in the United States of America

9 8 7 6 5 4 3 2 1

For more information on LearningExpress, other LearningExpress products, or bulk sales, please write to us at:
LearningExpress/An EBSCO Company
224 West 29th Street
3rd Floor
New York, NY 10001

CONTENTS ▶

CONTENTS

10/8

INTRODUCTION ▶

The math portion of the SAT exam often strikes fear into the hearts of test takers. It's timed, it covers the bulk of high school math, and it's tough—no doubt about it. And, as you might know, in recent years the format for the SAT Math exam has been revamped, with more of a focus on problem-solving and analytical skills. That means you not only need to know your math basics and how to solve problems, but you also need to understand word problems—you must break non-math language apart to understand what is being asked and then solve the problem presented.

If you have been panicking about the upcoming test and the thought of dealing with linear equations, polynomials, trigonometry, and statistics, then this book is just for you!

SAT Math Success in 20 Minutes a Day gives you quick, doable lessons that will review the most important concepts and skills you may have forgotten. Reviewing the lessons and questions in this book will give you a thorough overview of *all* the concepts you will see on the exam, along with practice questions that mirror the ones the SAT presents.

How to Use This Book

SAT Math Success in 20 Minutes a Day is organized into compact, manageable lessons. Most you can master in just 20 minutes a day. Some are longer and will take two or three 20-minute sessions. We will let you know at the start of a lesson if it should be broken down into multiple sessions.

Each lesson presents a small part of a task one step at a time. The lessons teach by example—rather than by theory—so you have plenty of opportunities for successful learning. You'll learn by understanding, not by memorization.

Each new lesson also contains practical, easy-to-follow examples. You'll also find lots of valuable memory "hooks" and shortcuts to help you retain what you're learning. Practice question sets, scattered throughout each lesson, typically begin with easy questions to help build your confidence. As the lessons progress, easier questions are interspersed with the more challenging ones, so that even readers who are having trouble can successfully complete many of the questions. A little success goes a long way!

Exercises found in each lesson give you the chance to practice what you learned and apply each lesson's topic to your daily life.

You should start by taking the pretest that begins on page 1. The pretest will tell you which lessons you should really concentrate on. At the end of the book, you'll find a posttest that will show you how much you've improved. You will find the lesson number that corresponds to each pretest and posttest question next to its correct answer. Visit that chapter to review the concepts giving you the most trouble.

This is a workbook, and as such, it's meant to be written in. Unless you checked it out from a library or borrowed it from a friend, write all over it! Get actively involved in doing each math problem—mark up the chapters boldly. You may also want to keep extra paper available because sometimes you could end up using two or three pages of scratch paper for one problem—and that's fine!

IF YOU NEED TO START WITH THE VERY BASICS . . .

Lesson 1 dives right in to reviewing SAT-level math. However, you might need a brush-up on your basics before beginning with more complex topics and problems.

If that's the case, begin your work in this book by making your way through Appendix A: Review of Numbers. It covers operations with whole numbers, integers, decimals and fractions, and much more. Appendix A is a great section to turn to for a reminder of basic math rules that come up in almost every SAT Math problem.

The goal of every book chapter is to get you ready to tackle the new math section for the SAT exam. Let's break down the new SAT exam before going any further.

What to Expect on the SAT Math Test

Unlike in past years, the new SAT Math section is more focused on the getting you ready for college, career, and personal goals. The content is real world and relevant to the situations you will face in your professional and personal life.

On test day, you will have 80 minutes to answer 58 total questions. The majority of questions are multiple-choice (with choices A–D), and the rest are "grid in" (where you will need to supply an answer on your own—no choices are given). In this book, you will learn tips on how to answer both types of questions efficiently to ensure that you finish the test on time.

Calculator Section vs. Non-Calculator Section

The new math section of the SAT has a calculator section and non-calculator section. The calculator section of the test will allow you to save time so you can focus on more complex problems and your reasoning skills to solve them. Although the calculator is a great tool and is needed at times to solve problems, you can always choose not to use it. In fact, students who use their reasoning abilities and their knowledge of how problems are structured will most likely finish the test before students who choose to use their calculator for every problem.

The non-calculator portion of the test consists of problems that can be done using your knowledge of math techniques and comfort level with numbers. These problems aim to test your fluency in the subject and your understanding of the concepts.

Sections on the Exam

There are four sections of math on the new SAT Math test:

- Heart of Algebra (covering linear equations and systems)
- Problem Solving & Data Analysis (covering quantitatively based problems)
- Passport to Advanced Math (covering complex equations)
- Additional Topics in Math (covering assorted topics in geometry and trigonometry)

The new math section of the SAT attempts to measure your "fluency" or ability to apply mathematics techniques and principles, your ability to understand math concepts and make connections within the context of problems, and your ability to solve real-world problems that require you to analyze a situation and determine appropriate solutions.

Overcoming Math Anxiety

Let's talk a moment about math anxiety and how it can affect your test taking. For those of you who find math concepts and problems too difficult to understand or too hard to solve and math exams incredibly scary, read this carefully.

If you're going to succeed on standardized tests, at work, or just in your daily life, you're going to have to be able to deal with math. You need some basic math literacy to do well in many different kinds of careers. So if you have math anxiety or if you are mathematically challenged, the first step is to try to overcome your mental block about math. Start by remembering your past successes (yes, everyone has them!). Then remember some of the nice things about math, things even a writer or artist can appreciate. Then, you'll be ready to tackle this book, which will make math as painless as possible.

Great Things about Math

Math has many positive aspects that you may not have thought about before. Here are just a few:

1. Math is steady and reliable. You can count on mathematical operations to be constant every time you perform them: 2 plus 2 always equals 4. Math doesn't change from day to day depending on its mood. You can rely on each math fact you learn and feel confident that it will always be true.
2. Mastering basic math skills will not only help you do well on your school exams, it will also aid you in other areas. If you work in fields such as the sciences, economics, nutrition, or business, you need math. Learning the basics now will enable you to focus on more advanced mathematical problems and practical applications of math in these types of jobs.
3. Math is a helpful, practical tool that you can use in many different ways throughout your daily life, not just at work. For example, mastering the basic math skills in this book will help you complete practical tasks, such as balancing your monthly budget, planning your retirement funds, or knowing the sale price of that new iPad that's been marked down 25%.
4. Mathematics is its own clear language. It doesn't have the confusing connotations or shades of meaning that sometimes occur in the English language. Math is a common language that is straightforward and understood by people all over the world.
5. Spending time learning new mathematical operations and concepts is good for your brain! You've probably heard this one before, but it's true. Working out math problems is good mental exercise that builds your problem-solving and reasoning skills. And that kind of increased brain power can help you in any field you want to explore.

These are just a few of the positive aspects of mathematics. Remind yourself of them as you work through this book. If you focus on how great math is and how much it will help you solve practical math problems in your daily life, your learning experience will go much more smoothly than if you keep telling yourself that math is terrible. Positive thinking really does work—whether it's an overall outlook on the world or a way of looking at a subject you're studying. Harboring a dislike for math could limit your achievement, so give yourself the powerful advantage of thinking positively about math.

Make a Commitment

You've got to take your SAT Math preparation further than simply reading this book. Improving your math skills takes time and effort on your part. You have to make the commitment. You have to carve time out of your busy schedule. You have to decide that improving your skills—improving your chances of doing well in almost any profession—is a priority for you.

If you're ready to make that commitment, this book will help you. If you follow the tips for continuing to improve your skills and do each of the exercises, you'll build a strong foundation. Use this book to its fullest extent—as a self-teaching guide and then as a reference resource—to get the fullest benefit.

Now that you're armed with a positive math attitude, it's time to take the pretest and dig into the first lesson. Go for it!

PRETEST

Lesson 1: Solving Linear Equations and Inequalities in One Variable

1. $8x + 5 = -3(x + 2)$
  a. -3
  b. -1
  c. 2
  d. 4

2. $2(x + 5) > 3(x - 2)$
  a. $x > -10$
  b. $x < 8$
  c. $x < 16$
  d. $x > 18$

Lesson 2: Problem-Solving with Linear Functions

3. You have been contracted to replace a countertop in a kitchen. You will get paid $1,000 to do the job. You can complete the job in 3 days, working 8 hours a day. You will need to pay the cost of the materials, which is $525, with the $1,000 you receive to do the job. How much will you be paid per hour for your time?
  a. $19.79 per hour
  b. $20.19 per hour
  c. $23.50 per hour
  d. $32.90 per hour

Lesson 3: Solving Systems of Linear Equations and Inequalities in Two Variables

4. Solve the following system of equations using any method:

$x + 2y = 10$

$2x - 2y = -4$

   a. $(-2,3)$
   b. $(0,2)$
   c. $(2,4)$
   d. $(3,7)$

Lesson 4: Understanding Equations and Their Graphs

5. Which of the following is the equation for this graph?

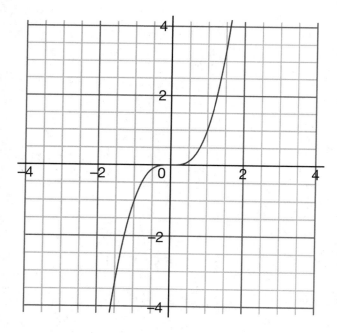

   a. $y = \frac{1}{x}$
   b. $y = x^2 + 7$
   c. $y = 4x - 5$
   d. $y = x^3$

6. Which is true about the following graph?

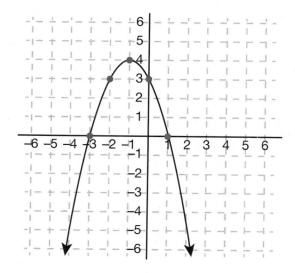

   a. The y-intercept is $(0,1)$.
   b. The maximum point is the vertex.
   c. There is only one x-intercept.
   d. The parabola is symmetric about the x-axis.

Lesson 5: Ratios, Proportions, and Scale

7. At a certain corporation, the ratio of clerical workers to executives is 7 to 2. If a combined total of 81 clerical workers and executives work for that corporation, how many clerical workers are there?

   a. 9
   b. 14
   c. 48
   d. 63

Lesson 6: Percent Problems

8. A certain car sells for $20,000, if it is paid for in full (the cash price). However, the car can be financed with a 10% down payment and monthly payments of $1,000 for 24 months. How much more money is paid for the privilege of financing, excluding tax, and what percent is this of the car's cash price?

   a. $3,500 and 25%

   b. $4,000 and 30%

   c. $6,000 and 30%

   d. $6,400 and 35%

Lesson 7: Unit Conversions

9. One gram of carbohydrates is 4 calories. A pastry has 1.3 ounces of carbohydrates. How many calories is the pastry if 1 ounce is approximately 28 grams? (Round to the nearest integer.)

   a. 37 calories

   b. 98 calories

   c. 112 calories

   d. 146 calories

Lesson 8: Analyzing Graphs and Scatter Plots

10. What kind of correlation does the scatter plot show?

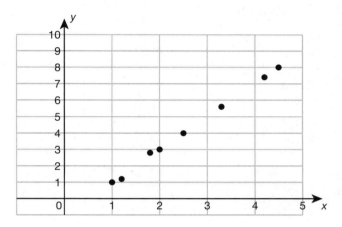

   a. Not enough information

   b. No correlation

   c. Perfect correlation

   d. Negative correlation

Lesson 9: Using Two-Way Tables to Analyze Data

11. The following table shows that out of 188 students, 48 took Algebra, 70 took English, and 60 took both courses.

	ALGEBRA	NO ALGEBRA	TOTAL
English	60	70	130
No English	48	10	58
Total	108	80	188

How many students took English and Algebra?

a. 60
b. 70
c. 48
d. 10

Lesson 10: Making Conclusions with Statistical Measures

Use the following sales chart, which shows February's new car and truck sales for the top five sales associates at Vero Beach Motors, to answer questions 12 and 13.

CAR AND TRUCK SALES				
	ARNIE	BOB	CALEB	DEBBIE	ED
Week 1	7	5	0	8	7
Week 2	4	4	9	5	4
Week 3	6	8	8	8	6
Week 4	5	9	7	6	8

12. The monthly sales award is given to the sales associate with the highest weekly average for the month. Who won the award in February?
a. Arnie
b. Bob
c. Caleb
d. Debbie

13. Based on the February sales figures, what was the most likely number of weekly sales for an associate?
a. 0
b. 4
c. 5
d. 8

Lesson 11: Problem-Solving with Quadratic and Exponential Functions

14. A dairy is required to have a waste holding pond for runoff. Ms. Van Beek plans to build a pond that will be 20 feet by 15 feet. There will be a border of equal length around the pond. The total area of the pond and the border is 500 square feet. How wide will the border be?
a. 1 foot
b. $1\frac{1}{4}$ feet
c. $2\frac{1}{2}$ feet
d. 3 feet

Lesson 12: Solving Quadratic Equations, Systems Involving Quadratic Equations, and Inequalities

15. Solve using the quadratic formula: $6x^2 + 1 = 5x$
 a. 3, 5
 b. 2, −5
 c. $\frac{1}{2}, \frac{1}{3}$
 d. $\frac{1}{4}, \frac{2}{3}$

Lesson 13: Polynomial, Radical, and Rational Expressions

16. Simplify $\frac{x^2 + 3x - 18}{x^2 - 9}$.
 a. $\frac{3x}{x-2}$
 b. $\frac{5x+1}{x-3}$
 c. 1
 d. $\frac{x+6}{x+3}$

17. Which of the following is equivalent to $\frac{3}{x^2+4x+4} - \frac{2}{x^2-4}$?
 a. $\frac{3(x-2)}{(x+2)(x+2)} - \frac{2(x+2)}{(x+2)(x-2)}$
 b. $\frac{(x+2)}{(x+2)(x+2)} - \frac{(x+2)}{(x+2)(x-2)}$
 c. $\frac{3}{(x+2)(x+2)} - \frac{2}{(x+2)(x-2)}$
 d. $\frac{2(x+2)}{(x+2)(x-1)} - \frac{3(x-2)}{(x+2)(x-1)}$

Lesson 14: Radical and Rational Functions in One Variable

18. Which of the following is the solution set for the equation $4 + 3\sqrt{x} = x$?
 a. {1,16}
 b. {3,8}
 c. {5}
 d. θ

19. Solve: $\frac{15}{x+4} = \frac{x-4}{x}$
 a. $x = 5$ or −4
 b. $x = 12$ or −3
 c. $x = 8$ or −2
 d. $x = 16$ or −1

Lesson 15: Factorable Polynomials and Non-Linear Functions

20. How many distinct real zeros does the polynomial $p(x) = x^4 - 4x^3 + 4x^2$ have?
 a. 0
 b. 1
 c. 2
 d. 5

Lesson 16: Transformations and Compositions of Functions

21. The graphs of $f(x)$ and $f'(x)$ are shown. Which of the following is the equation for $f'(x)$?

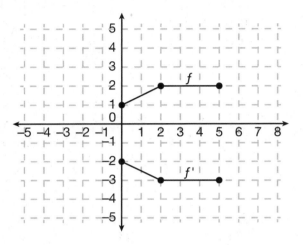

 a. $f'(x) = f(-x + 1)$
 b. $f'(x) = -f(x - 1)$
 c. $f'(x) = f(-x) - 1$
 d. $f'(x) = -f(x) - 1$

Lesson 17: Operations with Complex Numbers

22. For $i = \sqrt{-1}$, which of the following equals $(2 + 4i)^2$?
 a. $5 - 20i$
 b. $16i - 12$
 c. $10 - 24i$
 d. $4 - 22i$

Lesson 18: Using Trigonometry to Solve Problems Involving Lines, Angles, and Right Triangles

23. What angle would be supplementary to *ONP*?

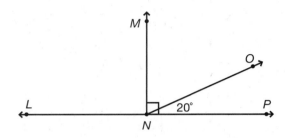

 a. $\angle MNO$
 b. $\angle MNP$
 c. $\angle MNL$
 d. $\angle LNO$

Lesson 19: Volume Problems

24. How much water would it take to completely fill the cylindrical tank shown?

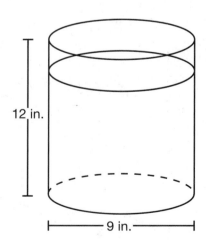

 a. 504 in.^{3}
 b. 630 in.^{3}
 c. 705 in.^{3}
 d. 763 in.^{3}

Lesson 20: Circles, Sector Area, and Arc Length

25. What is the length of the arc QR?

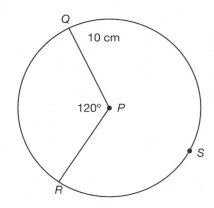

a. $\frac{10}{3}\pi$

b. $\frac{20}{3}\pi$

c. $\frac{1}{3}\pi$

d. $\frac{5}{3}\pi$

Answer Key

1. **b.** Lesson 1
2. **c.** Lesson 1
3. **a.** Lesson 2
4. **c.** Lesson 3
5. **d.** Lesson 4
6. **b.** Lesson 4
7. **d.** Lesson 5
8. **c.** Lesson 6
9. **d.** Lesson 7
10. **c.** Lesson 8
11. **a.** Lesson 9
12. **d.** Lesson 10
13. **d.** Lesson 10
14. **c.** Lesson 11
15. **c.** Lesson 12
16. **d.** Lesson 13
17. **a.** Lesson 13
18. **a.** Lesson 14
19. **d.** Lesson 14
20. **c.** Lesson 15
21. **b.** Lesson 16
22. **b.** Lesson 17
23. **d.** Lesson 18
24. **d.** Lesson 19
25. **b.** Lesson 20

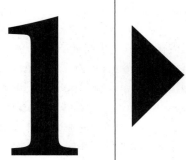

1 ▶ SOLVING LINEAR EQUATIONS AND INEQUALITIES IN ONE VARIABLE

For the things of this world cannot be made known without a knowledge of mathematics.

—ROGER BACON

LESSON SUMMARY

This first lesson teaches you how to solve different types of linear equations and inequalities. You will learn how to use addition, subtraction, multiplication, and division to solve the equations and check your answers, along with specific test-taking strategies for handling these types of questions on the SAT exam.

This is a longer lesson that you will likely have to break into two 20-minute sessions in order to fully absorb all of the concepts presented. A good place to stop for the day is after completing two full practice sets.

Algebra allows you to solve many real-life problems in the world around you. With variables, expressions, and equations, you can model situations and find solutions to problems. By knowing how to handle numbers such as integers, fractions, and decimals; algebraic expressions; and like terms, you can solve any type of equation that exists on the SAT.

What Is a Linear Equation?

In general, an equation expresses an equal relationship between two sides separated by an equal sign. A **variable** in an equation is an unknown quantity that can exist on the left side, right side, or both sides of the equation. A **linear equation** is one that has the following characteristics:

- It has two equal algebraic expressions.
- The degree or exponent on the variable is 1.
- Left side = right side.

The equations that we are considering in this lesson have only one variable or unknown quantity. When you solve any equation, you are finding the unknown quantity. Since linear equations can be simple or complicated, you need to know how to handle solving them.

SAT TEST-TAKING TIP

When you solve an equation, you are finding a value (or values) that makes the left side of the equation equal to the right side of the equation.

The basic rule for working with equations is that when you do something to one side of an equation, you must also do it to the other side. When you solve the equation, you need to isolate the variable by itself on one side, with a number on the other side. For instance, $x = 5$ is a solution to an equation. On the other hand, $-x = 5$ is not because $-1x$ is not the variable by itself.

Solving Equations Using Addition or Subtraction

You can solve equations using addition and subtraction by getting the variable on a side by itself. Think about how you would solve this equation: $x + 4 = 10$. Your goal is to get the variable x on a side by itself. How do you do that? To get x by itself, you need to get rid of the 4. How? If you subtract 4 from 4, the result is 0, and you have eliminated the 4 to get x on a side by itself. However, if you subtract 4 from the left side of the equation, then you must do the same to the right side of the equation. You would solve the equation this way:

> **Example:** $x + 4 = 10$
> Subtract 4 from both
> sides of the equation. $\qquad x + 4 - 4 = 10 - 4$
> Simplify both sides of
> the equation. $\qquad x + 0 = 6$
> Add 0 to x. $\qquad x = 6$

When you add zero to a number, the number does not change, so $x + 0 = x$. When you do this, you are using the **additive property of zero**, which states that a number added to zero equals that number.

Let's look at another equation: $x - 5 = 9$. What do you need to do to get the variable on a side by itself? You need to get rid of the 5. The equation says to subtract 5, so what undoes subtraction? If you said addition, you are right! In this problem, you need to add 5 to both sides of the equation to get rid of the 5.

> **Example:** $x - 5 = 9$
> Add 5 to both sides of the
> equation. $\qquad x - 5 + 5 = 9 + 5$
> Simplify both sides of the
> equation. $\qquad x + 0 = 14$
> Add 0 to x. $\qquad x = 14$

Example: $a + 6 = 7$
Subtract 6 from both sides
of the equation. $a + 6 - 6 = 7 - 6$
Simplify both sides of the
equation. $a + 0 = 1$
Add 0 to a. $a = 1$

Example: $y - 11 = 8$
Add 11 to both sides of
the equation. $y - 11 + 11 = 8 + 11$
Simplify both sides of
the equation. $y + 0 = 19$
Add 0 to y. $y = 19$

Example: $-r + 9 = 13$
Subtract 9 from both
sides of the equation. $-r + 9 - 9 = 13 - 9$
Simplify both sides of
the equation. $-r + 0 = 4$
Add 0 to $-r$. $-r = 4$
Are you finished? No! The variable r is not
alone on one side by itself. You can isolate it by
multiplying both sides of the equation by (-1).
$$(-1)(-r) = 4(-1)$$
$$r = -4$$

Solving Equations Using Multiplication and Division

In the equation $x + 10 = 2$, to get rid of the 10, you
would subtract 10, which is the opposite of adding 10.
In the equation $x - 5 = 6$, to get rid of the 5, you would
add 5, which is the opposite of subtracting 5. So in the
equation $5x = 10$, how do you think you would get rid
of the 5? What is the opposite of multiplying by 5? Yes,
the opposite of multiplying by 5 is dividing by 5. You
would solve these equations using division.

$5x = 10$ $4x = 12$
$\frac{5x}{5} = \frac{10}{5}$ $\frac{4x}{4} = \frac{12}{4}$
$x = 2$ $x = 3$

When you divide a number by itself, you always get 1,
so $5x$ divided by 5 equals $1x$.

Practice
Solve for x in the following equations.

1. $x - \frac{1}{2} = 4$
2. $x + 23 = 5$
3. $-3x = 39$
4. $5x = \frac{1}{2}$
5. $x + 2.3 = -4.7$

Solving More Complicated Linear Equations

Many equations on the SAT Math portion of the exam
are equations that require two or more steps to solve.
Be sure to remember the basic rule:

> What you do to one side of the equation, you
> must do to the other side.

You can add, subtract, multiply, or divide on both
sides of the equation to isolate the variable on one
side and a number on the other side. It should be said
that the variable can be isolated on the left or the
right side. So, for instance, $x = 5$ would be the same as
$5 = x$.

Can you guess what steps you would use to solve
$3x + 1 = 10$? Ask yourself which numbers you need to
get rid of so that the variable will be on a side by itself.
In other words, you need to isolate the variable. To
get the x on a side by itself or to isolate the variable,
you will need to eliminate the 3 and the 1. Does it
matter which number you get rid of first? Yes!

When isolating the variable in a more complicated equation, first circle the variable. Then eliminate what is farthest away from the variable. For

instance, consider the equation $3x + 1 = 10$. By circling the variable, you can see that $+1$ is farther away from the circle than 3. So, you would subtract 1 first from both sides. Here's how the solution looks:

Example: $3x + 1 = 10$
Subtract 1 from both
sides of the equation. $\qquad 3x + 1 - 1 = 10 - 1$
Simplify both sides of
the equation. $\qquad 3x = 9$
Divide both sides of
the equation by 3. $\qquad \frac{3x}{3} = \frac{9}{3}$
Simplify both sides
of the equation. $\qquad x = 3$

Here are more examples.

Example: $5x - 2 = 13$
Add 2 to both sides of
the equation. $\qquad 5x - 2 + 2 = 13 + 2$
Simplify both sides of
the equation. $\qquad 5x = 15$
Divide both sides of
the equation by 5. $\qquad \frac{5x}{5} = \frac{15}{5}$
Simplify both sides
of the equation. $\qquad x = 3$

Example: $18 = 9 - 3x$
Subtract 9 from both
sides of the equation. $\qquad 18 - 9 = 9 - 9 - 3x$
Simplify both sides of
the equation. $\qquad 9 = -3x$
Divide both sides of
the equation by -3. $\qquad \frac{9}{-3} = \frac{-3x}{-3}$
Simplify both sides
of the equation. $\qquad -3 = x$

Practice

6. $14x - 2 = 26$

7. $-2m - 20 = -32$

8. $2.2x + 1 = 3.2$

Solving Equations with Fractions in Front of the Variable

To solve equations, you always need to isolate the variable on one side. If there is a fraction in front of the variable, you need to use the multiplicative inverse or reciprocal of the fraction. You're probably wondering, "What is the multiplicative inverse of a number?" Take a look at these examples: The multiplicative inverse of 2, which can be written as $\frac{2}{1}$, is $\frac{1}{2}$. The multiplicative inverse of 5, which can be written as $\frac{5}{1}$, is $\frac{1}{5}$. The multiplicative inverse of $\frac{2}{3}$ is $\frac{3}{2}$. The multiplicative inverse of $-\frac{3}{4}$ is $-\frac{4}{3}$. You probably get the idea now—you get the multiplicative inverse of a number by inverting the number. In other words, just turn it upside down!

A number times its multiplicative inverse will always equal 1. Thus, $\frac{4}{5} \cdot \frac{5}{4} = 1$. Here's how you use the multiplicative inverse to solve equations with a fraction in front of the variable:

Example: $\frac{2}{3}x + 1 = 5$
Subtract 1 from both
sides of the equation. $\qquad \frac{2}{3}x + 1 - 1 = 5 - 1$
Simplify both sides
of the equation. $\qquad \frac{2}{3}x = 4$
Multiply both sides
of the equation by the
multiplicative inverse
of the coefficient. $\qquad \frac{2}{3}x \cdot \frac{3}{2} = 4 \cdot \frac{3}{2}$
Simplify both sides
of the equation. $\qquad x = 6$

Example: $\frac{3}{5}x - 2 = 7$
Add 2 to both sides of
the equation. $\qquad \frac{3}{5}x - 2 + 2 = 7 + 2$
Simplify both sides
of the equation. $\qquad \frac{3}{5}x = 9$
Multiply both sides of
the equation by $\frac{5}{3}$. $\qquad \frac{3}{5}x \cdot \frac{5}{3} = 9 \cdot \frac{5}{3}$
Simplify both sides
of the equation. $\qquad x = 15$

SAT TEST-TAKING TIP

Use the reciprocal to clear fractions.

Let's work through another example.

Example: $\frac{x}{2} + 1 = 9$ (Note, $\frac{x}{2}$ is the same as $\frac{1}{2}x$)

Strategy: Isolate the variable first by subtracting 1 from both sides.

$$\frac{x}{2} + 1 = 9 \rightarrow \frac{1}{2}x + 1 = 9 \rightarrow$$
$$\frac{1}{2}x + 1 - 1 = 9 - 1$$
$$\frac{1}{2}x = 8$$

Multiply both sides by the reciprocal of $\frac{1}{2}$ to clear the fraction from the variable.

$$(2)\frac{1}{2}x = 8(2)$$
$$x = 16$$

Practice

9. $\frac{5}{8}x + 3 = 3$

10. $\frac{2}{3}m + 8 = 20$

11. $\frac{2m}{5} + 16 = 24$

Working with Decimals in Equations

Many students are intimidated by using decimals. The easiest way to deal with decimals is to think of money as a reference. We calculate with money almost every day and often without the aid of calculators. So, applying this "mental memory" can actually help you complete problems involving decimals much faster.

Consider this example.

Example: $5x - 3.55 = 8.70$

Strategy: Use money as a reference point in dealing with decimals. Add $3.55 to both sides. So, on the right it's like adding $8.70 + $3.55, which is $12.25. Divide both sides by 5. This is like dividing $12.25 by 5, which is $2.45.

$$5x - 3.55 = 8.70 \rightarrow$$
$$5x - 3.55 + 3.55 = 8.70 + 3.55$$
$$5x = 12.25$$
$$5x = 12.25$$
$$x = \frac{12.25}{5}$$
$$x = 2.45$$

Solving Equations with Parentheses

To clear parentheses in equations, you should use the distributive property. The distributive property tells you to multiply the number outside the parentheses by each term inside the parentheses in equations like $2(x + 2) = 2x + 4$ and $3(a - b) = 3a - 3b$.

Example: $5x + 3 = 3(x + 5)$

Use the distributive property. $5x + 3 = 3x + 15$

Subtract 3 from both sides of the equation. $5x + 3 - 3 = 3x + 15 - 3$

Simplify both sides of the equation. $5x = 3x + 12$

Subtract $3x$ from both sides of the equation. $5x - 3x = 3x - 3x + 12$

Simplify both sides of the equation. $2x = 12$

Divide both sides of the equation by 2. $\frac{2x}{2} = \frac{12}{2}$

Simplify both sides
of the equation. $\qquad x = 6$

Example: $4x + 6 = -2(3x + 4)$
Use the distributive
property. $\qquad 4x + 6 = -6x - 8$
Subtract 6 from both
sides of the equation. $\qquad 4x + 6 - 6 = -6x - 8 - 6$
Simplify both sides
of the equation. $\qquad 4x = -6x - 14$
Add $6x$ to both sides
of the equation. $\qquad 4x + 6x = -6x + 6x - 14$
Simplify both sides
of the equation. $\qquad 10x = -14$
Divide both sides of
the equation by 10. $\qquad \frac{10x}{10} = \frac{14}{10}$
Simplify both sides
of the equation. $\qquad x = -\frac{14}{10} = -\frac{7}{5} = -1\frac{2}{5}$

Combining Like Terms in Equations

In longer equations, you may need to combine like terms BEFORE you actually isolate the variable on one side. Like terms have the same variable with the same exponent. So, for instance, $3x$ and $10x$ are like terms. Numbers are considered like terms and should also be combined.

Example: $2x + 3 + 3x = 4x - 7 + 9$
Combine similar
terms on both sides
of the equation. $\qquad 5x + 3 = 4x + 2$
Subtract 3 from
both sides of
the equation. $\qquad 5x + 3 - 3 = 4x + 2 - 3$
Simplify both sides
of the equation. $\qquad 5x = 4x - 1$
Subtract $4x$ from
both sides of
the equation. $\qquad 5x - 4x = 4x - 4x - 1$

Simplify both sides
of the equation. $\qquad x = -1$

Example: $5x + 3 - 2x = 2(x - 3) + 5$
Use the distributive
property. $\qquad 5x + 3 - 2x = 2x - 6 + 5$
Combine similar
terms on both sides
of the equation. $\qquad 3x + 3 = 2x - 1$
Subtract 3 from
both sides of
the equation. $\qquad 3x + 3 - 3 = 2x - 1 - 3$
Simplify both sides
of the equation. $\qquad 3x = 2x - 4$
Subtract $2x$ from
both sides of
the equation. $\qquad 3x - 2x = 2x - 2x - 4$
Simplify both sides
of the equation. $\qquad x = -4$

> ### SAT TEST-TAKING TIP
>
> Use the distributive property to clear parentheses from equations. Also, look for like terms to combine on either or both sides.

Example: $x + 2x + 1 = 2(x - 2)$
Strategy: Use the
distributive property
to remove the
parentheses right
away. Also, combine
the like terms on
the left side. $\qquad x + 2x + 1 = 2(x - 2) \rightarrow$
$\qquad\qquad\qquad 3x + 1 = 2x - 4$
Subtract $2x$ from $\qquad 3x - 2x + 1 = 2x - 2x - 4$
both sides. $\qquad\qquad 1x + 1 = -4$
Subtract 1 from $\qquad 1x + 1 - 1 = -4 - 1$
both sides. $\qquad\qquad x = -5$

Checking Your Answers

You can use the answer key at the end of the lesson to check your answers. However, in the real world there is no answer key to tell you if you got the correct answer to an equation. But, there is a way to check your answer. When you replace the variable with your answer, you should get a true statement. If you get a false statement, then you do not have the right answer.

To check the solution to the last equation, you would follow these steps:

Check: $x = -5$ in $x + 2x + 1 = 2(x - 2)$
Substitute $x = -5$
in the original equation. $\quad x + 2x + 1 = 2(x - 2) \rightarrow$
$(-5) + 2(-5) + 1 = 2((-5) - 2)$
Simplify the left side by adding $-5, -10,$ and $+1$. $\quad -5 + -10 + 1 = 2(-7)$
Then, multiply 2 and -7 on the right side. $\quad -5 + -10 + 1 = -14$
The solution is correct because the left side = the right side. $\quad -14 = -14$

What Is an Inequality?

An **inequality** consists of two numbers or expressions connected by an inequality symbol. The inequality symbols are < (less than), > (greater than), ≤ (less than or equal to), ≥ (greater than or equal to), and ≠ (not equal to). Here are some examples of inequalities:

$2 < 5$ (two is less than five)
$9 > 3$ (nine is greater than three)
$4 \leq 4$ (four is less than or equal to four)
$2 + 5 \neq 11$ (two plus five is not equal to eleven)

Solving Inequalities

You can solve inequalities involving variables just like you can solve equations with variables. Use what you already know about solving equations to solve inequalities. Like equations, you can add, subtract, multiply, or divide both sides of an inequality with the same number. In other words, what you do to one side of an inequality, you must do to the other side.

Example: $2x + 3 < 1$
Subtract 3 from both sides of the inequality. $\quad 2x + 3 - 3 < 1 - 3$
Simplify both sides of the inequality. $\quad 2x < -2$
Divide both sides of the inequality by 2. $\quad \frac{2x}{2} < \frac{-2}{2}$
Simplify both sides of the inequality. $\quad x < -1$

Notice from this example that you use the same steps to solve an inequality that you would use to solve an equation. However, there are two important differences:

1. Remember that the solution for an inequality is most often an inequality itself. For instance, in solving the inequality $x + 5 > 1$, you get $x + 5 - 5 > 1 - 5$ or $x > -4$, which is itself another inequality.
2. Whenever you multiply or divide an inequality by a negative number, you need to reverse the inequality symbol.

Example

$2 < 5$
$(-2) \times 2 < 5 \times (-2)$
$-4 < -10$

Notice that when you multiply the inequality 2 < 5 by −2 on both sides, the resulting inequality

$-4 < -10$ is not true. So, you have to correct the resulting inequality by changing the sign to $-4 > -10$.

Practice

Solve for x in the following inequalities.

12. $x \div 8 - 1 < -2$

13. $4x + 2(x + 1) \geq -4$

14. $\frac{x}{-5} + 2 > 2$

15. $-2x - 8 > 3(x + 4)$

Checking Your Answers in Inequalities

There is a way to check your answer to an inequality. Just follow the steps shown in the following example.

> **Example:** $x + 4 < 10$
> Subtract 4 from both
> sides of the inequality. $x + 4 - 4 < 10 - 4$
> Simplify both sides
> of the inequality. $x < 6$

The answer is the inequality, $x < 6$. This means that any number less than 6 is an answer. To check your answer, pick a number less than 6 and substitute that number into the original problem. Let's use the number 2 to check the answer.

> **Check:** $x + 4 < 10$
> Substitute 2 in place of
> the variable. $2 + 4 < 10$
> Simplify. $6 < 10$

Yes, 6 is less than 10. When your result is a true statement, you know you have worked the problem correctly.

SAT TEST-TAKING TIP

When working with linear inequalities, remember the following:

1. You solve these in the same way that you would solve linear equations.
2. If you multiply or divide by a negative number on both sides of an inequality, you must change the inequality sign. For instance, $-3x > 9$ becomes $x < -3$ because you must divide by -3 on both sides.
3. The direction sign of the inequality indicates less than or greater than. For instance, if your answer is $x < -3$, this means that all values less than -3 will work as answers; -3 is not included because there is no equal sign under the inequality sign. If the answer is $a \geq 9$, this means that all values greater than or equal to 9 will work as answers.

Solving Linear Equations (and Inequalities) on the SAT

In this lesson, you have learned how to solve different linear equations (and inequalities). When solving complicated equations with fractions and decimals in them, look to remove them as soon as possible. The same is true for equations with parentheses in them. Use the distributive property to remove parentheses. Note that while some questions on the SAT may require the actual solution for the linear equation, other questions may ask you to USE the equation's solution to answer the question. These types of questions test your "fluency" in knowing how to solve for the equation's unknown but also test your ability to use what you know (or find out) to solve a problem.

Look at these examples.

Example: Given the equation $2(x-9) = 3x-1$, what is the value of x^2?

Solution: $x^2 = 289$

Use the distributive property to remove the parentheses from the left side.

$2(x-9) = 3x-1 \rightarrow$
$2x - 18 = 3x - 1$

Subtract $3x$ from both sides.

$2x - 3x - 18 = 3x - 3x - 1$
$-1x - 18 = -1$

Add 18 on both sides.

$-1x - 18 + 18 = -1 + 18$
$-1x = 17$

Divide both sides by -1.

$(\frac{-1}{-1})x = (\frac{17}{-1})$
$x = -17$

Square -17 to get 289.

$(-17)^2 = (-17)(-17)$
$x^2 = 289$

Example: Which is a characteristic of the solution to $3x - 15 > 20$?

a. It is greater than 12.
b. It is a multiple of 3.
c. It is between 11 and 12.
d. It is equal to 12.

Solution: c

Add 15 to both sides.

$3x - 15 > 20$
$3x - 15 + 15 > 20 + 15$
$3x > 35$

Divide by 3 on both sides.

$\frac{3}{3}x > \frac{35}{3}$

Divide $\frac{35}{3}$ to get the mixed number $11\frac{2}{3}$ to solve the problem. The answer $11\frac{2}{3}$ is between 11 and 12.

$x > 11\frac{2}{3}$

Answers and Explanations

1. $4\frac{1}{2}$. Add $\frac{1}{2}$ to both sides of the equation.
2. -18. Subtract 23 from both sides of the equation.
3. -13. Divide both sides of the equation by -3.
4. $\frac{1}{10}$. Divide both sides of the equation by 5.
5. -7. Subtract 2.3 from both sides of the equation.
6. 2. Add 2 to both sides of the equation. Then divide both sides by 14.
7. 6. Add 20 to both sides of the equation. Then divide both sides by -2.
8. 1. Subtract 1 from both sides of the equation. Then divide both sides by 2.2.
9. 0. Subtract 3 from both sides of the equation. Then multiply both sides by $\frac{8}{5}$.
10. 18. Subtract 8 from both sides of the equation. Then multiply by $\frac{3}{2}$.
11. 20. Subtract 16 from both sides of the equation. Then multiply by $\frac{5}{2}$.
12. $x < -8$. Add 1 to both sides of the inequality. Then multiply both sides of the inequality by 8.
13. $x \geq -1$. Multiply 2 and $(x+1)$ on the left side to get $2x + 2$. Next, add $4x$ and $2x$. Subtract 2 on both sides of the inequality. Divide both sides of the inequality by 6.
14. $x < 0$. Subtract 2 on both sides of the inequality. Multiply both sides by -5. Since you multiply both sides by a negative number, you must change the direction of the inequality sign.
15. $x < -4$. Multiply $3(x+4)$ on the right side to get $3x + 12$. Subtract $3x$ from both sides. Next, add 8 to both sides of the inequality. Divide both sides of the inequality by -5. Since you multiply both sides by a negative number, you must change the direction of the inequality sign.

LESSON

2 ▶ PROBLEM-SOLVING WITH LINEAR FUNCTIONS

There is no branch of mathematics, however abstract, which may not someday be applied to phenomena of the real world.

—NIKOLAI IVANOVICH LOBACHEVSKY

LESSON SUMMARY

In this lesson, you will learn how to create linear functions that model given situations in the real world. We'll cover how to define independent and dependent variables and interpret them in the context of a given problem, and you'll acquire helpful tips for assigning variables, solving for them, and expressing their meaning.

Linear equations can be used to model many situations in the real world. Using functions allows you to solve problems in the real world by using variables to represent quantities you are interested in studying.

What Are Linear Functions?

Linear functions are a special type of equation that describes a relationship between two or more quantities or variables. Equations have solutions that are based on what a variable is equal to, like $x = 5$. On the other hand, functions can have many solutions. You can think of a function as having three parts:

$$\text{INPUT} \rightarrow \text{EQUATION} \rightarrow \text{OUTPUT}$$

Values get INPUT into the function's EQUATION, which results in values that are OUTPUT.

Independent vs. Dependent Variables

In a linear function with two variables, one variable is independent (x) and the other is dependent (y). The dependent variable, y, is the result of the other variable and thus depends upon it. The other variable is referred to as the independent variable, x, because it occurs on its own and is not the result of another value. Using the previous example:

INPUT (independent variable) → EQUATION (function) → OUTPUT (dependent variable)

We can say that values from the independent variable are INPUT into the equation for the FUNCTION, which results in values for the dependent variable, which are the OUTPUT.

In a function, variable y is dependent because it "depends on" or is affected by the independent variable, x. In a function, every x value has one unique y variable.

Setting Up Equations for Word Problems

Equations can be used to solve real-life problems. In an equation, the variable often represents the answer to a real-life problem. For example, suppose you know that you can earn twice as much money this month as you did last month. You made $1,200 last month. How much will you earn this month? You can use the variable x to represent the answer to the problem. You want to know how much you can earn this month.

Let x = how much you can earn this month.
$1,200 = amount earned last month
$x = 2 \cdot 1,200$
$x = \$2,400$

You might be wondering why you should use algebra to solve a problem when the answer can be found using arithmetic. Good question! If you practice using equations for simple problems, then you will find it easier to write equations for problems that can't be solved using arithmetic.

Take a look at these examples of setting up equations for word problems.

Example: A silk-screening company charges $150 to create a printing screen from your artwork and print a minimum of 25 T-shirts. Each additional shirt is $5. Which function expresses the cost (C) of x shirts if a 6.5% sales tax applies?
First, assign variables.
Let x = the total number of shirts.
Let C = cost of printing shirts with sales tax.
Then, translate the information from the problem into expressions.
The cost of printing shirts is $150 for the first 25 T-shirts. There is an additional charge of $5 each for the number of shirts over 25, which is $(x - 25)$. Putting this together, we have that the cost is $150 + $5(x - 25)$. Then there is the tax rate of 6.5% for the cost of the T-shirts. This makes the function $C = (1.065)$ $[\$150 + \$5(x - 25)]$.

Now, try one on your own.

Practice
1. The cost to rent a tandem bike at the boardwalk includes a flat fee of $20 plus a charge of $4.50 for every half hour of use. Which of the following functions describes the total cost, in dollars, for a rental lasting x hours?
   a. $C(x) = 9x + 20$
   b. $C(x) = 4.5x$
   c. $C(x) = 29x$
   d. $C(x) = 4.5x + 20$

When setting up equations, always assign the independent variable to the unknown quantity. The unknown quantity is what you are trying to find out. In the preceding example, the independent variable was the number of T-shirts because this value occurred on its own and was not dependent on any other value. On the other hand, the cost was dependent on the number of shirts printed. So, we assign the amount that is earned in a month to the independent variable x.

Using Function Notation

We can express functions by using function notation. In function notation, you express the dependent variable, y, in terms of x by writing $f(x)$, which is read as "f of x." So, $f(x) = x + 5$ means that the independent variable is x and the dependent variable is y or $f(x)$. To find y when $x = 5$, you write $f(5) = (5) + 5$ or $f(5) = 10$. When $x = -3$, what is the value of $f(-3)$? To find y when $x = -3$, you write $f(-3) = (-3) + 5 = 2$ or $f(-3) = 2$.

Creating and Using Linear Function Questions on the SAT

Some questions on the SAT will require you to set up linear functions from word problems, just as you have looked at in the examples. Other problems may give you a linear function and ask you to use it to solve a problem.

Example: Cherie is going to a charity book sale at her local library. Every book costs 40 cents, but only after you pay $8 to enter the sale. Which of the following functions describes the total dollar amount that Cherie will spend at the library to take home b number of books?

  a. $C(b) = 8 + 40b$
  b. $C(b) = 8 + 0.40b$
  c. $C(b) = 0.40 + 8b$
  d. $C(b) = 8.40b$

The cost to enter the book sale, even if you buy nothing, is $8. Once you're inside, the cost to purchase b books is $0.40b$. So the total dollar amount you need to spend for b books is $8 + 0.40b$. Therefore, the correct answer is **b**.

Now, try one on your own.

Practice

  2. When installing windows, a local contractor generally charges $450 per window for installation, plus a flat recycling fee of $200 for the project. He decides to give Miguel a 6% discount on the whole job. Which of the following expressions represents Miguel's total bill, in dollars, for buying w windows?

  a. $1.06(200 + 450w)$
  b. $0.94(650w)$
  c. $0.94(450w + 200)$
  d. $(200 + 450w) - 0.06(450w)$

For problems that give you a linear function, be sure to understand what the given variable represents in the scenario. Then, carefully read the question to determine what information is being asked for. Often, these types of questions will be fill-in responses requiring you to supply an answer.

Let's walk through some more examples together.

Example: The equation $C = 11m + 400$ describes the relationship between the number of calories, C, burned in a given day and the number of minutes, m, spent jogging. How many minutes would one need to spend jogging in order to burn 895 calories in one day? Substitute 895 for C, and then solve for m:

$$895 = 11m + 400$$
$$495 = 11m$$
$$m = 45$$

So, 45 minutes must be spent jogging to burn the desired number of calories.

Example: When Kim works 40 hours in a week, she earns $560. Which function could be used to compute Kim's pay, P, when she works more than 40 hours?

Kim works 40 hours per week at $560. When she works more than 40 hours, the quantity is $(x - 40)$ times the pay per hour. To find her hourly rate, divide $560 by 40 to get $14.

So, Kim's pay can be represented by the function $P = \$560 + \$14(x - 40)$.

Finally, try one last practice problem on your own.

Practice

3. During the first three months of its life, a breed of exotic fish is born with one stripe and then develops two new stripes every five days. What is the number of stripes, s, that the fish has at t days after its birth?

   a. $t = \frac{2}{5}s$

   b. $s = 5t + 1$

   c. $s = \frac{2}{5}t + 1$

   d. $s = \frac{5}{2}t + 1$

Answers and Explanations

1. **a.** Since it costs $4.50 to rent the bike for 30 minutes, the charge for an hour is $9. So, the cost for x hours would be $9x$. This, plus the flat fee of $20, means the total cost is $9x + 20$. Choice **b** is incorrect because $4.50 is the cost for half an hour, not an hour. You need to multiply x by 9 instead of by 4.5. Also, you forgot to include the flat fee of $20 in the total cost. Choice **c** is incorrect because you incorporated the flat fee into the hourly rate, which isn't accurate. Choice **d** is incorrect because $4.50 is the cost for half an hour, not an hour. You need to multiply x by 9 instead.

2. **c.** The standard cost of a job involving w windows is $450w + 200$. A 6% discount on this would be $0.06(450w + 200)$. To get the special bill for Miguel, subtract the discount from the standard cost, which gives you $0.94(450w + 200)$ dollars. In choice **a**, the bill represents 6% more than the original total, not 6% less. In choice **b**, the $200 recycling fee is charged for each window, but the question says that it's a flat fee for the whole project. Choice **d** would be the right expression if the contractor gave Miguel a 6% discount on the window installation only, not on the recycling fee. But according to the question, the discount applies to the entire job.

3. c. The information "2 stripes every 5 days" is a rate of change, $\frac{2}{5}$. Since we are starting with 1 stripe, that is the y-intercept. So, the equation is $s = \frac{2}{5}t + 1$. In choice **a**, you interchanged t and s and forgot to include the one stripe with which the fish is born. Choice **b** would imply the fish gets 5 stripes each day. In choice **d**, you used the reciprocal of the correct answer.

SOLVING SYSTEMS OF LINEAR QUATIONS AND INEQUALITIES IN TWO VARIABLES

The book of nature is written in the language of mathematics.

—GALILEO GALILEI

LESSON SUMMARY

This lesson teaches you how to solve systems of two or more linear equations and inequalities. You will learn about the substitution and elimination methods and how they are helpful in solving systems of equations. In addition, you will practice interpreting the solutions you find in the context of the problem.

You might want to break apart this lesson into two 20-minute sessions. If you do, stop right before Dealing with Systems of Linear Inequalities.

n a previous lesson, you learned how to solve linear equations in two variables. A system of linear equations consists of two or more equations with the same variables. If you have two different variables, you need at least two equations. There are several methods of solving systems of linear equations.

Solutions of Systems of Linear Equations

The solution to a system of linear equations will satisfy both equations by making them true. There are three possibilities for any given system of equations.

In the first case, the system can have one solution. This means that there is one value for x and one value for y that satisfies both equations in the system. For example, consider the following:

$$y = x + 1$$
$$y = 2x + 1$$

Can you think of a value of x and a value of y that would make both equations true? If you thought of $x = 0$ and $y = 1$, you are correct. The solution to the system is $(0,1)$ because for $y = x + 1$, we get $(1) = (0) + (1)$, which is true. For the second equation, $y = 2x + 1$, we get $(1) = 2(0) + 1$, which is also true.

In the second case, the system may have no solution. In other words, there is no pair of x and y that makes both equations in the system true. For example, can you think of a pair of values for x and y that makes the equations $y = x + 1$ and $y = x + 3$ true? There is no such set of numbers.

SAT TEST-TAKING TIP

A quick way to spot a system with no solution is to look at the numbers in front of the x. If they are the same in both equations, then there is no solution.

In the third case, the system may have many pairs of x and y that satisfy both equations. For example, look at the following solution:

$$y = x + 2$$
$$2y = 2x + 4$$

If you try any pair of values for x and y, all of them will work.

Example: When $x = 1$ and $y = 3$, then

$$y = x + 2 \rightarrow (3) = (1) + 2 \rightarrow 3 = 3$$
$$2y = 2x + 4 \rightarrow 2(3) = 2(1) + 4 \rightarrow 6 = 6$$

Example: When $x = 5$ and $y = 7$, then

$$y = x + 2 \rightarrow (7) = (5) + 2 \rightarrow 7 = 7$$
$$2y = 2x + 4 \rightarrow 2(7) = 2(5) + 4 \rightarrow 14 = 14$$

And there are even more pairs that satisfy this equation.

SAT TEST-TAKING TIP

A good way to spot a system of equations with many solutions is to check to see if one equation is a multiple of the other. In the preceding examples, one equation was multiplied by a number to get the other equation.

How to Use the Elimination Method

Graphs serve many useful purposes, but using algebra to solve a system of equations can be faster and more accurate than graphing a system. A system of equations consists of equations often involving more than one variable. When you use the elimination method of solving systems of equations, the strategy is to eliminate all the variables except one. When you have only one variable left in the equation, then you can solve it.

Example

Solve the system: $x + y = 10$
$$x - y = 4$$

Add the equations. $(x + y) + (x - y) = 10 + 4$
$$2x - 0y = 14$$

Drop the $0y$. $2x = 14$

Divide both sides of
the equation by 2. $\frac{2x}{2} = \frac{14}{2}$

Simplify both sides
of the equation. $x = 7$

You have solved for
the variable x. To
solve for the
variable y, substitute
the value of the x
variable into one of
the original equations.
It does not matter
which equation
you use. $x + y = 10$

Substitute 7 in place
of the x variable. $7 + y = 10$

Subtract 7 from
both sides of
the equation. $7 - 7 + y = 10 - 7$

Simplify both sides
of the equation. $y = 3$

You solve a system of equations by finding the value of all the variables. In the previous example, you found that $x = 7$ and $y = 3$. Write your answer as the ordered pair (7,3). To check your solution, substitute the values for x and y into *both* equations.

Check: $x + y = 10$
Substitute the values
of the variables into
the first equation. $7 + 3 = 10$
Simplify. $10 = 10$
$$x - y = 4$$
Substitute the values
of the variables into
the second equation. $7 - 3 = 4$
Simplify. $4 = 4$

Did you get the right answer? Because you got true statements when you substituted the value of the variables into both equations, you solved the system of equations correctly. Try another example.

Example

Solve the system: $x + y = 6$
$$-x + y = -4$$

Add the two equations. $0x + 2y = 2$

Drop the $0x$. $2y = 2$

Divide both sides of
the equation by 2. $\frac{2y}{2} = \frac{2}{2}$

Simplify both sides
of the equation. $y = 1$

Use one of the original
equations to solve for x. $x + y = 6$

Substitute 1 in place
of y. $x + 1 = 6$

Subtract 1 from both
sides of the equation. $x + 1 - 1 = 6 - 1$

Simplify both sides
of the equation. $x = 5$

Write the solution of the system as an ordered pair: (5,1).

Check: $x + y = 6$
Substitute the values of
x and y into the
first equation. $5 + 1 = 6$
Simplify. $6 = 6$
$$-x + y = -4$$
Substitute the values
of x and y into the
second equation. $-(5) + 1 = -4$
Simplify. $-4 = -4$

Did you get the right answer? Yes! You got true statements when you substituted the value of the variables into both equations, so you can be confident that you solved the system of equations correctly.

Try the next problems on your own. Follow along with the steps.

Practice

1. $3x + 4y = 8$

$-3x + y = 12$

2. $4x + 2y = 12$

$-4x + y = 3$

3. $3x = 5 - 7y$

$2y = x - 6$

When You Can't Easily Eliminate a Variable

Sometimes, you can't easily eliminate a variable by simply adding the equations. Take a look at the following example. What should you do?

Example

Solve the system: $x + y = 24$

$\qquad\qquad\qquad 2x + y = 3$

If you were to add this system of equations the way it is, you would be unable to eliminate a variable. However, if one of the y variables were negative, you would be able to eliminate the y variable. You can change the equation to eliminate the y variable by multiplying one of the equations by -1. You can use either equation. Save time by choosing the equation that looks easier to manipulate.

Multiply both sides of
the first equation by -1. $\quad -1(x + y) = -1 \cdot 24$

Simplify both sides
of the equation. $\qquad\qquad -x - y = -24$

Add the second $\qquad\qquad 2x + y = 3$

equation to the $\qquad\qquad\; x = -21$

modified first equation. $\quad x + y = 24$

Substitute the value
of x into one of the
original equations. $\qquad -21 + y = 24$

Add 21 to both
sides of the equation. $\quad -21 + 21 + y = 24 + 21$

Simplify both sides
of the equation. $\qquad\qquad\; y = 45$

The solution to the system of equations is $(-21, 45)$.

Rearranging Equations

Sometimes, it is necessary to rearrange an equation before you can solve it using the elimination method. Take a look at this example.

Example

Solve the system: $2x = 2y + 6$

$\qquad\qquad\qquad 3x = -3y + 3$

Rearrange the
first equation. $\qquad\qquad 2x = 2y + 6$

Subtract $2y$ from both
sides of the equation. $\quad 2x - 2y = 2y - 2y + 6$

Simplify. $\qquad\qquad\qquad 2x - 2y = 6$

Rearrange the second
equation. $\qquad\qquad 3x = -3y + 3$

Add $3y$ to both sides
of the equation. $\qquad 3x + 3y = -3y + 3y + 3$

Simplify. $\qquad\qquad\qquad 3x + 3y = 3$

Your system has
been altered to
these equations. $\qquad\quad 2x - 2y = 6$

$\qquad\qquad\qquad\qquad 3x + 3y = 3$

Multiply the first
equation by 3. $\qquad\quad 3(2x - 2y) = 3 \cdot 6$

Multiply the second
equation by 2. $\qquad\quad 2(3x + 3y) = 2 \cdot 3$

Simplify both
equations. $\qquad\qquad\; 6x - 6y = 18$

Add both equations. $\quad \underline{6x + 6y = 6}$

Divide both sides of $\qquad 12x = 24$

the equation by 12. $\qquad \dfrac{12x}{12} = \dfrac{24}{12}$

Simplify both sides. $x = 2$

Substitute 2 in place
of x in one of the $2x = 2y + 6$
original equations. $2 \cdot 2 = 2y + 6$

Simplify. $4 = 2y + 6$

Subtract 6 from both
sides of the equation. $4 - 6 = 2y + 6 - 6$

Simplify both sides
of the equation. $-2 = 2y$

Divide both sides by 2. $\frac{-2}{2} = \frac{2y}{2}$

Simplify. $-1 = y$

The solution of the system is $(2, -1)$.

Practice

4. $2x + 4y = 10$
$-3x + 3y = -6$

5. $8x - 4y = 16$
$4x + 5y = 22$

6. $-5x + 2y = 10$
$3x + 6y = 66$

How to Use the Substitution Method

Some systems of equations are easier to solve using the substitution method instead of the elimination method. Study the following examples.

Example

Solve the system: $y = 2x$
                 $2x + y = 12$

The first equation says
that $y = 2x$. If you
substitute $2x$ in place
of y in the second
equation, you can
eliminate a variable. $2x + 2x = 12$

Combine similar terms. $4x = 12$

Divide both sides of
the equation by 4. $\frac{4x}{4} = \frac{12}{4}$

Simplify both sides
of the equation. $x = 3$

Substitute 3 in place $y = 2x$
of x in one of the $y = 2 \cdot 3$
original equations. $y = 6$

The solution of the system is $(3, 6)$.

Example

Solve the system: $x = 2y + 1$
                 $x + 3y = 16$

Substitute $2y + 1$ in
place of x in the
second equation. $2y + 1 + 3y = 16$

Simplify. $5y + 1 = 16$

Subtract 1 from both
sides of the equation. $5y + 1 - 1 = 16 - 1$

Simplify both sides
of the equation. $5y = 15$

Divide both sides of
the equation by 5. $\frac{5y}{5} = \frac{15}{5}$

Simplify both sides
of the equation. $y = 3$

Substitute 3 in place
of y in one of the $x = 2y + 1$
original equations. $x = 2 \cdot 3 + 1$
                         $x = 7$

The solution for the system is $(7, 3)$.

Practice

7. $y = 2x + 1$
$3x + 2y = 9$

8. $y = 3x + 2$
$2x - 3y = 8$

9. $x + 6y = 11$
$x - 3 = 2y$

WHEN TO USE WHICH METHOD

Much of the SAT Math section is about using your time wisely. So, when you need to solve systems of linear equations, you will want to choose the method that allows you to solve the equation the quickest. Some students choose one method and stick with it no matter what the given equations are, but this can waste valuable time.

- First, check to see if the system has no solution.
- Then, check to see if the system has many solutions.
- If neither of these is the case, arrange the terms in each equation so that the variables line up in columns.
- Then, if you have inverse coefficients on a variable, such as $3x$ in one equation and $-3x$ in another equation, use the elimination method.
- If there are no inverse coefficients in the equations, use the substitution method.

Dealing with Systems of Linear Inequalities

Systems of linear inequalities are not as popular but are worth a mention here. Since linear inequalities are solved in the same manner as linear equations, systems of linear inequalities are solved in the same manner as systems of linear equations. The main fact to remember with inequalities is that your answer will be constrained. Many questions on the SAT exam involving inequalities ask you about the constraint on the answer.

Here is such a question:

Example: Consider the inequality $\frac{9}{4} \leq 1 - 2t \leq \frac{21}{8}$. Which of the following is a possible value of $16t$?
  a. -11
  b. $-\frac{11}{16}$
  c. 12
  d. $-\frac{13}{16}$

First, solve the double inequality for t by getting t in the middle by itself and the constants on either side.

To do so, multiply through by 8 to clear the fractions: $18 \leq 8 - 16t \leq 21$.

Next, subtract 8 from all parts of the inequality, and then divide through by -16, making certain to reverse both inequality signs:

$$10 \leq -16t \leq 13$$

$$-\frac{10}{16} \geq t \geq -\frac{13}{16}$$

This is equivalent to $-\frac{13}{16} \leq t \leq -\frac{10}{16}$.

Next, multiply through by 16 to get the expression $16t$ in the middle of the double inequality:

$$-13 \leq 16t \leq -10$$

This means that any value between -13 and -10, inclusive, is a possible value of $16t$. The number -11 (choice **a**) falls in this range.

Systems of Linear Equations on the SAT Exam

Most questions on the SAT involve solving and using linear equations. However, you will sometimes encounter word problems and will need to set up the system first and then solve it to answer the question.

SAT TEST-TAKING TIP

When creating a system of linear equations
1. assign the variables.
2. interpret one sentence at a time.
3. line up the variables in the system (this makes it easier to determine what method to use when solving).

Take a look at this question. To answer it, you will need to create a linear equation and then solve it.

Example: Joel is installing a new kitchen floor using two different size tiles. The larger tiles each cost $12, and the smaller tiles each cost $8. If a total of 192 tiles are used, and the total cost is $2,096, how many smaller tiles are used in the project?

Let x be the number of larger tiles used and y be the number of smaller tiles used. Create the following system of linear equations based on the information in the problem:

$$\begin{cases} x + y = 192 \\ 12x + 8y = 2,096 \end{cases}$$

Now, solve the first equation for y: $y = 192 - x$.

Next, substitute $192 - x$ for y in the second equation, and then solve for x:

$$12x + 8(192 - x) = 2,096$$
$$12x + 1,536 - 8x = 2,096$$
$$4x = 560$$
$$x = 140$$

Now that you know the value of x, you can easily find the value of y. Substitute 140 for x as follows:

$$y = 192 - x$$
$$y = 192 - 140$$
$$y = 52$$

In this next practice question, you are being asked to pick the appropriate system of linear equations. You still need to assign the variables and then interpret each sentence.

Practice

10. A local nursery charges $40.50 for a tree and $20.75 for a bush. A gardener wants to buy a combination of 22 trees and bushes so that he spends $614.50. Solving which of the following systems of linear equations would yield the number of trees, t, and bushes, b, that the gardener must purchase?

a. $\begin{cases} t + b = 22 \\ 20.75t + 40.50b = 614.50 \end{cases}$

b. $\begin{cases} t + b = 22 \\ 40.50t + 20.75b = 614.50 \end{cases}$

c. $\begin{cases} t + b = 22 \\ 61.25(t + b) = 614.50 \end{cases}$

d. $\begin{cases} t + b = 22 \\ 61.25 + t + b = 614.50 \end{cases}$

SAT TEST-TAKING TIP

Sometimes, you will be asked to complete systems of linear equations given some information about the solution. In this type of question, you will work backwards using your knowledge of the three types of solutions: one solution, no solution, and many solutions.

Let's look at another example together.

Example

Let k be a real number, and consider the following system:

$$\begin{cases} 5 - 3x = 2y \\ kx - 8y = -20 \end{cases}$$

For which value of k does the system have more than one solution?

a. $\frac{16}{3}$

b. -3

c. 4

d. -12

The two equations must be constant multiples of each other in order for the system to have more than one solution. If you multiply both sides of the first equation by 4, you get $20 - 12x = 8y$, which you can rearrange as $-12x - 8y = -20$. This means that if you identify k as -12, both equations in the system will be constant multiples of each other and the system will have more than one solution. The correct answer is therefore **d**.

Answers and Explanations

1. $(-\frac{8}{3}, 4)$. Add the equations to eliminate the x variable. In the resulting equation, $5y = 20$, divide both sides by 5 to get $y = 4$. Substitute 4 for y in the first equation to solve for x.

2. $(\frac{1}{2}, 5)$. Add the equations to eliminate the x variable. In the resulting equation, $3y = 15$, divide both sides by 3 to get $y = 5$. Substitute 5 for y in the first equation to solve for x.

3. $(4, -1)$. Rewrite the first equation as $7y = -3x + 5$ so that the variables from both equations line up. Multiply the second equation by 3 to get $6y = 3x - 18$. Add the equations to eliminate the x variable. In the resulting equation, $13y = -13$, divide both sides by 13 to get $y = -1$. Substitute -1 for y in the first equation to solve for x.

4. $(3, 1)$. Multiply the first equation by 3 to get $6x + 12y = 30$. Multiply the second equation by 2 to get $-6x + 6y = -12$. Add the two equations to eliminate the x variable. In the resulting equation, $18y = 18$, divide both sides by 18 to get $y = 1$. Substitute 1 for y in the first equation to solve for x.

5. $(3, 2)$. Multiply the second equation by -2 to get $-8x - 10y = -44$. Add the two equations to eliminate the x variable. In the resulting equation, $-14y = -28$, divide both sides by -2 to get $y = 2$. Substitute 2 for y in the first equation to solve for x.

6. $(2, 10)$. Multiply the first equation by -3 to get $15x - 6y = -30$. Add the two equations to eliminate the y variable. In the resulting equation, $18x = 36$, divide both sides by 18 to get $x = 2$. Substitute 2 for x in the first equation to solve for y.

7. **(1,3).** Substitute $(2x + 1)$ for y in the second equation to get $3x + 2(2x + 1) = 9$. Multiply 2 and $(2x + 1)$ to get a resulting equation of $3x + 4x + 2 = 9$. Add $3x$ and $4x$ on the left side to get $7x + 2 = 9$. Subtract 2 on both sides. Divide both sides by 7 to get $x = 1$. Substitute 1 for x in the first equation to solve for y.

8. **(−2,−4).** Substitute $(3x + 2)$ for y in the second equation to get $2x − 3(3x + 2) = 8$. Multiply −3 and $(3x + 2)$ to get a resulting equation of $2x − 9x − 6 = 8$. Add $2x$ and $−9x$ on the left side to get $−7x − 6 = 8$. Add 6 to both sides. Divide both sides by −7 to get $x = −2$. Substitute −2 for x in the first equation to solve for y.

9. **(5,1).** In the second equation, add 3 to both sides to get $x = 2y + 3$. Substitute $(2y + 3)$ for x in the first equation to get $2y + 3 + 6y = 11$. Add $2y$ and $6y$ on the left side. Subtract 3 from both sides to get $y = 1$. Substitute 1 for y in the first equation to solve for x.

10. **b.** The first equation is the symbolic interpretation of the condition "he wants a combination of 22 trees and bushes," and the second equation is the symbolic interpretation of how to compute the cost of buying t trees and b bushes. Choice **a** is incorrect—you likely interchanged the price of one bush and the price of one tree in the second equation. Choice **c** is incorrect because you mistakenly added the costs of one tree and one bush and applied it to both t trees and b bushes. You should have multiplied the cost of a single tree by t and the cost of a single bush by b to get the left side of the second equation. Choice **d** is incorrect because the second equation does not correctly describe how the cost is computed for t trees and b bushes. You should have multiplied the cost of a single tree by t and the cost of a single bush by b to get the left side of the second equation.

UNDERSTANDING EQUATIONS AND THEIR GRAPHS

We cannot solve problems with the same thinking we used when we created them.

—ALBERT EINSTEIN

LESSON SUMMARY
In this fourth lesson, you will gain a better understanding of the relationship between algebraic equations and their graphs. This ability is tested in algebra and advanced math questions on the SAT. This lesson will teach you ways to read a graph for information about its equation, and vice versa.

Equations such as linear, quadratic, and exponential ones each have special features that make their graphs unique. Each equation has a unique shape and characteristics that are well known. When you encounter an equation, knowing about its graph may help solve a problem. On the other hand, given a graph, knowing the associated equation can help solve other types of problems.

Graphs of Linear Equations (Lines)

Linear functions are equations that have the highest degree of one, such as y or $f(x) = x + 1$. The graph of a linear equation is a line in the point-slope form $y = mx + b$, where m is the slope or slant of the line and $(0,b)$ is the y-intercept, where the line crosses the y-axis.

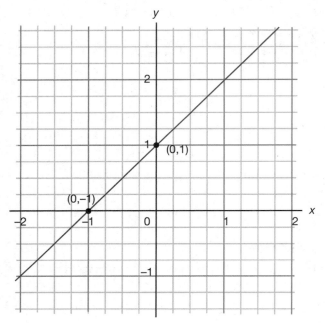

In the linear equation for $y = x + 1$, the y-intercept is $(0,1)$, which is where the line intersects with the y-axis. The line leans to the right side and thus has a positive slope of 1.

Graphs of Quadratic Equations (Parabolas)

A quadratic function is an equation in the form $f(x) = ax^2 + bx + c$, which can be used to model a rate of change that increases, reaches a high point called a **maximum**, and then decreases. Also, the rate of change can decrease, reach a low point called a **minimum**, and then increase.

The graph of a quadratic is called a **parabola**. The minimum or maximum point of a parabola is called the **vertex** or middle of the set of points that comprise the parabola.

The parabola will have **symmetry** on either side of the vertex point. That is, the parabola will be exactly the same size and shape but reversed on either side of the vertex.

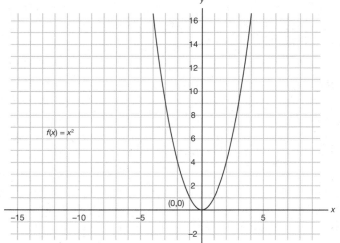

For instance, in the equation $f(x) = ax^2$, where $b = 0$ and $c = 0$, the y-axis runs through the center of the parabola and is called the **axis of symmetry**. All parabolas have an axis of symmetry, a line in the form of $y = a$, where a is a real number.

For quadratics in the form of $f(x) = ax^2 + bx + c$, the parabola crosses the x-axis at points called **zeros** in the form $(0,a)$, where a is a real number. These are the **roots** or solutions obtained from solving the quadratic equation. Most quadratics in the form $ax^2 + bx + c$ can be solved by factoring them into two binomials $(x \pm a)(x \pm b)$ and then solving for x.

Graphs of Exponential Functions

An exponential function is appropriate to use when the rate of change increases or decreases very rapidly. The exponential function is an equation in the form y or $f(x) = b^x$, where b is the **base** (a real number) raised to the power or exponent x.

The graph of an exponential function is a slightly curved line.

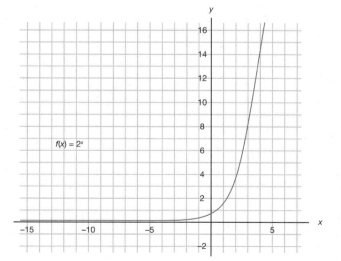

In the exponential function $f(x) = 2^x$, the left side gets smaller and approaches the x-axis but never touches while the right side gets wider as the x-values approach positive infinity.

In this example, the x-axis is called an **asymptote**. An asymptote is a line that a graph comes close to but never touches. Asymptotes can be horizontal ($y = a$, where a is a real number) or vertical ($x = a$, where a is a real number).

An exponential equation can be solved by using logarithms to rewrite the exponents in the equation. Recall that $y = b^x$ can be rewritten with $x = \log_y b$. The resulting equation is then solved by taking the log, which is an operation that can be computed by hand or on a calculator.

Problem Types Involving Equations and Their Graphs on the SAT

One of the most common types of SAT questions that you'll notice is to observe a graph and then choose its corresponding equation. This type of question requires that you know about the key features of each type of graph.

SAT TEST-TAKING TIP

Take the time to memorize the basic graphs of linear, quadratic, and exponential equations. Each equation has key features that are often tested on the SAT. By knowing the basic graphs and their equations, you can answer these types of questions more efficiently. In most cases, you can observe the feature on the graph and answer the question without taking too much time.

Example: Which of the following is the equation for the line graphed here?

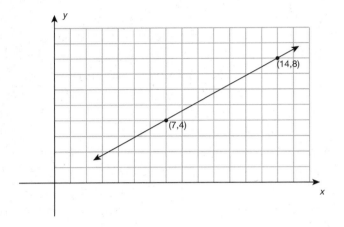

a. $4y = 7x$
b. $4x + 7y = 0$
c. $7y = 4x$
d. $4x - 7y = 4$

Using the two points on the line, (7,4) and (14,8), you can find the slope: $\frac{8-4}{14-7} = \frac{4}{7}$. Then write the equation for the line in point-slope form: $y - 4 = \frac{4}{7}(x - 7)$, which simplifies to $7y = 4x$.

Here is a problem involving a quadratic equation and the graph of a parabola.

Example: Which x-value would appear as the lowest point in the graph of $2x^2 + 8x = -12$?

Since this is a quadratic equation, its graph is a parabola. Also, this equation in standard form is $2x^2 + 8x + 12 = 0$, with $a = +2$. Since a is positive, we know that this parabola is an open "U" shape and thus the lowest point is the vertex, $x = -\frac{b}{2a}$.
Computing the vertex, we get $x = \frac{-8}{2(2)} = \frac{-8}{4} = -2$.
The answer is $x = -2$.

Look at this problem involving an exponential equation and its graph.

Example: Consider the graph of the function $f(x) = 2^x$. What is the y-intercept of the graph if the base were doubled?

The answer is (0,1). The y-intercept point indicates where a graph intersects the y-axis. In an exponential function, $x = 0$ and so $f(0) = $ (base)^0, which is always 1. So, no matter what happens to the base of the exponential function, the y-intercept will always be (0,1).

Some questions on the SAT are straightforward but contain some type of complexity in the equation for the graph. Try one such question on your own.

Practice

1. Suppose w is a real number larger than 2. Which of the following could be the graph of $wy + 2x = w(x + 3)$ in the xy-plane?

a.

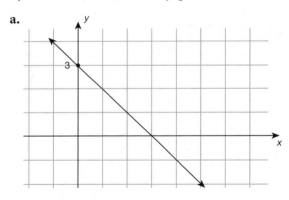

b.

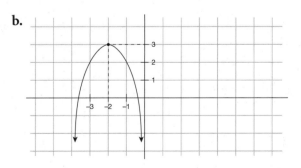

c.

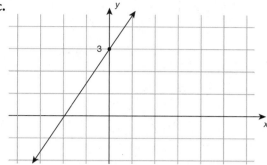

d.

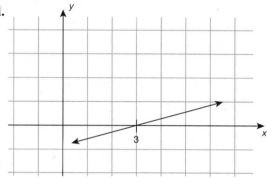

2. Which of the following is the graph of $2x + 3y = -3$?

a.

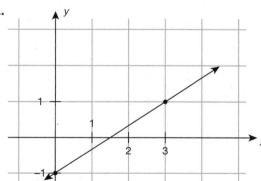

b.

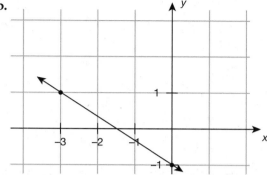

c.

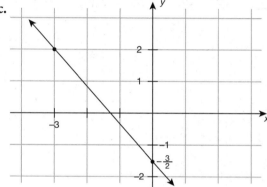

d.

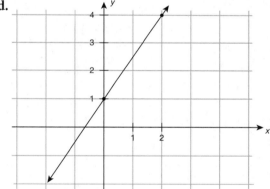

3. The graph of the line $\frac{4}{3}x - y = \frac{1}{2}$ passes through the point $(b, -b)$. What is the value of b?

a. $\frac{3}{14}$

b. $\frac{7}{6}$

c. $\frac{3}{2}$

d. $-\frac{3}{2}$

4. Determine the slope of the line in the xy-plane that has x-intercept $-\frac{3}{4}$ and passes through the point $(-2, \frac{1}{3})$.

    a. $-\frac{13}{14}$

    b. $-\frac{14}{13}$

    c. $-\frac{4}{15}$

    d. $-\frac{15}{4}$

SAT TEST-TAKING TIP

Knowing about equations and their corresponding graphs is essential to answering most questions involving graphs on the SAT exam. Practice memorizing the basic standard forms and graphs for linear, quadratic, and exponential functions by folding a piece of paper in half and listing the function on the left side and its graph on the right side. You must also remember the key features for each graph and what they mean. Go back and review the graphs with the key features presented here and copy the information onto your practice sheet for easy reference.

Answers and Explanations

1. c. The equation can be written equivalently as $y = (\frac{w-2}{w})x + 3$, a linear equation. Since $w > 2$, the slope is positive, so its graph must rise from left to right. Moreover, its y-intercept is 3, so it must cross the y-axis at $(0,3)$. This graph has these characteristics. Choice **a** is incorrect because the graph pictured has a negative slope. Choice **b** is incorrect because the given equation is linear, while the one graphed is not linear (in fact, it's probably quadratic). Choice **d** is incorrect because while this does show a line with positive slope, the y-intercept is not 3. The marked point $(3,0)$ is the x-intercept.

2. b. Write the given equation in slope-intercept form: $y = -\frac{2}{3}x - 1$. The y-intercept is -1, indicating a negative slope. Also notice that the point $(-3,1)$ satisfies the equation. This graph possesses all of the necessary characteristics to be the graph of the given equation. Choices **a** and **d** are incorrect because the equation has a *negative* slope, but these graphs have a positive slope (meaning it rises from left to right). Choice **c** is incorrect because it solved the given equation for x instead of y but then graphed it in the xy-plane as if it were solved for y.

3. a. Since $(b,-b)$ is on the line, it must satisfy the equation. Substituting $x = b$ and $y = -b$ yields the following:

$$\tfrac{4}{3}(b) - (-b) = \tfrac{1}{2}$$
$$\tfrac{4}{3}b + b = \tfrac{1}{2}$$
$$\tfrac{7}{3}b = \tfrac{1}{2}$$
$$b = \tfrac{1}{2} \cdot \tfrac{3}{7} = \tfrac{3}{14}$$

Choice **b** is incorrect because after substituting $(b,-b)$ into the equation, in the final step of solving for b you multiplied both sides by the coefficient of b instead of dividing. Choice **c** is incorrect because when substituting $(b,-b)$ into the equation, you made a mistake with signs when simplifying the expression $\tfrac{4}{3}(b) - (-b)$. This is equivalent to $\tfrac{4}{3}b + b$, not $\tfrac{4}{3}b - b$. Choice **d** is incorrect because you substituted in $(-b,b)$, not $(b,-b)$.

4. c. Since the x-intercept is $-\tfrac{3}{4}$, we know the line goes through the point $(-\tfrac{3}{4},0)$. Using this information plus the other point on the line, we can compute the slope:

$$\frac{\tfrac{1}{3} - 0}{-2 - (-\tfrac{3}{4})} = \frac{\tfrac{1}{3}}{-\tfrac{5}{4}} = \tfrac{1}{3} \times (-\tfrac{4}{5}) = -\tfrac{4}{15}$$

Choice **a** is incorrect because the x-intercept of $-\tfrac{3}{4}$ is the point $(-\tfrac{3}{4},0)$, not $(0,-\tfrac{3}{4})$. Choice **b** is incorrect because it incorrectly identified the x-intercept of $-\tfrac{3}{4}$ as the point $(0,-\tfrac{3}{4})$ instead of $(-\tfrac{3}{4},0)$, and it also computed the slope as "run over rise" instead of "rise over run." Choice **d** is incorrect because it is the reciprocal of the slope. Remember, slope is "rise over run," not "run over rise."

L E S S O N

5 ▶ RATIOS, PROPORTIONS, AND SCALE

Not everything that can be counted counts, and not everything that counts can be counted.

—ALBERT EINSTEIN

LESSON SUMMARY

In this lesson, you will gain valuable tips on using ratios and proportions in word problems. You will also practice using scales to solve real-world problems.

Many word problems on the SAT deal with ratios, proportions, and scales. These types of problems are generally straightforward and require you to set up the solution and then apply algebraic techniques to solve.

What Are Ratios?

A **ratio** is a comparison of two numbers. For example, let's say that there are 3 men for every 5 women in a particular club. That means that the ratio of men to women is 3 to 5. It doesn't necessarily mean that there are exactly 3 men and 5 women in the club, but it does mean that for *every group of 3 men, there is a corresponding group of 5 women*. The following table shows some of the possible sizes of this club.

BREAKDOWN OF CLUB MEMBERS; 3 TO 5 RATIO			
# OF GROUPS	# OF MEN	# OF WOMEN	TOTAL MEMBERS
1	???	/////	8
2	??? ???	///// /////	16
3	??? ??? ???	///// ///// /////	24
4	??? ??? ??? ???	///// ///// ///// /////	32
5	??? ??? ??? ??? ???	///// ///// ///// ///// /////	40

In other words, the number of men is **3 times the number of *groups***, and the number of women is **5 times that same number of *groups***.

⚠ CAUTION

The order in which you write the numbers is important. Saying "3 to 5" is not the same as saying "5 to 3."

A ratio can be expressed in several ways:

- using **"to"** (3 **to** 5)
- using **"out of"** (3 **out of** 5)
- using a **colon** (3:5)
- as a **fraction** ($\frac{3}{5}$)
- as a **decimal** (0.6)

Like a fraction, a ratio should always be reduced to lowest terms. For example, the ratio of 6 to 10 should be reduced to 3 to 5 (because the fraction $\frac{6}{10}$ reduces to $\frac{3}{5}$).

Here are some examples of ratios in familiar contexts:

- Last year, it snowed 13 out of 52 weekends in New York City. The ratio *13 out of 52* can be reduced to lowest terms (*1 out of 4*) and expressed as any of the following:

$\left. \begin{array}{l} \text{1 to 4} \\ \text{1:4} \\ \frac{1}{4} \\ 0.25 \end{array} \right\}$ Reducing to lowest terms tells you that it snowed 1 out of 4 weekends ($\frac{1}{4}$ of the weekends or 25% of the weekends)

- Lloyd drove 140 miles on 3.5 gallons of gas, for a ratio (or gas *consumption rate*) of 40 *miles per gallon*:

$$\frac{\overset{40}{\cancel{140}} \; miles}{\underset{1}{\cancel{3.5}} \; gallons} = \frac{40 \; miles}{1 \; gallon} = 40 \; miles \; per \; gallon$$

- The student-teacher ratio at Clarksdale High School is 7 to 1. That means for every 7 students in the school, there is 1 teacher. For example, if Clarksdale has 140 students, then it has 20 teachers. (There are 20 groups, each with 7 students and 1 teacher.)

In word problems, the word *per* means to divide. For example, 30 miles *per* hour is equivalent to $\frac{30 \; miles}{1 \; hour}$. Phrases with the word *per* are ratios with a bottom number of 1, like these:

24 miles per gallon $= \frac{24\ miles}{1\ gallon}$

$12 per hour $= \frac{12\ dollars}{1\ hour}$

3 meals per day $= \frac{3\ meals}{1\ day}$

4 cups per quart $= \frac{4\ cups}{1\ quart}$

SAT TEST-TAKING TIP

Ratios can also be used to relate more than two items, but then they are not written as fractions. Example: If the ratio of infants to teens to adults at a school event is 2 to 7 to 5, it is written as 2:7:5.

A ratio usually tells you something about the *total* number of things being compared. In our first ratio example of a club with 3 men for every 5 women, the club's total membership is a **multiple of 8** because each group contains 3 men and 5 women. The following example illustrates some of the *total* questions you could be asked about a particular ratio:

Example: Wyatt bought a total of 12 books, purchasing two $5 books for every $8 book.
- How many $5 books did he buy?
- How many $8 books did he buy?
- How much money did he spend in total?

The total number of books Wyatt bought is a multiple of 3 (each group of books contained **two** $5 books **plus one** $8 book). Since he bought a total of 12 books, he bought 4 groups of books (4 groups × 3 books = 12 books in total).

Total books: **8 $5 books + 4 $8 books =**
                 12 books

Total cost: $40 + $32 = **$72**

SAT TEST-TAKING TIP

Set up a "ratio chart" for ratios involving more than two quantities.

Example: A molecule of sucrose contains carbon, hydrogen, and oxygen atoms in the ratio of 12:22:11. If a pinch of table sugar contains 1,800 total atoms, how many carbon atoms does it contain?

First, let's set up a ratio chart:

	CARBON	HYDROGEN	OXYGEN	TOTAL
Ratio:	12	22	11	
Real:				1,800

Now that everything's set up, we're going to try to fill one column completely. We can add 12, 22, and 11 to get a total in the ratio column:

	CARBON	HYDROGEN	OXYGEN	TOTAL
Ratio:	12	22	11	45
Real:				1,800

Once we have a full column, we look for our multiplier. The total ratio is 45:1,800, or $\frac{45}{1,800}$ which is $\frac{1}{40}$. This means that the ratios for carbon, hydrogen, and oxygen must also be $\frac{1}{40}$. Thus, we need to multiply all of our numbers in the ratio row by 40 to get the numbers in the real column.

	CARBON	HYDROGEN	OXYGEN	TOTAL
Ratio:	12	22	11	45
Real:	480	880	440	1,800

So, our answer for the number of carbon atoms in the sugar is 480.

SAT TEST-TAKING TIP

Most ratio problems on the SAT are easy in that they ask you to observe a situation in a word problem and then record the ratio as you've just learned. Some ratio problems give you a graph or scatter plot and ask you to observe the ratio from there. No matter what form the information is given in, be careful to note the two quantities you are making a ratio from.

Try this SAT-type problem on your own.

Practice

1. A botanist studying red chili peppers created the following scatter plot to examine the relationship between the number of days it takes to harvest a chili pepper and its heat intensity (measured in Scoville heat units):

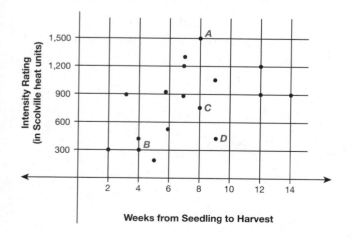

Weeks from Seedling to Harvest

Of the labeled points, which represents the pepper for which the ratio of intensity to harvest time is least?

a. A
b. B
c. C
d. D

Proportions

A **proportion** states that two ratios are equal to each other. For example, have you ever heard someone say something like this?

> Nine out of ten professional athletes suffer at least one injury each season.

The phrase *nine out of ten* is a ratio. It tells you that $\frac{9}{10}$ of professional athletes suffer at least one injury each season. But there are more than 10 professional athletes. Suppose that there are 100 professional athletes. Then $\frac{9}{10}$ of the 100 athletes, or 90 out of 100 professional athletes, suffer at least one injury per season. The two ratios are equivalent and form a proportion:

$$\frac{9}{10} = \frac{90}{100}$$

Here are some other proportions:

$$\frac{3}{5} = \frac{6}{10} \qquad \frac{1}{2} = \frac{5}{10} \qquad \frac{2}{5} = \frac{22}{55}$$

Notice that a proportion reflects equivalent fractions: each fraction reduces to the same value.

Cross Products

As with fractions, the cross products of a proportion are equal.

$$\frac{3}{5} \diagup\!\!\!\!\!\diagdown \frac{6}{10}$$

$$3 \times 10 = 5 \times 6$$

> ⚠ **CAUTION**
>
> In each fraction, the units must be written in the same order.

Solving Proportion Problems

Many proportion word problems are easily solved with fractions and cross products. For example, let's say we have two ratios (ratio #1 and ratio #2) that compare red marbles to white marbles. When you set up the proportion, both fractions must be set up the same way—with the red marbles on top and the corresponding white marbles on the bottom, or with the white marbles on top and the corresponding red marbles on the bottom:

$$\frac{red_{\#1}}{white_{\#1}} = \frac{red_{\#2}}{white_{\#2}} \quad or \quad \frac{white_{\#1}}{red_{\#1}} = \frac{white_{\#2}}{red_{\#2}}$$

Alternatively, one fraction may compare the red marbles while the other fraction compares the white marbles, with both comparisons in the same order:

$$\frac{red_{\#1}}{red_{\#2}} = \frac{white_{\#1}}{white_{\#2}} \quad or \quad \frac{red_{\#2}}{red_{\#1}} = \frac{white_{\#2}}{white_{\#1}}$$

Here is another proportion example.

Example: Wyatt bought two $5 books for every $8 book he bought. If he bought eight $5 books, how many $8 books did Wyatt buy? How many books did Wyatt buy in total? How much money did Wyatt spend in total?

The ratio of books Wyatt bought is 2:1, or $\frac{2(\$5\ books)}{1(\$8\ book)}$. For the second ratio, the eight $5 books goes on top of the fraction to correspond with the top of the first fraction, the number of $5 books. Therefore, the unknown b (the number of $8 books) goes on the bottom of the second fraction. Here's the proportion:

$$\frac{2(\$5\ books)}{1(\$8\ book)} = \frac{8(\$5\ books)}{b(\$8\ book)}$$

Solve it using cross products:

$$\frac{2}{1} \diagdown\!\!\!\!\diagup \frac{8}{b}$$

$$2 \times b = 1 \times 8$$

$$2 \times 4 = 8$$

Thus, Wyatt bought **4** $8 books and **8** $5 books, for a total of **12** books, spending **$72** in total:

$$(8 \times \$5) + (4 \times \$8) = \$72$$

Check: Reduce $\frac{8}{4}$, the ratio of $5 books to $8 books that Wyatt bought, to ensure getting back $\frac{2}{1}$, the original ratio.

Scale

A scale is a simple ratio that is used to convert an actual measurement to an easier one. For example, if you are drawing a map of the state you live in using miles, it would be impossible to draw that on paper. Instead, by using a scale, you can convert the miles into a smaller measurement, say, inches. The scale factor is usually given as a ratio, like 1 inch = 100 miles or 1:100.

Problems with Ratios, Proportion, and Scale on the SAT Exam

Sometimes the SAT will require you to come up with equations or models to describe situations involving ratios, proportions, or scale factors. Of these, scale questions are the easiest, as the test generally tells you what the scale factor is, such as 2 inches = 20 miles, and then asks you to convert one unit into another.

Example: A map of your neighborhood is drawn to scale so that every 2 inches on the map represents 1 city block. If every city block is perfectly square and 300 yards long, how many inches would you use to indicate the trip from your house to your job, which is 1,500 yards away?

To solve a question like this, you want to first set up two fractions, both with the same units in their numerators and denominators:

$$\frac{2 \text{ inches}}{1 \text{ city block}} = \frac{x \text{ inches}}{1{,}500 \text{ yards}}$$

The problem here is that our denominators do not have the same units. So, let's change 1,500 yards to city blocks using a stoichiometry table:

$$\frac{1{,}500 \text{ yards}}{1} = \frac{1 \text{ city block}}{300 \text{ yards}} = 5 \text{ city blocks}$$

Now replace the 1,500 yards. Since we have the same units, we can cross multiply and solve our equation for our answer:

$$\frac{2 \text{ inches}}{1 \text{ city block}} = \frac{x \text{ inches}}{5 \text{ city blocks}}$$

$$2 \times 5 = 1 \times x$$

$$x = 10$$

So, our answer is 10 inches.

SAT TEST-TAKING TIP

Remember that ratio and proportion problems on the SAT can be solved by setting up a pair of equivalent fractions and cross multiplying, just as the previous scale factor problem did.

Let's work through another example together.

Example: In a new videogame, the number of level points and the number of coins that a player earns is directly proportional to the number of hidden objects he or she finds during the game.

When Margaret tried out the game, she was too busy playing to pay attention to how many level points and coins she had at all times, but she did notice that when she found 3 objects, she earned 78 coins and that when she found 4 objects, she earned 228 level points.

If Margaret finds 11 objects, how many level points will she earn?
 a. 627
 b. 235
 c. 2,508
 d. 836

Let x = number of level points a player earns for finding 11 objects. Then set up the following proportion:

$$\frac{228 \text{ level points}}{4 \text{ objects}} = \frac{x}{11 \text{ objects}}$$

Now, solve for x:

$$x = \frac{228(11)}{4} = 627$$

So, the correct answer is **a**.

Try the following SAT Math problems on your own.

Practice

2. Sam's wedding photo measures $1\frac{3}{8}$ inches $\times$ $2\frac{3}{4}$ inches. He wants to create a larger copy of it to give as a gift and then frame the original to put on his desk. If the enlarged copy of the photo measures 8 inches, what is the length, in inches, of the copy's shorter side? _____

3. Christopher can make enough iced coffee for one person by mixing two teaspoons of espresso with water. How many tablespoons of espresso would he need to make enough iced coffee for 24 people? (3 teaspoons = 1 tablespoon)
 a. 12
 b. 16
 c. 48
 d. 144

4. If 15 chairs cost j dollars, which of the following equations would help determine the cost, k, of 3 chairs?

   a. $\frac{15}{j} = \frac{3}{k}$

   b. $\frac{15}{k} = \frac{3}{j}$

   c. $\frac{15}{3} = \frac{k}{j}$

   d. $\frac{k}{j} = \frac{15}{3}$

SAT TEST-TAKING TIP

When you are setting up proportions, be sure you match the units of the numerators and the denominators in your ratios. In the previous example, notice that the ratios were listed as $\frac{\text{chairs}}{\text{dollars}}$.

Answers and Explanations

1. d. This ratio is $\frac{450}{9} = 50$, which is the lowest of the four labeled points. Choice **a** is incorrect because this ratio is $\frac{1,500}{8} = 187.5$, which is the highest of the four labeled points. Choice **b** is incorrect because this ratio is $\frac{300}{4} = 75$, which is the second lowest of the four labeled points. Choice **c** is incorrect because this ratio is $\frac{750}{8} = 93.75$, which is the second highest of the four labeled points. Note: Did you notice the busyness of the points on the scatter plot? The only points you needed were **a**, **b**, **c**, and **d**, though!

2. 4. Let s be the length of the shorter side of the enlarged photo. Since the lengths are proportional, we have the following:

$$\frac{1\frac{3}{8} \text{ inches}}{2\frac{3}{4} \text{ inches}} = \frac{s \text{ inches}}{8 \text{ inches}}$$

Solving for s, we have

$$\frac{1\frac{3}{8} \text{ inches}}{2\frac{3}{4} \text{ inches}} = \frac{s \text{ inches}}{8 \text{ inches}}$$

$$\frac{(1\frac{3}{8} \text{ inches})(8 \text{ inches})}{2\frac{3}{4} \text{ inches}} = s \text{ inches}$$

$$\frac{\frac{11}{8} \times 8}{\frac{11}{4}} = s \text{ inches}$$

$$\left(\frac{11}{8} \times 8 \times \frac{4}{11}\right) \text{ inches} = s \text{ inches}$$

$$s = 4 \text{ inches}$$

3. b. Christopher can make a 1-person serving of iced coffee with 2 teaspoons. So, the first ratio is 1 person: 2 teaspoons or $\frac{1}{2}$. The next ratio given to you is that 3 teaspoons = 1 tablespoon. So, we can set up the following proportion to solve as

$$\frac{1 \text{ person}}{2 \text{ teaspoons}} = \frac{24 \text{ people}}{x \text{ teaspoons}}$$

Cross multiplying yields $x = (2)(24) = 48$ teaspoons. If it takes 48 teaspoons for 24 people, how many tablespoons is that? We are given that 3 teaspoons = 1 tablespoon, so 48 teaspoons would be $\frac{48}{3}$, or 16 tablespoons.

4. a. We can get a proportion from the two ratios that are described. The first ratio gives $\frac{15 \text{ chairs}}{j \text{ dollars}}$, and the second ratio is $\frac{3 \text{ chairs}}{k \text{ dollars}}$. Create a proportion by putting them together:

$$\frac{15 \text{ chairs}}{j \text{ dollars}} = \frac{3 \text{ chairs}}{k \text{ dollars}}$$

6 ▶ PERCENT PROBLEMS

Can you do Division? Divide a loaf by a knife—what's the answer to that?

—LEWIS CARROLL

LESSON SUMMARY

In this lesson, you will work with decimals and percents. This lesson will strengthen skills you may already have but also give you some tips for completing any SAT problem that involves percents and converting them to decimals (or mixed numbers).

Percent problems are very common on the SAT, and so your knowledge of them must be fluent. Most likely you will encounter percents in word problems, so in this lesson we will focus on percentages in the context of a situation.

What Is a Percent?

A percent is a special kind of fraction. The bottom number (the **denominator**) is always 100. For example, 5% is the same as $\frac{5}{100}$. Literally, the word *percent* means *per 100 parts*. The root *cent* means 100: A *cent*ury is 100 years; there are 100 *cents* in a dollar. Thus, 5% means 5 parts out of 100. Fractions can also be expressed as decimals: $\frac{5}{100}$ is equivalent to 0.05 (five-hundredths). Therefore, 5% is also equivalent to the decimal 0.05.

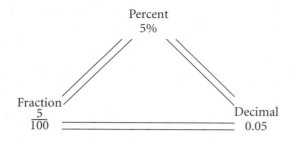

Percent
5%

Fraction
$\frac{5}{100}$

Decimal
0.05

SAT TEST-TAKING TIP

Percentages are used only in writing and are never used in calculations. The percent symbol (%) looks like a jumbled-up "100," so that should help remind you to always change your percentages to a fraction over 100 before doing any algebraic calculations! Example: $37.5\% = \frac{37.5}{100}$ or $\frac{375}{1,000}$.

Changing Percents to Decimals

To change a percent to a decimal, drop the percent sign and move the decimal point two digits to the left. Remember: If a number doesn't have a decimal point, it's assumed to be at the right. If there aren't enough digits to move the decimal point, add zeros on the left before moving the decimal point.

> **Example:** Change 20% to a decimal.
> 1. Drop the percent sign: 20
> 2. There's no decimal point, so put it at the right: 20.
> 3. Move the decimal point two digits to the left: 0.20.

Thus, 20% is equivalent to 0.20, which is the same as 0.2.
(Remember: Zeros at the right of a decimal don't change its value.)

Now you try these sample questions. The step-by-step solutions are at the end of this lesson.

Practice

1. Change 75% to a decimal. _____

2. Change 142% to a decimal. _____

Changing Decimals to Percents

To change a decimal to a percent, move the decimal point two digits to the right. If there aren't enough digits to move the decimal point, add zeros on the right before moving the decimal point. If the decimal point moves to the very right of the number, don't write the decimal point. Finally, tack on a percent sign (%) at the end.

> **Example:** Change 0.3 to a percent.
> 1. Move the decimal point two digits to the right after adding one zero on the right so there are enough decimal digits: 0.30.
> 2. The decimal point moved to the very right, so remove it: 30
> 3. Tack on a percent sign: 30%
> Thus, 0.3 is equivalent to 30%.

⚠ CAUTION

$0.3 \neq 3\%$. Don't forget to move the decimal point two digits to the right.

SAT TEST-TAKING TIP

When changing decimals to percentages, remember that a mixed decimal is always going to be more than 100%. Example: 1 = 100% and 2.75 = 275%.

Practice

3. Change 0.875 to a percent. _____

4. Change 0.7 to a percent. _____

Changing Percents to Fractions

To change a percent to a fraction, remove the percent sign and write the number over 100; then reduce if possible.

Example: Change 20% to a fraction.
1. Remove the % and write the fraction 20 over 100: $\frac{20}{100}$

2. Reduce: $\frac{20 \div 20}{100 \div 20} = \frac{1}{5}$

Example: Change $16\frac{2}{3}$% to a fraction.
1. Remove the % and write the fraction $16\frac{2}{3}$ over 100: $\frac{16\frac{2}{3}}{100}$

2. Since a fraction means "top number divided by bottom number," rewrite the fraction as a division problem: $16\frac{2}{3} \div 100$

3. Change the mixed number $(16\frac{2}{3})$ to an improper fraction $(\frac{50}{3})$: $\frac{50}{3} \div \frac{100}{1}$

4. Flip the second fraction $(\frac{100}{1})$ and multiply: $\frac{\overset{1}{\cancel{50}}}{3} \times \frac{1}{\underset{2}{\cancel{100}}} = \frac{1}{6}$

Practice

5. Change $33\frac{1}{3}$% to a fraction. _____

Changing Fractions to Percents

To change a fraction to a percent, there are two techniques. Each is illustrated by changing the fraction $\frac{1}{5}$ to a percent.

Technique 1: Multiply the fraction by 100.

Multiply $\frac{1}{5}$ by 100: $\frac{1}{\underset{1}{\cancel{5}}} \times \frac{\overset{20}{\cancel{100}}}{1} = 20\%$

Note: Change 100 to its fractional equivalent, $\frac{100}{1}$, before multiplying.

Technique 2: Divide the fraction's bottom number into the top number; then move the decimal point two digits to the **right** and tack on a percent sign (%).

Divide 5 into 1, move the decimal point two digits to the right, and tack on a percent sign: $5\overline{)1.00}^{\,0.20} \rightarrow 0.20. \rightarrow 20\%$

Note: You can get rid of the decimal point because it's at the extreme right of 20.

Practice

6. Change $\frac{1}{9}$ to a percent. _____

SAT TEST-TAKING TIP

Since many percent problems on the SAT should be calculated quickly and without a calculator, it would help if you memorized the more common decimals, percents, and fractions that are equivalent.

CONVERTING DECIMALS, PERCENTS, AND FRACTIONS

DECIMAL	PERCENT	FRACTION
0.25	25%	$\frac{1}{4}$
0.5	50%	$\frac{1}{2}$
0.75	75%	$\frac{3}{4}$
0.1	10%	$\frac{1}{10}$
0.2	20%	$\frac{1}{5}$
0.4	40%	$\frac{2}{5}$
0.6	60%	$\frac{3}{5}$
0.8	80%	$\frac{4}{5}$
$0.\overline{3}$	$33\frac{1}{3}\%$	$\frac{1}{3}$
$0.\overline{6}$	$66\frac{2}{3}\%$	$\frac{2}{3}$
0.125	12.5%	$\frac{1}{8}$
0.375	37.5%	$\frac{3}{8}$
0.625	62.5%	$\frac{5}{8}$
0.875	87.5%	$\frac{7}{8}$

Types of Percent Problems

Word problems involving percents come in three main varieties:

1. Find a percent of a whole.
   Example: What is 15% of 50? (50 is the whole.)
2. Find what percent one number (the "part") is of another number (the "whole").
   Example: 10 is what percent of 40? (40 is the whole.)
3. Find the whole when the percent of it is given as a part.
   Example: 20 is 40% of what number? (20 is the part.)

While each variety has its own approach, there is a single shortcut formula you can use to solve each of these:

$$\frac{part}{whole} = \frac{\%}{100}$$

part   The number that usually follows (but can precede) the word **is** in the question.

whole   The number that usually follows the word **of** in the question.

%   The number in front of the **%** or word **percent** in the question.

To solve each of the three main varieties of percent questions, use the fact that the **cross products** are equal. The cross products are the products of the quantities diagonally across from each other. Remembering that *product* means *multiply*, here's how to create the cross products for the percent shortcut:

$$\frac{part}{whole} \diagdown \frac{\%}{100}$$

$$part \times 100 = whole \times \%$$

It's also useful to know that when you have an *equation* like the one previously mentioned—a number sentence that says that two quantities are equal—you can do the same thing to both sides and the results will still be equal. You can add, subtract, multiply, or divide both sides by the same number and still have equal numbers. You'll see how this works in this lesson.

SAT TEST-TAKING TIP

Remember, when you are solving for a percentage using the $\frac{part}{whole} = \frac{\%}{100}$ method, you will get the answer in the form of a decimal. You must then change it into a percent by moving the decimal to the right two times and adding the percent symbol.

Finding a Percent of a Whole

Plug the numbers you're given into the percent shortcut to find the percent of a whole.

Example: What is 15% of 40?
1. 15 is the **%**, and 40 is the **whole**:
$$\frac{part}{40} = \frac{15}{100}$$
2. Cross multiply and solve for **part**:
$$part \times 100 = 40 \times 15$$
$$part \times 100 = 600$$
Thus, **6 is** 15% of 40. $$6 \times 100 = 600$$
Note: If the answer didn't leap out at you when you saw the equation, you could have divided both sides by 100, leaving **part** = 6.

Example: Twenty percent of the 25 students in Mr. Mann's class failed the test. How many students failed the test?
1. The **percent** is 20 and the **whole** is 25, since it follows the word **of** in the problem.
$$\frac{part}{25} = \frac{20}{100}$$

2. Cross multiply and solve for **part**:
$$part \times 100 = 25 \times 20$$
$$part \times 100 = 500$$
$$5 \times 100 = 500$$
Thus, 5 students failed the test. Again, if the answer doesn't leap out at you, divide both sides of **part** × 100 = 500 by 100, leaving **part** = 5.

Now you try finding the percent of a whole with the following sample question. The step-by-step solution is at the end of this lesson.

Practice

7. Ninety percent of the 300 dentists surveyed recommended sugarless gum for their patients who chew gum. How many dentists did NOT recommend sugarless gum? _____

Finding What Percent a Number Is of Another Number

Use the percent shortcut and the fact that cross products are equal to find what percent one number is of another number.

Example: 10 is what percent of 40?
1. 10 is the **part** and 40 is the **whole**:
$$\frac{10}{40} = \frac{\%}{100}$$
2. Cross multiply and solve for %:
$$10 \times 100 = 40 \times \%$$
Thus, 10 is **25%** of 40.
$$1{,}000 = 40 \times \%$$
If you didn't know offhand what to multiply by 40 to get 1,000, you could divide both sides of the equation by 40:
$$1{,}000 = 40 \times 25$$
$$1{,}000 \div 40 = 40 \times \% \div 40$$
$$25 = \%$$

Example: Thirty-five members of the 105-member marching band are girls. What percent of the marching band is girls?

1. The **whole** is 105 because it follows the word **of** in the problem: $\frac{35}{105} = \frac{\%}{100}$ Therefore, 35 is the **part** because it is the other number in the problem, and we know it's not the percent because that's what we must find:

$$35 \times 100 = 105 \times \%$$

$$3{,}500 = 105 \times \%$$

2. Divide both sides of the equation by 105 to find out what % is equal to:

$$3{,}500 \div 105 =$$
$$105 \times \% \div 105$$

Thus, $33\frac{1}{3}\%$ of the marching band is girls.

$$33\frac{1}{3} = \%$$

Practice

8. The quality control step at the Light Bright Company has found that 2 out of every 1,000 lightbulbs tested are defective. Assuming that this batch is indicative of all the lightbulbs they manufacture, what percent of the manufactured lightbulbs is defective? _____

Finding the Whole When a Percent Is Given

Once again, you can use the percent shortcut to determine the whole when you're given a percentage.

Example: 20 is 40% of what number?

1. 20 is the **part** and 40 is the %: $\frac{40}{whole} = \frac{40}{100}$

2. Cross multiply and solve for the **whole**:

$$20 \times 100 = \textbf{whole} \times 40$$
$$2{,}000 = \textbf{whole} \times 40$$

Thus, 20 is 40% **of 50**. $\quad 2{,}000 = 50 \times 40$

Note: You could instead divide both sides of the equation by 40 to leave 50 on one side and **whole** on the other.

Example: John left a $3 tip, which was 15% of his bill. How much was his bill?

In this problem, $3 is the **part**, even though there's no **is** in the actual question; instead, there's *was*, the past tense of *is*. You know this for two reasons: (1) It's the **part** John left for his server, and (2) the word **of** appears later in the problem: *of the bill*, meaning that the amount **of** the bill is the **whole**. And, obviously, 15 is the **%** since the problem states **15%**.

So, here's the setup and solution:

$$\frac{3}{whole} = \frac{15}{100}$$
$$3 \times 100 = \textbf{whole} \times 15$$
$$300 = \textbf{whole} \times 15$$
$$300 = 20 \times 15$$

Thus, John's bill was $20.

Note: Some problems may ask you a different question. For instance, what was the total amount that John's lunch cost? In that case, the answer is the amount of the bill **plus** the amount of the tip, or $23 ($20 + $3).

Practice

9. The combined city and state sales tax in Bay City is $8\frac{1}{2}\%$. The Bay City Boutique collected $600 in sales tax for sales on May 1. What was the total sales figure for that day, excluding sales tax? _____

Problems Involving Percent of Change (% Increase and % Decrease)

Another type of percent problem on the SAT involves calculating percent of change.

You can use the $\frac{part}{whole}$ technique to find the percent of change, whether it's an increase or a decrease. The *part* is the amount of the increase or decrease, and the *whole* is the **original amount**.

> **Example:** If a merchant puts his $10 pens on sale for $8, by what percent does he decrease the selling price?
> 1. Calculate the decrease, the *part*: $10 − $8 = $2
> 2. The *whole* is the **original amount**: $10
> 3. Set up the $\frac{part}{whole}$ formula and solve for the **%** by cross multiplying:
> $$\frac{2}{10} = \frac{\%}{100}$$
> $$2 \times 100 = 10 \times \%$$
> $$200 = 10 \times \%$$
> $$200 = 10 \times 20$$

Thus, the selling price is decreased by **20%**. If the merchant later raises the price of the pens from $8 back to $10, don't be fooled into thinking that the percent increase is also 20%! It's actually more, because the increase amount of $2 is now based on a lower **original price** of only $8 (since he's now starting from $8):

$$\frac{2}{8} = \frac{\%}{100}$$
$$2 \times 100 = 8 \times \%$$
$$200 = 8 \times \%$$
$$200 = 8 \times 25$$

Thus, the selling price is increased by **25%**.

Practice

10. Chris spent 208 hours jogging and 78 hours playing racquetball this year. Next year, he plans to increase his racquetball playing by 50% and decrease his jogging by 10%. By what percentage will the total time spent on these two activities change if Chris follows his plan?

a. 40%

b. 18.2%

c. 6.4%

d. 70.2%

Answers and Explanations

1 and 2. 0.75 and 1.42.

Drop the percent sign:	75	142

There's no decimal point,
so put one at the right: 75.   142.

Move the decimal point
two digits to the left: 0.75.   1.42

Thus, 75% is equivalent to 0.75, and 142% is equivalent to 1.42.

3. 87.5%.

Move the decimal point
two digits to the right: 0.87.5

Tack on a percent sign: 87.5%

Thus, 0.875 is equivalent to 87.5%.

4. 70%.

Move the decimal point
two digits to the right after
tacking on a zero: 0.70.

Remove the decimal point
because it's at the
extreme right: 70

Tack on a percent sign: 70%

Thus, 0.7 is equivalent to 70%.

5. $\frac{1}{3}$.

Remove the % and write
the fraction $33\frac{1}{3}$ over 100: $\frac{33\frac{1}{3}}{100}$

Since a fraction means
"top number divided by
bottom number," rewrite
the fraction as a division
problem: $33\frac{1}{3} \div 100$

Change the mixed
number ($33\frac{1}{3}$) to an
improper fraction ($\frac{100}{3}$): $\frac{100}{3} \div \frac{100}{1}$

Flip the second fraction
($\frac{100}{1}$) and multiply: $\frac{\overset{1}{\cancel{100}}}{3} \times \frac{1}{\underset{1}{\cancel{100}}} = \frac{1}{3}$

Thus, $33\frac{1}{3}\%$ is equivalent to the fraction $\frac{1}{3}$.

6. $11\frac{1}{9}\%$.

Technique 1:

Multiply $\frac{1}{9}$ by 100%: $\frac{1}{9} \times \frac{100}{1}\% = \frac{100}{9}\%$

Convert the improper
fraction ($\frac{100}{9}$) to a decimal: $\frac{100}{9} = 11.\overline{1}\%$

Or, change it to a mixed
number: $\frac{100}{9}\% = 11\frac{1}{9}\%$

Thus, $\frac{1}{9}$ is equivalent to both $11.\overline{1}\%$ and $11\frac{1}{9}\%$.

Technique 2:

Divide the fraction's bottom number (9) into the top number (1):

$$\begin{array}{r} 0.111 \text{ etc.} \\ 9)\overline{1.000} \text{ etc.} \\ \underline{0} \\ 10 \\ \underline{9} \\ 10 \\ \underline{9} \\ 10 \end{array}$$

Move the decimal point in the quotient two digits to the **right** and tack on a percent sign (%): $11.\overline{1}\%$

Note: $11.\overline{1}\%$ is equivalent to $11\frac{1}{9}\%$.

7. 30. Calculate the number of dentists who recommended sugarless gum using the $\frac{part}{whole}$ technique, and then subtract that number from the total number of dentists surveyed to get the number of dentists who did NOT recommend sugarless gum.

The **whole** is 300, and the **%** is 90: $\frac{part}{300} = \frac{90}{100}$

Cross multiply and solve for **part**: $part \times 100 = 300 \times 90$

$part \times 100 = 27,000$

Thus, **270** dentists recommended sugarless gum.

$270 \times 100 = 27,000$

Subtract the number of dentists who recommended sugarless gum from the number of dentists surveyed to get the number of dentists who did NOT recommend sugarless gum: $300 - 270 = 30$

8. 0.2.

2 is the **part** and 1,000 is the **whole**: $\frac{2}{1,000} = \frac{\%}{100}$

Cross multiply and solve for **%**: $2 \times 100 = 1,000 \times \%$

Thus, **0.2%** of the lightbulbs are assumed to be defective. $200 = 1,000 \times \%$

$200 = 1,000 \times 0.2$

9. $7,058.82. Since this question includes neither the word **is** nor **of**, it takes a little more effort to determine whether 600 is the **part** or the **whole**! Since $600 is equivalent to $8\frac{1}{2}\%$ tax, we can conclude that it is the **part**. The question is asking this: "$600 tax **is** $8\frac{1}{2}\%$ **of** what dollar amount of sales?"

Thus, 600 is the **part**, and $8\frac{1}{2}$ is the **%**: $\frac{600}{whole} = \frac{8\frac{1}{2}}{100}$

Cross multiply and solve for the **whole**: $600 \times 100 = whole \times 8\frac{1}{2}$

You must divide both $60,000 = whole \times 8\frac{1}{2}$

sides of the equation $60,000 \div 8\frac{1}{2} = whole \times$

by $8\frac{1}{2}$ to get the $8\frac{1}{2} \div 8\frac{1}{2}$

answer: $7,058.82 \cong whole$

Thus, $600 is $8\frac{1}{2}\%$ of approximately **$7,058.82** (rounded to the nearest cent), the total sales on May 1, excluding sales tax.

10. c. The amount of time Chris plans to spend playing racquetball next year is $78 + 0.50(78) = 117$ hours. The amount of time he plans to spend jogging next year is $208 - 0.10(208) = 187.2$ hours. So, the total time he plans to spend on these two activities next year is 304.2 hours. Since the time spent this year is 286 hours, the percent change is

$$\frac{304.2 - 286}{286} = 0.064 = 6.4\%$$

Choice **a** is incorrect because you must apply the two percentages to each activity separately: take 10% of 208 hours jogging and 50% of 78 hours playing racquetball. You instead added the percentages (50% + 10% = 60%) and applied the same percentage to the hours jogging and to the hours playing racquetball. Choice **b** is the *total number of hours* more that Chris plans to spend exercising next year over his exercise time this year. But the question asks for a percent change. Choice **d** is the number of hours (not percent) more that he plans to spend jogging next year than playing racquetball.

7

UNIT CONVERSIONS

The essence of mathematics is not to make simple things complicated, but to make complicated things simple.

—S. GUDDER

LESSON SUMMARY

This lesson covers unit conversions, which involve working with different quantities. You'll practice with different types of measurement problems that involve converting units, work with problems most often used on the SAT, and learn ways to solve them quickly.

This is a breather lesson—a short break from the more complex topics we've covered so far. If you have more stamina when you've finished it, you can combine it with the next lesson!

Unit conversion in mathematics is important when solving measurement problems in real-world situations. Many questions on the SAT will involve changing one unit of measurement to another. So, you will need to know about the unit conversion process to solve these types of problems.

What Is Unit Conversion?

For math problems that involve measurement, you will sometimes have to convert from one unit of measurement to another within the same problem. For instance, if you need to know the number of feet but are given yards, you will need to know how to convert feet to yards. This process is called **unit conversion**.

How Do Unit Conversions Work?

To compete a unit conversion, you need to multiply by a **conversion factor** or a rate. This will usually be given to you within a word problem. Calculating conversions involves rates, ratios, and proportions. Conversions can be very simple or one-step.

> **Example:** A typical car weighs 2,880 pounds. If 1 ton is 2,000 pounds, what is its weight in tons? To solve this, set up the proportion:
>
> $$\frac{1 \text{ ton}}{2,000 \text{ pounds}} = \frac{x \text{ tons}}{2,880 \text{ pounds}}$$
>
> Cross multiplying and solving for x yields
>
> $$2,000x = 2,880$$
> $$x = 1.44 \text{ tons}$$

On the other hand, multi-step unit conversions involve performing more than one unit conversion.

> **Example:** One gram of carbohydrates is 4 calories. A pastry has 1.3 ounces of carbohydrates. How many calories is the pastry if 1 ounce is approximately 28 grams? (Round to the nearest integer.)
>   This problem requires two unit conversions. There are
>
> $$1 \text{ gram of carbohydrate} = 4 \text{ calories}$$
> $$1 \text{ ounce} = 28 \text{ grams}$$

What we need to know:

$$1.3 \text{ ounces} = x \text{ calories}$$

These problems are relatively simple if you use the **chart method**. Setting up a chart is an easy and convenient way of keeping track of the multiple conversions. Start by sketching a chart as shown here:

Start by putting your initial unit of measure in the left-hand side of the chart. Notice how in the chart method we place similar units on opposite lines. For instance, we placed the grams on opposite lines of the chart. This is because we need to cancel out old units of measure to form new ones.

4 calories	28 grams	
1 gram	1 ounce	

The next step is to use the conversion factor to convert each old unit into the required unit.

4 calories	28 ~~grams~~	
1 ~~gram~~	1 ounce	

Now we can continue in the chart with the next ratio, which is what we want to find:

$$1.3 \text{ ounces} = x \text{ calories}$$

Again, we place the ounces on opposite lines so that we can cancel them.

4 calories	28 ~~grams~~	1.3 ounces
1 ~~gram~~	1 ounce	x calories

So, multiplying across the top and bottom yields

$$x = (4)(28)(1.3)$$
$$x = 145.6 \text{ or } 146 \text{ calories}$$

So, the pastry with 1.3 ounces of carbohydrates has about 146 calories in it.

Let's work on another multi-step conversion problem using the chart method.

Example: If the speed of light in a vacuum is 983,571,056 feet per second, what is the speed of light in a vacuum in miles per hour? (Hint: 1 mile = 5,280 ft.)

We're starting with an easier one, so let's set up our chart first:

983,571,056 ft	1 mile	3,600 s
s	5,280 ft	1 hr

After multiplying across the top and dividing by the bottom, we get a final answer:

(983,571,056)(3,600) mi/5,280 hr = 670,616,629 miles per hour

Here are some more conversion problems to practice with.

Practice

1. The typical human heart beats at 60 beats per minute. How many beats is this in a day?

2. A chair lift takes 8 minutes to transport 4 skiers at a time. How many hours would it take to transport 50 skiers? (Approximate to the nearest hour.)

3. A secretary types 90 words per minute (wpm). If the average page contains 500 words, how many pages per hour can the secretary type? (Round to the nearest whole number.)

4. A race car can travel 4 laps around a 2-mile racetrack in 1 minute. How many feet would the car travel for 1 lap?

SAT TEST-TAKING TIP

When you encounter SAT unit conversion questions, always be aware of what you're given and what you are trying to solve for. Always set up a chart so that it's clear which unit conversion factors you need to multiply by and which you need to divide by.

The following are some important unit conversions that show up frequently on the SAT. If you don't know these already, you should memorize them.

Length:
1 mile (mi.) = 5,280 feet (ft.)
1 mile (mi.) = 1,780 yards (yd.)
1 yard (yd.) = 3 feet (ft.)
1 foot (ft.) = 12 inches (in.)

1 kilometer (km) = 1,000 meters (m)
1 meter (m) = 100 centimeters (cm)
1 meter (m) = 1,000 millimeters (mm)
1 millimeter (mm) = 1,000 micrometers (μm)

Mass:
1 ton (T.) = 2,000 pounds (lb.)
1 pound (lb.) = 16 ounces (oz.)
1 kilogram (kg) = 1,000 grams (g)
1 gram (g) = 1,000 milligrams (mg)
1 milligram (mg) = 1,000 micrograms (μg)

Volume:
1 gallon (gal.) = 4 quarts (qt.)
1 quart (qt.) = 2 pints (pt.)
1 pint (pt.) = 16 ounces (oz.)

Answers and Explanations

1. 86,400. Using the chart method:

60 beats	60 ~~minutes~~	24 ~~hours~~
1 ~~minute~~	1 ~~hour~~	1 day

Cross out the common units from top and bottom. Multiply the numbers from all of the numerators and then multiply the numbers from all of the denominators. Notice that you are left with the units that are unknown. From doing this, you have that 1 day is $(60)(60)(24) =$ 86,400 beats.

2. 2 hours. Using the chart method:

4 skiers	60 ~~minutes~~	x hours
8 ~~minutes~~	1 hour	50 skiers

Cross out the common units from top and bottom. Multiply the numbers from all of the numerators and then multiply the numbers from all of the denominators. Notice that you are left with the units that are unknown. From doing this, you get $(8)(50) = (4)(60)(x)$, which leaves $400 = 240x$. Solving for x, you get that it takes 1.6 hours, which is approximately 2 hours to lift 50 skiers.

3. 11 pages. Using the chart method:

90 ~~words~~	1 page	60 ~~minutes~~	1 hour
1 ~~minute~~	500 ~~words~~	1 hour	x pages

Cross out the common units from top and bottom. Multiply the numbers from all of the numerators and then multiply the numbers from all of the denominators. Notice that you are left with the units that are unknown. From doing this, you get $(90)(60) = (500)(x)$. Solving for x yields $x = 10.8$, or approximately 11 pages.

4. 2,640. Using the chart method:

4 ~~laps~~	1 ~~mile~~	x feet
2 ~~miles~~	5,280 feet	1 ~~lap~~

Cross out the common units from top and bottom. Multiply the numbers from all of the numerators and then multiply the numbers from all of the denominators. Notice that you are left with the units that are unknown. From doing this, you get $4x = (2)(5,280)$. Solving for x yields $x = 2,640$ feet.

8 ▶ ANALYZING GRAPHS AND SCATTER PLOTS

Mathematics possesses not only truth, but supreme beauty.

—BERTRAND RUSSELL

LESSON SUMMARY
This lesson teaches you how to analyze graphs and scatter plots to solve word problems. You will focus on how the variables described are related based on the graphs or plots and learn easy tips for reading graphs or plots for the information you need.

Graphs are a visual representation of equations. Equations express the relationship between two real-world quantities. So, we can get a sense of how two quantities are related by looking at a graph. Similarly, scatter plots are used to visually represent values from a set of data. So, in a very quick way, you can get an idea as to how data values in a study are related to one another.

Analyzing Linear Graphs

Linear graphs are most often used to model a rate of change between two variables that is constant. The graph of a linear equation is a line in the standard form $y = mx + b$, where m is the slope or slant of the line and $(0,b)$ is where the line crosses the y-axis and is the y-intercept. A line can also cross the x-axis at an x-intercept point in the form $(a,0)$.

Lines can be slanted toward the left or toward the right. If you move along the x-axis from left to right, you can determine the slant of the line as positive (increasing) or negative (decreasing).

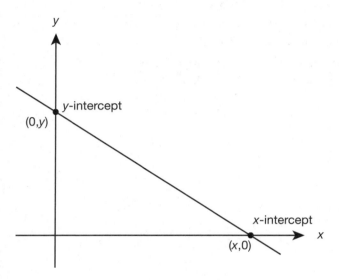

For linear graphs, the intercepts can tell you much about the relationship between the variables involved.

Example: The following linear graph displays the relationship between cellphone usage in hours per day and the corresponding amount of data given in GB data storage by a customer. Notice how as the number of hours used by the customer goes up, the amount of GB data storage given to the customer also increases. How much data storage is given to the customer when he or she uses no hours?

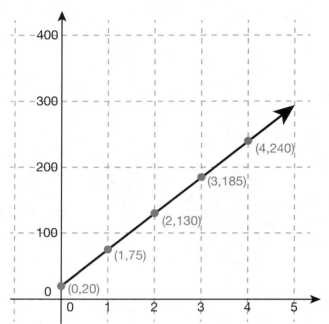

The y-intercept at $(0,20)$ of the graph in this context would mean that the customer used 0 minutes but still received 20 GB free of charge from the carrier company.

Example: The following linear graph shows a decline in the subscriber base of regular users for a new blog. The variable x gives the month of new subscribership within a two-year period (where 0 is January of the first year and 24 is December of the second year). The y-value gives the number of new social media subscribers to the blog.

What do the intercepts say about the variables here?

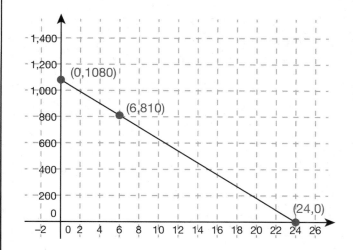

The point (0,1080) would represent the beginning of the blog's life, when the subscriber base is high at 1,080 regular users. But by the 24th month (24,0), the graph shows that there are 0 regular subscribers to the blog.

How to Interpret the Slope of a Line

The slope of a line represents the rate of change between points on the line. By calculating the change in the *y*-coordinates divided by the change in the *x*-coordinates of two data points, you can determine by how much the data is changing.

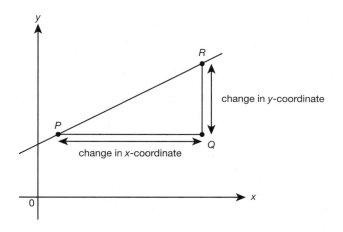

For linear graphs, the slant or direction of the line (positive or negative) tells about the variables being modeled in the situation in question. In addition, the actual slope value can tell you the rate of change of the data being modeled in the situation.

Let's look at some examples of linear graphs in which you can get information by looking at the slope of the graph.

Example: The following graph represents the number of coupons earned from purchasing a certain amount of groceries at a local supermarket.

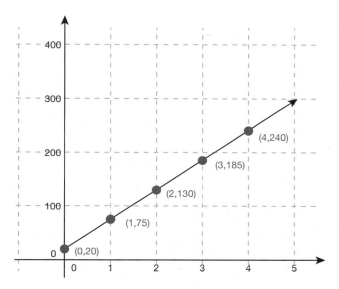

The positive direction of the line (toward the right side of the *x*-axis) indicates that as you purchase more, you receive more coupons. This is a good incentive, right? To find the actual rate of change, we take any two points (0,20) and (2,130) and calculate $\frac{130-20}{2-0} = \frac{110}{2}$, or 55.

Therefore, a slope of 55 in this situation means that for every $55 you spend, you'll get 1 coupon from the supermarket.

SAT TEST-TAKING TIP

When analyzing a line graph, pay attention to the general direction of the line to interpret a positive or negative relationship. Then, pay attention to the actual slope using the slope formula $\frac{\text{change in } y}{\text{change in } x}$ using points from the line.

Try these practice questions that involve interpreting the slope of a line.

Practice

1. The following graph represents sales in a local cupcake shop. Use the direction of the line and slope to find the cost per cupcake.

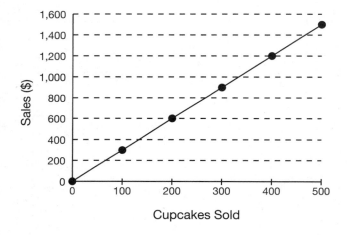

2. If the following graph represents the money earned by a 7-year-old for doing his chores over a period of 16 days, what can you say about his earnings, according to the slope and direction of the line?

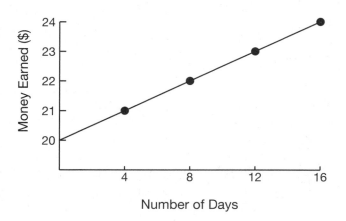

Analyzing Scatter Plots

A **scatter plot** is a collection of data points plotted on a graph. A scatter plot is used to show the relationship or correlation between two variables—its purpose is to show a visual picture of what the entire set of points looks like and how close the points are to each other.

Scatter plots can show a variety of relationships between two variables.

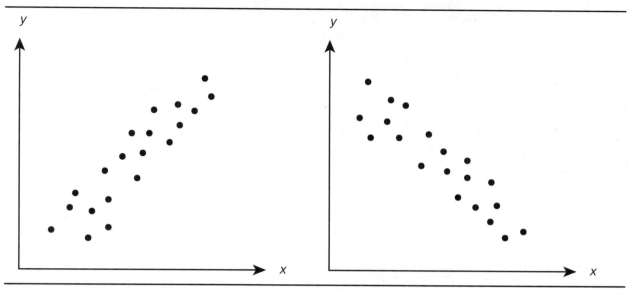

Positive Correlation. Notice how for each value of x that increases, the corresponding y value also increases. Also, the general direction of the scatter plot with a positive correlation looks like the points travel together toward the right side of the x-axis.

Negative Correlation. In this case, the overall scatter plot will show points that travel toward the left side of the x-axis. Also, as each individual x-value increases, the corresponding y-value decreases.

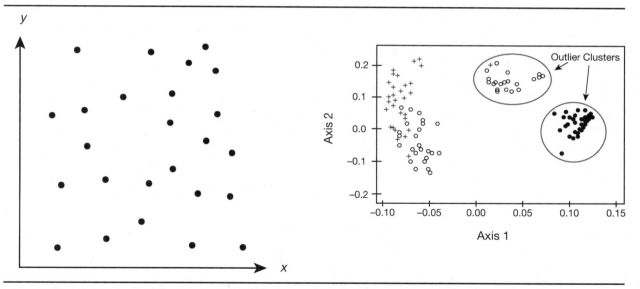

Non-Linear Patterns. On the other hand, if the variables are not related and do not influence each other's values, the scatter plot will show no correlation. In the case of no correlation, the points on the graph will "scatter" all over in a random-looking order, with no line shape at all. In this case, we say that there is a non-linear pattern.

Clustering Outliers. In a scatter plot, an outlier is a data point located outside the normal pattern of values. If you have a group of outliers, then you have what is called a **clustering outlier**. In the scatter plot above, you'll notice that there are many data points but that there are two groups on the right side that seem separate from the mass of data points on the left side. This is an example of clustering outlier groups that can exist within a set of data points.

On the SAT exam, questions that deal with scatter plots can range from choosing the appropriate scatter plot to combine other areas such as percents and functions such as linear, quadratic, and exponential functions.

Example: Which of the following graphs best shows a strong, positive, non-linear association between p and z?

a.

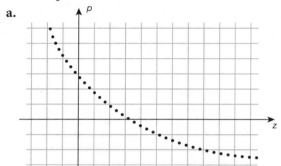

b.

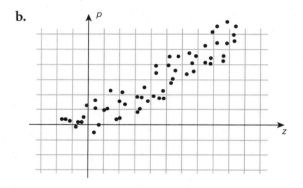

c.

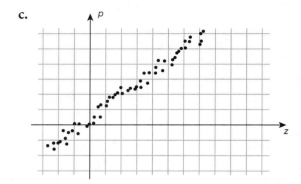

d.

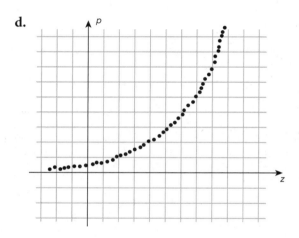

The relationship is strong because the points are tightly packed together. It is positive because the values rise from left to right. And it is non-linear because there is a discernible curve to the growth as you move from left to right. In fact, this would be best described by a function of the form $p = b \times a^z$, where a is positive and $b > 1$. Therefore, the correct answer is **d**.

Try some examples on your own.

Practice

3. The following scatter plot shows the average weekly counts of whale sightings off the coast of Alaska from 1998 to 2014.

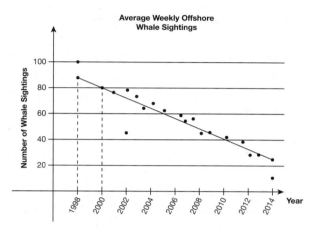

Average Weekly Offshore Whale Sightings

Using the line of best fit for the data shown, choose the answer that is the closest to the average yearly rate of decrease in the number of whale sightings.

a. 60
b. 5.6
c. 0.2
d. 5

4. Which of the following scatter plots shows a relationship that is approximately modeled by the equation $y = a \times b^x$, where $0 < b < 1$?

a.

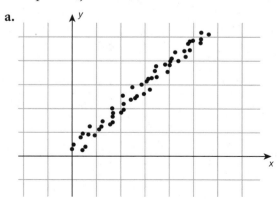

b.

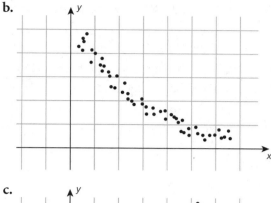

c.

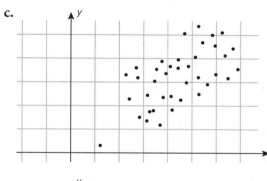

d.

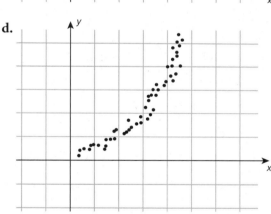

When answering questions on scatter plots, remember the types of associations (positive correlations, negative correlations, non-linear, outlier) and what they mean. Also, remember that scatter plot questions often combine with other areas, such as percents and linear, quadratic, and exponential functions.

Answers and Explanations

1. $3. According to the graph, the line has a positive slant, which means that the more cupcakes the shop sells, the more money it will make. Using the points (200,600) and (400,1200), find the slope by calculating change of y divided by change of x:

$$\frac{1{,}200-600}{400-200} = \frac{600}{200} = 3$$

This means that for every 1 cupcake sold, sales will increase by $3.

2. The direction of the line is positive, so the child is earning money over the 16 months. Also, using the points (4,21) and (8,22), we have that slope as change in y divided by change in x:

$$\frac{22-21}{8-4} = \frac{1}{4}$$

That means for every day, the child will earn $0.25 in allowance.

3. d. To estimate the slope of the line, use two points that clearly lie on the line (or very close to it). Using the points (1998,90) and (2000,80), we find that the slope is

$$\frac{90-80}{1998-2000} = -5$$

Since the slope is negative, we can conclude that the whale sightings are decreasing over time (which we already knew) and that the rate of this decrease is 5 weekly whale sightings per year. Choice **a** is the net difference (decrease) in the number of weekly whale sightings over this period, obtained using the points on the line at 1998 and 2014. This is not a *rate* of decrease. Choice **b** uses the highest point at 1998 (with value 100) and the lowest point at 2014 (with value 10) to compute the slope. But these choices are not on the best fit line, so they can't be used to compute its slope. Choice **c** is the reciprocal of the correct slope. You should divide the change in whale sightings by the change in year, not the other way around.

4. b. Viewed together, the points resemble an exponential curve that falls from left to right, which would have the equation $y = a \cdot b^x$, where $0 < b < 1$. Choice **a** is incorrect because this scatter plot would be best modeled by a straight line with equation $y = a + bx$, where $b > 0$. There is no clear association between x and y in choice **c**. In choice **d**, while the points do conform to a nonlinear curve, they rise from left to right, so they couldn't be modeled by the equation $y = a \cdot b^x$, where $0 < b < 1$, which describes a decaying exponential.

9 ▶ USING TWO-WAY TABLES TO ANALYZE DATA

Numbers are the highest degree of knowledge. It is knowledge itself.

—PLATO

LESSON SUMMARY

In this lesson, you will learn about categorical data and how to summarize it using relative frequencies. You will also calculate probabilities based on the data. This lesson presents common SAT questions in this area and tips for finding the answers from data tables given to you.

ave you ever wondered how many people your age have the same interests as you do? How would you ever find this out? You may think that you would have to ask the whole group, right? Statistics are about getting information from a group.

What Do Statistics Tell Us?

Through statistics, you can learn how to observe things about a group you are interested in. You can also make guesses or predictions about the members of a group. Your **observations** can be summarized by counting the number of times you observe an event that occurs. For example, if you wanted to find out how many males and females in your class use their computers to do their homework, you could survey your entire class. For each person who is a female and uses a computer, you would add 1 to your count. By the end of your survey, you would have the number of females, the number of males, and the number of people in each group who use a computer to do homework.

Using Categorical Data and Two-Way Tables

There are two variables in this survey—gender (female or male) and computer use for homework (yes or no). In this case, your variables have choices or categories and so the tallies you collect for them would be called categorical data. For **categorical data**, you can create an easy-to-use table with rows and columns to help you display the tallies that you counted during the surveys. This table is known as a **two-way table**.

What Is a Relative Frequency?

For your survey, you are observing the number of times each categorical variable occurs under its choices. For instance, you are counting the number of times the gender of the person in your class is a female and how many times a female uses a computer (yes). In statistics, these are called **frequencies**. On the other hand, if we count the number of times the gender of a person is a certain gender in "relation" to the total number of people in the class, we have a **relative frequency**.

Example: A survey of 100 students who were smartphone users was conducted to determine whether they stored pictures and their home address on their phones. The following two-way table was created from the data.

	HOME ADDRESS STORED	NO HOME ADDRESS STORED	TOTAL
Pictures stored	30/100	40/100	70/100
No pictures stored	20/100	10/100	30/100
Total	50/100	50/100	100/100

What information could you get from the table? (Notice that to get the relative frequencies, all of the entries of the table have been divided by the total number of students in the survey, 100.)

By considering each number and then tracing it back to the row header and column, we can learn about how the variables in the table are associated. For instance, just reading across the first row of the table we know that

- 30/100 students had both their pictures and their home address stored in their phones.
- 40/100 students had only their pictures stored in their phones.

By reading across the second row of the table, we know that

- 20/100 students had only their home address stored in their phones.
- 10/100 students had neither their pictures nor their home address stored in their phones.

By reading across the total row, we know that

- 50/100 students had their home address stored in their phones.
- 50/100 students did not have their home address in their phones.

By reading down the total column, we know that

- 70/100 students had their pictures stored in their phones.
- 30/100 students did not have their pictures stored in their phones.

Notice how both the total row and total column add up to 100, which is the number of students surveyed in the original problem.

Calculating Probabilities from Two-Way Tables

A probability is the chance or likelihood that an event will occur. With a probability, you are making an "educated guess" based on data that you already have. Probabilities can be calculated by looking at $\frac{event}{total \text{ \# of occurrences}}$.

Here is an example of computing probabilities from a two-way table.

Example: A car dealership asks 200 of its customers what color car they like. Fifty answer blue, 30 answer red, 25 like both blue and red, and the rest do not like either color.

Here is the data shown in a two-way table of frequencies.

	LIKES BLUE CARS	DOES NOT LIKE BLUE CARS	TOTAL
Likes red cars	25	30	55
Does not like red cars	50	95	145
Total	75	125	200

If a customer is randomly selected, what is the probability that if she likes red cars, she also likes blue cars?

In this case, the number of customers who like red cars is 55. Out of 55, the number of customers who also like blue cars is 25. So, the probability that a customer will like red and blue cars is 25/55, or 0.45, which is 45%.

What is the probability that a customer surveyed will like blue cars?

Out of the 200 customers surveyed, there are 75 who like blue cars. The probability is 75/200, which is 0.375, or 37.5%.

SAT Problems Involving Two-Way Tables

Problems that involve two-way tables come in the following varieties:

1. those that ask you to fill in missing values of a table,
2. those that ask you to calculate probabilities from the table, and
3. those that ask you to do both!

In this example, notice that some values from the two-way table are missing.

> **Example:** A coffee shop has introduced a new style of mug for its customers. The customers from the morning and evening shifts were asked if they liked the new mug. The following table shows the responses from their interviews.

	LIKES MUG	DOES NOT LIKE MUG	TOTAL
Morning shift	89		100
Evening shift	54	46	100
Total	143		200

Here are some typical questions the SAT test might ask about the table.

1. Complete the missing values in the table.

	LIKES MUG	DOES NOT LIKE MUG	TOTAL
Morning shift	89	100 − 89 = 11	100
Evening shift	54	46	100
Total	143	200 − 143 = **57**	200

2. How many customers showed up for the morning shift? Evening shift?

There are 100 customers in the shop during the morning shift and 100 customers in the evening shift.

3. How many customers like the mug?

A total of 143 customers like the mug.

4. Based on this data, what is the probability that customers who visit the shop during the evening shift will NOT like the new mug?

Out of the 100 customers who came during the evening, 46 did not like the new mug. So, the probability is 46/100, or 46%, that customers in the evening will not like the new mug.

5. Based on this data, what is the probability that customers who like the mug will be there during the morning?

Out of the 143 customers who like the mug, 89 of them are there in the morning. So, the probability is 89/143, which is 0.62, or 62%.

Now, try some on your own.

Practice

1. The following table shows the "varsity athlete" status of all sophomores, juniors, and seniors at a high school one year.

	IS A VARSITY ATHLETE	IS NOT A VARSITY ATHLETE	TOTAL
Sophomore			
Junior	40	95	
Senior		80	135
Total	130		370

Of the students classified as varsity athletes, what proportion are sophomores?
a. 7/26
b. 13/37
c. 7/74
d. 7/20

Use the following information to answer questions 2–4.

Data from a survey of the news sources for 160 freshmen and sophomore students in a community college is presented in the following table. It shows the proportion of freshman and sophomore students who get their news from TV and/or the Internet.

	TV	INTERNET	TOTAL
Freshman	50		62
Sophomore		78	98
Total	70	90	160

2. Complete the table with the missing values.

3. What percentage of students who get their news from TV are freshmen? _____

4. What percentage of students who get their news from the Internet are sophomores?

_____

SAT TEST-TAKING TIP

Pay attention to what the question is asking.
- If the question gives a table that has missing values, you should add or subtract from existing table values.
- If the question asks for the probability, then you should calculate $\frac{event}{total\ \#\ of\ occurrences}$.
- If the question asks for a proportion, then you need to answer "How many out of a total?"

Let's walk through another example together.

Example: The following table summarizes the test results of 500 high school students who wish to become qualified as a lifeguard.

	PASSED LIFEGUARD TEST	FAILED LIFEGUARD TEST
Member of the high school swim team	110	30
Not a member of the high school swim team	80	280

If one of these students is selected at random, what is the probability that the person chosen passed the test and does not belong to the high school swim team?
a. 0.72
b. 0.84
c. 0.16
d. 0.38

The criteria are satisfied by the students indicated in the lower left cell of the table. Since there are 500 students total and 80 of them satisfy the criteria, the probability is 80/500 = 0.16. Therefore, choice **c** is correct. Choice **a** is the probability that the student selected is not on the high school swim team. It doesn't account for him or her passing the lifeguard test. Choice **b** is the probability of the complement, namely "either failed the test or belongs to the high school swim team." Choice **d** is the probability that the chosen student passed the lifeguard test. It does not account for whether the student belongs to the high school swim team.

Practice

5. A school superintendent proposed a change to the daily schedule that would extend the school day by 15 minutes. Two hundred faculty members, staff, and students from high schools in her district were asked to provide their opinions. The following table shows their responses:

	OPPOSE	FAVOR	NEUTRAL	TOTAL
Faculty	20	55	5	80
Staff	32	8	30	70
Students	40	10	0	50
Total	92	73	35	200

If a person is chosen at random from those who were not neutral on the issue, what is the probability that the person was a faculty member?

a. 5/11
b. 15/16
c. 2/5
d. 33/40

Compound Probability

Some two-way table problems may ask you to calculate "compound" probabilities. These are probabilities that would involve adding up numbers in two or more columns. Take a look at the following example.

Example: Joanna wanted to get a sense of the performance of three major airlines when it came to flights being on time or delayed. To compare the airlines, she randomly selected 200 flights and charted their arrival times in the following table:

NO. OF FLIGHTS BY ARRIVAL TIME					
AIRLINE	ON TIME OR EARLY	LATE BY LESS THAN 15 MINUTES	LATE BY 15 TO 30 MINUTES	LATE BY MORE THAN 30 MINUTES	TOTAL
A	7	42	0	11	60
B	7	18	25	33	83
C	30	12	5	10	57
Total	44	72	30	54	200

If a flight selected at random comes from either Airline A or Airline C, what is the probability that the flight is at least 15 minutes late?

Since we're told that the flight is operated by Airline A or Airline C, look at those rows only: the total number of flights under consideration is 117. Now, since we want to know the proportion of these 117 flights that are at least 15 minutes late, add the third and fourth columns in the first and third rows to get

$$\frac{0 + 11 + 5 + 10}{117} = \frac{26}{117} = \frac{2}{9}$$

The probability is $\frac{2}{9}$.

Practice

6. The following table shows the distribution of the gender of 50 online shoppers and their answers to the question, "Do you routinely preorder paper goods from an online retailer?"

	YES	NO	TOTAL
Male	8	3	11
Female	12	27	39
Total	20	30	50

If a shopper is selected at random, what is the probability that the shopper will either be female or answer "yes" to this question? Enter your answer as a decimal. _____

Answers and Explanations

1. a. First, you need to fill in the missing information in the table, as follows:

	IS A VARSITY ATHLETE	IS NOT A VARSITY ATHLETE	TOTAL
Sophomore	35	65	100
Junior	40	95	135
Senior	55	80	135
Total	130	240	370

Since we are asked about varsity athletes, we restrict our attention to the first column, so that the number of students of concern is 130, not the entire 370 with which we began. Of these students, 35 are sophomores. So, the desired proportion is 35/130 = 7/26. Choice **b** is the proportion of the entire sample (including juniors and seniors) who are varsity athletes. Choice **c** is incorrect because the phrase "Of the students classified as varsity athletes" indicates that you need to restrict your attention to only those students as your new sample space. As such, divide 35 by 130, not 370. Choice **d** restricts attention to the wrong subset from the beginning. This is the proportion of sophomores who are varsity athletes, not the proportion of varsity athletes who are sophomores.

2.

	TV	INTERNET	TOTAL
Freshmen	50	90 − 78 = **12**	62
Sophomores	70 − 50 = **20**	78	98
Total	70	90	160

3. 31% (50/160) of the students who get their news from TV are freshmen.

4. 49% (78/160) of students who get their news from the Internet are sophomores.

5. a. Since the selection is being made from those sampled who did not remain neutral, we must restrict our attention to the first two columns, so the sample space of interest has 165 (not 200) people. Of these, there are 75 faculty members, so the desired probability is 75/165 = 5/11. Choice **b** is the proportion of faculty members who had an opinion. Choice **c** is the probability that a randomly chosen person from this sample was a faculty member. Choice **d** is the probability that a randomly chosen person from this sample did not remain neutral.

6. 0.94. The event for which we're computing the probability is "Female or Yes." To do so, we must use the addition formula:

$$P(\text{Female or Yes}) = P(\text{Female}) + P(\text{Yes}) - P(\text{Female and Yes})$$

$$= \frac{39}{50} + \frac{20}{50} - \frac{12}{50}$$

$$= \frac{47}{50} = 0.94$$

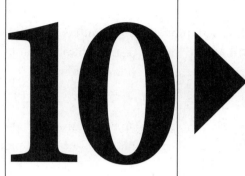

10 ▶ MAKING CONCLUSIONS WITH STATISTICAL MEASURES

Anyone who has never made a mistake has never tried anything new.

—ALBERT EINSTEIN

LESSON SUMMARY

This lesson teaches you about statistical measures for the center and spread of data. You'll learn the difference between mean, median, mode, interquartile range (IQR), range, and standard deviation. We'll also cover how to infer and justify conclusions from the statistics you calculate.

Using statistical measures to summarize data is important when studying real-life situations. When given a set of numerical data, information about the center values of the data set can be found by calculating the mean, median, and mode, which together are referred to as the **measures of central tendency.** By knowing about the center values of a data set, we can learn what the "typical" value is like and use it to then describe the entire data set.

Measuring the Center of Data

Let's look at a group of numbers, such as the number of students in a classroom at the Chancellor School, and compute these three measures of central tendency.

ROOM #	1	2	3	4	5	6	7	8	9
# of students	15	15	11	16	15	17	16	30	18

Mean (Average)

The mean (average) of a group of numbers is the sum of the numbers divided by the number of numbers:

$$\text{Average} = \frac{\text{sum of the numbers}}{\text{number of numbers}}$$

Example: Find the **average** number of students in a classroom at the Chancellor School.

Solution

$$\textit{Average} = \frac{15 + 15 + 11 + 16 + 15 + 17 + 16 + 30 + 18}{9}$$
$$= \frac{153}{9}$$
$$\textit{Average} = 17$$

The **average** (**mean**) number of students in a classroom at the Chancellor School is **17**. Do you find it curious that only two classrooms have more students than the average or that the average isn't right smack in the middle of the list of numbers being averaged? Read on to find out about a measure that is right in the middle of things.

Median

The median of a group of numbers is the number in the middle when the numbers are arranged in order.

When there is an even number of numbers, the median is the average of the two middle numbers.

Example: Find the **median** number of students in a classroom at the Chancellor School.

Solution: Simply list the numbers in order (from low to high or from high to low) and identify the number in the middle:

11   15   15   15 $\boxed{16}$ 16   17   18   30

Had there been an even number of classrooms, then there would have been two middle numbers:

$$15\tfrac{1}{2}$$
$$\downarrow$$

9   11   15   15 $\boxed{15}$ $\boxed{16}$ 16   17   18   30

With ten classrooms instead of nine, the median is the average of 15 and 16, or $15\tfrac{1}{2}$, which is also halfway between the two middle numbers.

If a number above the median is increased significantly or if a number below the median is decreased significantly, the *median* is not affected. On the other hand, such a change can have a dramatic impact on the *mean*—as did the one classroom with 30 students in the previous example. Because the median is less affected by quirks in the data than the mean, the median tends to be a better measure of central tendency for such data.

Consider the annual income of the residents of a major metropolitan area. A few multimillionaires could substantially raise the *average* annual income, but they would have no more impact on the *median* annual income than a few above-average wage earners. Thus, the *median* annual income is more representative of the residents than the *mean* annual income. In fact, you can conclude that the annual income for half the residents is greater than or equal to the *median*, while the annual income for the other half is less than or equal to the *median*. The same cannot be said for the *average* annual income.

> ⚠ **CAUTION**
>
> You *must* arrange the numbers in order when computing a median, but not a mean or mode.

Mode

The mode of a group of numbers is the number(s) that appears most often.

Example: Find the **mode**, the most common classroom size, at the Chancellor School.

Solution: Scanning the data reveals that there are more classrooms with 15 students than any other size, making **15** the mode:

11 $\boxed{15}$ $\boxed{15}$ $\boxed{15}$ 16 16 17 18 30

Had there also been three classrooms of, say, 16 students, the data would be **bimodal**—both **15** and **16** are the modes for this group:

11 $\boxed{15}$ $\boxed{15}$ $\boxed{15}$ $\boxed{16}$ $\boxed{16}$ $\boxed{16}$ 17 18 30

On the other hand, had there been an equal number of classrooms of each size, the group would NOT have a mode—no classroom size appears more frequently than any other:

11 11 13 13 15 15 17 17 19 19

Example: The data set {4, 5, 3, 5, 1, 4, 6, 1, 3, 2} represents the number of hits Johnny made in his last 10 baseball games. The hits made by his teammate Paulo are given by {4, 2, 1, 7, 3, 5, 5, 2, 2, 3}. Compare and contrast the measures of central tendency for the players.

For Johnny {4, 5, 3, 5, 1, 4, 6, 1, 3, 2}:

1. The mean is $\frac{4+5+3+5+1+4+6+1+3+2}{10}$ = 3.4.
2. The median is {4, 5, 3, 5, 1, 4, 6, 1, 3, 2} = (1, 1, 2, 3, 3, 4, 4, 5, 5, 6) = $\frac{3+4}{2}$ = 3.5.
3. The modes are 1, 3, 4, and 5, which all appear twice.

For Paulo {4, 2, 1, 7, 3, 5, 5, 2, 2, 3}:

1. The mean is $\frac{4+2+1+7+3+5+5+2+2+3}{10}$ = 3.4.
2. The median is {4, 2, 1, 7, 3, 5, 5, 2, 2, 3} = (1, 2, 2, 2, 3, 3, 4, 5, 5, 7) = $\frac{3+3}{2}$ = 3.
3. The mode is 2, which appears three times.

In summary, both Johnny and Paulo have the same average number of hits per game. For Johnny, the average number of hits is closer to the true middle of his data than the mean for Paulo is.

> **SAT TEST-TAKING TIP**
>
> Most SAT questions involving measuring central tendency include a chart or table of data values to use. Don't be thrown off by how the data is presented. Remember the definition of mean, median, and mode.
>
> | Mean = Average |
> | --- |
> | Median = Middle |
> | Mode = Most frequent |

Try the following practice question on your own.

Practice

1. Consider the following bar chart:

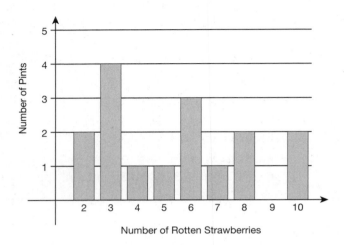

Number of Rotten Strawberries

Based on this information, what is the median number of rotten strawberries per pint?

2. The following graph shows the frequency distribution of the number of minutes an employee spends on his or her meeting with a supervisor to discuss the annual performance review.

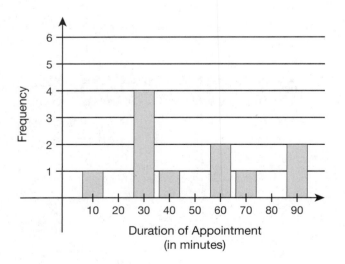

Duration of Appointment
(in minutes)

What is the approximate mean duration of these meetings?
a. 40 minutes
b. 49 minutes
c. 30 minutes
d. 54 minutes

3. The following bar graph describes the amount of wood burned (measured in cords) for a sample of 16 neighbors.

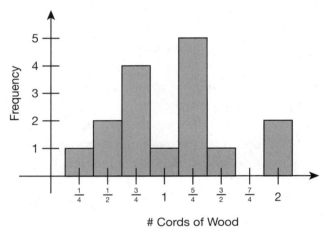

Cords of Wood

Based on this information, what is the median amount of wood burned? _____

Measuring the Spread of Data

Measures that are used to summarize the spread of the values in data sets are called **measures of variability**. The range and interquartile range (IQR) each give information on how numbers in a data set spread out from the center. Different than the central tendency measures, variability measures give a different view of a distribution of data values.

The **range** is the highest minus the lowest value of a data set. This measure of variability tells you how spread out the values in a data set are. The higher the number for the range, the more spread or variability within a data set. This means that the values in the set are all over the spectrum and not consistently close to each other.

For example, for the data set {96, 75, 80, 88, 90, 93, 79, 70, 82, 86}, the range is 96 − 70 = 26. This number is somewhat low, which means that the values are pretty close together.

Take a look at another example of data that represents the weight in pounds of dogs at a dog show, given by {65, 70, 76, 80, 70, 88, 88, 70, 90}. Another measure of variability is called the **interquartile range**, or **IQR**. It tells us about the values in the middle 50% of the data set.

- The range gives the difference between the lowest (65) and highest (90) weight (range = 25).
- IQR gives the middle 50% of the data when it is ordered from smallest to largest.

To find the IQR, first put the data values in order. Then, follow these steps:

1. Find the median (middle) of the data set → 65, 70, 70, 70, **76**, 80, 88, 88, 90.
2. Find the middle value of the data to the left of the middle ("left-middle") and to the right of the middle ("right-middle") → 65, **70, 70**, 70, **76**, 80, **88, 88**, 90
   - Left-middle = $\frac{70+70}{2}$ = 70
   - Right-middle = $\frac{88+88}{2}$ = 88
3. Subtract the two middle values → 88 − 70 = 18. This is the IQR of the data set.

   Example: Compare the following data sets by looking at the range and IQR.

   Set A = {18, 16, 35, 20, 24, 66, 35}
   Set B = {24, 18, 30, 22, 21, 25, 37}

For Set A = {18, 16, 35, 20, 24, 66, 35}:
Range = 66 − 16 = 50
For the IQR:
Ordered set = {16, 18, 20, 24, 35, 35, 66}
Upper quartile = 35
Lower quartile = 18
IQR = 35 − 18 = 17

For Set B = {24, 18, 30, 22, 21, 25, 37}:
Range = 37 − 18 = 19
For the IQR:
Ordered set = {18, 21, 22, 24, 25, 30, 37}
Upper quartile = 30
Lower quartile = 21
IQR = 30 − 21 = 9

In summary, data set A has a much higher range, which means that values are spread out more. An IQR confirms this because it too is much higher than the IQR for data set B.

Practice

4. At a sporting equipment store, every employee receives a $1,000 bonus in addition to his or her salary. How does adding this bonus impact the mean and the range of employee salaries at the company?
   a. The mean and range remain the same.
   b. Both the mean and range increase.
   c. The mean remains the same, but the range increases.
   d. The mean increases, but the range remains the same.

Standard Deviation

The standard deviation of a set of data tells you, on average, how far each number is away from the mean value. Think of the standard deviation as an indicator of the "distance" each number is away from the mean.

Calculating the standard deviation for a set of data values is easy if you remember four steps.

Given a set of numbers, {1, 2, 3, 4, 5}:

1. Find the mean: $\frac{15}{5} = 3$.
2. Find the distances of each number from the mean (ignore positive or negative numbers; just think of distance):

$$(1 - 3) = 2$$
$$(2 - 3) = 1$$
$$(3 - 3) = 0$$
$$(4 - 3) = 1$$
$$(5 - 3) = 2$$

3. Find the mean of the distances squared:

$$\frac{4 + 1 + 0 + 1 + 4}{5} = \frac{10}{5} = 2$$

4. Take the square root: $\sqrt{2}$. _____

SAT TEST-TAKING TIP

Some students think of the standard deviation as a longer calculation that requires setting up tables and using big formulas. On the SAT exam, the standard deviation does not make up the majority of questions, so you should not spend much time on the actual calculations. If you remember the four steps, you can round a bit and still arrive at an answer close to the actual standard deviation. Also, a good number of the questions for standard deviation will be multiple choice, so you will be able to quickly eliminate answers that do not make any sense.

Use your shortcut to finding the standard deviation to answer the following question.

Practice

5. The following tables show the distribution of the number of reported power outages each day of the week for two Internet providers, Company X and Company Y.

COMPANY X	
DAY	NUMBER OF REPORTED OUTAGES
Monday	1
Tuesday	2
Wednesday	1
Thursday	0
Friday	2
Saturday	10
Sunday	2

COMPANY Y	
DAY	NUMBER OF REPORTED OUTAGES
Monday	2
Tuesday	10
Wednesday	2
Thursday	0
Friday	1
Saturday	2
Sunday	1

Which of the following statements is true?

a. The standard deviation of the number of reported outages for one week for Company X is larger.
b. The standard deviation of the number of reported outages for one week for Company Y is larger.

c. Company Y and Company X have the same standard deviation of the number of reported outages for one week.

d. The standard deviations cannot be calculated using the data provided.

6. A Halloween specialty store discounts all costumes by $10 two days before Halloween to encourage customers to purchase them. If the store sells 150 costumes as a result, how does the discount impact the mean and standard deviation of the profit data had the discount never been applied to these 150 costumes?

a. The mean decreases and standard deviation increases.

b. The mean decreases and standard deviation remains the same.

c. The mean and standard deviation both remain unchanged.

d. The mean and standard deviation both decrease.

SAT TEST-TAKING TIP

Remember the shortcut definitions for each of the statistical measures: mean, median, mode, range, and standard deviation. This will give you a hint on what steps you need to find them.

mean = average
median = middle
mode = most frequent
range = beginning − end
standard deviation = distance from mean

Answers and Explanations

1. **5.5.** Since there are 16 data points, we must identify the 8th and 9th values of the ordered data set and then average them. The 8th value is 5 and the 9th value is 6. The median of 5 and 6 is 5.5.

2. **b.** Add all 11 times (obtained from the bar graph) and divide the sum by 11:

$$\frac{10 + 30(4) + 40 + 60(2) + 70 + 90(2)}{11} = \frac{540}{11} \approx 49$$

Choice **a** is the median time, not the mean time. Choice **c** is the mode (or most frequently occurring) time. In choice **d**, you divided the sum of all times by 10, not 11.

3. $\frac{9}{8}$ **cords.** Since there are 16 data points, we must identify the 8th and 9th values of the ordered data set (which is already the case because the x-values along the x-axis increase from left to right) and average them. The 8th value is 1, and the 9th value is $\frac{5}{4}$. The median is the average of these two numbers, namely $\frac{1 + \frac{5}{4}}{2} = \frac{\frac{9}{4}}{2} = \frac{9}{8}$ cords.

4. **d.** The mean must increase because all of the data values being summed have increased. In fact, it will increase by $1,000. Also, the range remains the same since the bonus is added to everyone's salary. So, if m represented the smallest salary and M represented the largest salary before the bonus, the range would be $M - m$. After the bonus, $m + 1,000$ and $M + 1,000$ would be the new minimum and maximum salaries, but the difference between these is also $M - m$. Choice **a** is incorrect because the mean must increase since all of the data values being summed have increased. Choice **b** is incorrect because the range remains the same since the bonus is added to everyone's salary. Choice **c** is incorrect because the mean goes up by $1,000 and the range remains the same.

5. c. We are interested in the numerical data sets {1, 2, 1, 0, 2, 10, 2} and {2, 10, 2, 0, 1, 2, 1}. Since the two sets are identical (the order in which elements of a set are listed is irrelevant), the means and standard deviations of the sets are identical. Choices **a** and **b** are incorrect because although the actual values occur on different days of the week for the two companies, the standard deviation is calculated only from the values in the data set, and order does not affect the values. So they have the same standard deviation. Choice **d** is incorrect because the standard deviation can be determined.

6. b. The mean must decrease because all of the data values being summed have decreased. In fact, it will decrease by $10. Also, the spread of the data remains unchanged because the same number is subtracted from all values in the data set; as such, the standard deviation remains the same. Choices **a** and **d** are incorrect because while the mean does indeed decrease, the spread of the data remains unchanged because the same number is subtracted from all values in the data set; as such, the standard deviation remains the same. Choice **c** is incorrect because the mean must decrease because all of the data values being summed have decreased.

11 ▶ PROBLEM-SOLVING WITH QUADRATIC AND EXPONENTIAL FUNCTIONS

I think, therefore I am.

—RENÉ DESCARTES

LESSON SUMMARY

For this lesson, you will work with quadratic and exponential functions. The lesson covers their equations and how to set them up in word problems. You'll see how both types of functions are appropriate for modeling different types of situations. You will learn when to use which type of equations and the strategies for solving problems involving the use of quadratic and exponential functions on the SAT exam.

While linear equations are great for modeling any situation that involves a quantity that is changing at a constant rate, they are not sufficient for situations that involve other rates of change. A quadratic function is an equation in the form $f(x) = ax^2 + bx + c$. It can be used to model a rate of change that increases, reaches a high point called a **maximum**, and then decreases. It can also be used to model the reverse situation, decreasing to a low point and then increasing again. The highest (or lowest) point for a quadratic function $f(x) = ax^2 + bx + c$ can be found by computing $x = -\frac{b}{2a}$.

On the other hand, an exponential function is appropriate to use when the rate of change increases or decreases very rapidly. For example, if you saved money at a compounding interest rate, the money would grow rapidly in the bank. An exponential function is perfect for this situation because the rate of change is constantly increasing. The reverse is also true, however. Exponential functions can also be used to model decaying situations in that the rate of change could be negative or decreasing rapidly. The exponential function is an equation in the form y or $f(x) = b^x$, where b is the **base** (a real number) raised to the power or exponent x.

Problem Solving with Quadratic and Exponential Functions

When working with quadratic and exponential functions in word problems, it is important to know how to set them up and how to work with them. So, first take a look at the quadratic equation and how it is solved to answer the question.

Take a look at the following example.

Example: You have a patio that is 8 ft. by 10 ft. You want to increase the size of the patio to 168 square ft. by adding the same length to both sides of the patio. Let x = the length you will add to each side of the patio.

You find the area of a rectangle by multiplying the length by the width. The new area of the patio will be 168 square ft.

	$(x + 8)(x + 10) = 168$
FOIL the factors $(x + 8)(x + 10)$.	$x^2 + 10x + 8x + 80 = 168$
Simplify.	$x^2 + 18x + 80 = 168$
Subtract 168 from both sides of the equation.	$x^2 + 18x + 80 - 168 = 168 - 168$
Simplify both sides of the equation.	$x^2 + 18x - 88 = 0$
Factor.	$(x + 22)(x - 4) = 0$
Set each factor equal to zero.	$x + 22 = 0$ and $x - 4 = 0$
Solve the equation.	$x + 22 = 0$
Subtract 22 from both sides of the equation.	$x + 22 - 22 = 0 - 22$
Simplify both sides of the equation.	$x = -22$
Solve the equation.	$x - 4 = 0$
Add 4 to both sides of the equation.	$x - 4 + 4 = 0 + 4$
Simplify both sides of the equation.	$x = 4$

Because this is a quadratic equation, you can expect two answers. The answers are 4 and −22. However, −22 is not a reasonable answer. You cannot have a negative length. Therefore, the correct answer is 4.

Check: The original dimensions of the patio were 8 ft. by 10 ft. If you were to add 4 to each side, the new dimensions would be 12 ft. by 14 ft. When you multiply 12 times 14, you get 168 square ft., which is the new area you wanted.

Now, try the following problems. In each one, set up the appropriate quadratic equation. Do not solve the quadratic equation—we'll focus on methods of solving these equations in the next lesson.

Practice

1. An ice cream manufacturer has daily production costs of $C(x) = 70{,}000 - 120x + 0.055x^2$, where C is the total cost (in dollars) and x is the number of units produced. Write an equation that can be used to find the number of units needed to produce \$4,546. _____

2. A water fountain sprouts water into the fountain basin at a speed of 10 inches per second. The function $d(x) = 4 + vx - 10x^2$ can be used to model this situation, where d is the distance (in inches) the water travels, v is the speed of the water, and x is time in seconds. Write an equation that can be used to model the flow of water from the time it leaves the spout to the time it hits the fountain basin.

_____

Let's look at a tougher one together.

Example: A golf ball is hit at a velocity of 100 feet per second at an angle of 45 degrees. The path of the golf ball can be modeled by $f(x) = -0.0032x^2 + x + 3$, where x is distance from the next golf hole in feet and $f(x)$ is the height of the golf ball in feet. What equation would be used to determine if the golf ball traveled higher than a 10-foot lookout tower located 300 feet from the next golf hole?

In this scenario, variable x is the distance from the next golf hole in feet and the $f(x)$ is the height of the golf ball. The question asks how to find out $f(x)$ when x is 300 feet.

So, the equation should be $f(300)$ or $f(x) = -0.0032(300)^2 + (300) + 3$.

Working with Exponential Functions

Exponential functions are perfect for modeling growth and decay in real-life situations. Equations for modeling growth and decay can also be derived from a general exponential growth model. An exponential function has the general form of $f(x) = b^x$, where b represents the base number and x is the power or exponent to which the base number is raised. A common exponential function is the one used for compounding interest:

$$A = P\left(1 + \frac{r}{n}\right)^{rt}$$

In this equation, A is the account balance, P is the principal, r is the interest rate, and n is the number of compounding periods (usually in years).

Example: John and Heather have deposited their house savings of \$26,600 into a savings account at a bank that compounds interest at a rate of 3% annually. Write an equation that represents the savings plan that compounds interest at a rate of 3% annually. If an alternative CD plan has the same terms but a rate of 2.5% quarterly, what is the equation that represents the change in the savings plan?

For 3% annually:

Use the compound interest formula,
$A = P(1 + \frac{r}{n})^{rt}$, to represent the savings plan.

$$A_1 = P(1 + \frac{r}{n})^{rt}$$
$$A_1 = 26{,}600(1.03)^{(0.03)(3)}$$
$$A_1 = 26{,}600(1.03)^{0.09}$$

The equation $A_1 = 26{,}600(1.03)^{0.09}$ represents the savings plan that compounds interest at a rate of 3% annually.

For 2.5% quarterly:

Again, use the compound interest formula,
$A = P(1 + \frac{r}{n})^{rt}$, to represent the savings plan.

$$A_2 = P(1 + \frac{r}{n})^{rt}$$
$$A_2 = 26{,}600(1.006)^{0.025(12)}$$
$$A_2 = 26{,}600(1.006)^3$$

The equation $A_2 = 26{,}600(1.006)^3$ represents the savings plan that compounds interest at a rate of 2.5% quarterly.

Practice

3. The exponential equation $A = 108.3e^{0.012t}$ describes the population of a country in millions of people for t years after 2003. What function models the population in the year 2030? _____

4. The value of a laptop diminishes by 8% each year. If the initial cost of the laptop is $2,150, which of the following expressions represents how much the laptop's value decreases in dollars between years n and $n + 1$?
   a. $2{,}150(0.92)^{n+1} - 2{,}150(0.92)^n$
   b. $2{,}150(0.92)^{n+1/n}$
   c. $2{,}150(0.92)^{n-(n+1)}$
   d. $2{,}150[(0.92)^n - (0.92)^{n+1}]$

5. An employee's salary increases by 2.6% annually. If the starting salary is $42,500, which of the following functions models the salary (in dollars) n years later?
   a. $f(n) = 42{,}500(1.026)^n$
   b. $f(n) = 1.026(42{,}500)^n$
   c. $f(n) = 42{,}500(0.026)^n$
   d. $f(n) = 0.026(42{,}500)^n$

Answers and Explanations

1. **$4{,}546 = 70{,}000 - 120x + 0.055x^2$.** x is the number of units needed to produce. $C(x)$ is the total cost (in dollars) from x number of units produced. If the cost is \$4,546, this means that $C(x) = 4{,}546$. So, the equation would be $4{,}546 = 70{,}000 - 120x + 0.055x^2$.

2. **$d = 4 + 10x - 10x^2$.** The original function $d = 4 + vx - 10x^2$ states that v represents the speed of the water. The problem also states that the water travels at a speed of 10 in./sec. Therefore, substitute 10 for v.

   $$d = 4 + vx - 10x^2 \qquad \text{Original equation}$$
   $$d = 4 + 10x - 10x^2 \qquad \text{Substitute 10 for } v.$$

   The function $d = 4 + 10x - 10x^2$ can be used to model the flow of the water.

3. **$A = 108.3e^{0.324}$.** The question is asking for the equation for the value of t that represents the year 2030. To find the value of t, subtract $2030 - 2003$, which is 27. So, $t = 27$ in the equation $A = 108.3e^{0.012t}$, which is $108.3e^{0.324}$.

4. **d.** The value of the laptop in year n is $2{,}150(0.92)^n$, and the value in year $n + 1$ is $2{,}150(0.92)^{n+1}$. So the amount by which the value decreases from year n to year $n + 1$ is $2{,}150(0.92)^n - 2{,}150(0.92)^{n+1}$, which is equivalent to $2{,}150[(0.92)^n - (0.92)^{n+1}]$. Choice **a** is incorrect because this quantity is negative, which doesn't make sense in this scenario. You used the correct expressions but subtracted them in the wrong order. Choice **b** is incorrect because $(0.92)^{n+1} - (0.92)^n \neq (0.92)^{n+1/n}$. Choice **c** is incorrect because $(0.92)^n - (0.92)^{n+1} \neq (0.92)^{n-(n+1)}$.

5. **a.** Since the employee's salary increases by 2.6% each year, to find next year's salary, multiply the current year's salary by 1.026. Doing this n times will give the salary for year n. Multiplying the base salary 42,500 by 1.026 n times is equivalent to multiplying 42,500 by $(1.026)^n$. Choice **b** is incorrect because you interchanged the starting salary and the percentage applied to the current year's salary to get the next year's salary. Choice **c** is incorrect because 0.026 is the percentage of the salary used to get the raise, not the multiple used to get the actual salary. Choice **d** is incorrect because you interchanged the starting salary and the percentage applied to get the yearly raise.

12 ▶ SOLVING QUADRATIC EQUATIONS, SYSTEMS INVOLVING QUADRATIC EQUATIONS, AND INEQUALITIES

But in my opinion, all things in nature occur mathematically.

—RENÉ DESCARTES

LESSON SUMMARY

This lesson covers methods for solving quadratic equations and quadratic inequalities and dealing with quadratic equations in a system of equations. You'll learn how to factor quadratics and use the square root property to solve these equations. For quadratics that are not factorable, you will learn how the quadratic formula can be used to solve them.

Quadratic equations are the most common higher-order equation that you will encounter on the SAT. You need to know how to create these in word problems and solve them by using various techniques. Once quadratic equations are factored, they are broken into factors, which, when set to zero, lead to solutions.

What Is a Quadratic Equation?

A **quadratic equation** is an equation of the form $ax^2 + bx + c = 0$, where a, b, and c are numbers. The graph of a quadratic equation will be a smooth U-shaped curve, unlike a linear equation, whose graph is always a straight line.

Here are some examples of quadratic equations:

$$x^2 = 4$$
$$x^2 + 3 = 0$$
$$2x^2 + 5 = 10$$
$$x^2 + 4x + 4 = 0$$
$$5x^2 - 1 = 0$$

Solutions to quadratic equations can be integer, real, or complex numbers. For this lesson, we will focus on integer and real solutions only.

In solving quadratic equations, it is essential to know various factoring techniques.

Factoring Using the Greatest Common Factor Method

To factor an expression like $2x + 6$, find the greatest common factor of both terms. In this expression, the factors of $2x$ are 2 and x, and the factors of 6 are 2 and 3, so the greatest common factor is 2. To factor the expression, put the greatest common factor outside the parentheses and put what is left inside the parentheses.

Example: $2x + 6 = 2(x + 3)$

Factoring Using the Difference of Two Squares Method

The second type of factoring is the difference of two squares. You will find this method easy to do. But before you learn this method, you need to review the concept of squares. What is a square? A number or expression multiplied by itself equals a **perfect square**. Examples of perfect squares are:

4 because $2 \cdot 2 = 4$
9 because $3 \cdot 3 = 9$
25 because $5 \cdot 5 = 25$
a^2 because $a \cdot a = a^2$
$16b^2$ because $4b \cdot 4b = 16b^2$
d^{10} because $d^5 \cdot d^5 = d^{10}$

The method of factoring using the difference of two squares is an easy pattern to remember. The pattern is $(x + y)(x - y)$, where x is the square root of the first term and y is the square root of the second term.

Example: $x^2 - 4$

Both x^2 and 4 are perfect squares, and they are connected by a subtraction sign, which is why the expression is called the *difference* of two squares. To factor the expression, take the square root of the first term and the square root of the second term. Write it like this: $(x + 2)(x - 2)$.

SAT TEST-TAKING TIP

The sum of two squares cannot be factored. Example: $x^2 + 4$ is prime. It cannot be factored.

Here are two more examples:

Example: $y^2 - 9$
$$= (y + 3)(y - 3)$$

Example: $16a^2 - 25b^2$
$$= (4a + 5b)(4a - 5b)$$

Factoring Using the Trinomial Method

You may have found that the process of factoring has been fairly simple so far. The trinomial method of factoring is a little more involved. This section will challenge you, but you can do it!

You have already learned that a trinomial is an algebraic expression with three terms. You must have three terms in your expression before you can consider using the trinomial method of factoring.

When the Sign in Front of the Third Term Is Positive

Here are some examples of how you factor using the trinomial method when the sign in front of the third term is positive.

Example: $x^2 + 2x + 1$

The pattern for the factors of a trinomial looks like this:

$$([\quad] \pm [\quad])([\quad] \pm [\quad])$$

To factor this expression, you need to determine what the missing numbers or expressions are and whether the problem needs a positive or negative sign. To begin, look at the first term in the trinomial, which is x^2. What are the factors of x^2? You have only one choice: $x \cdot x$, so you will place an x in the first term of each factor.

$$(x \pm [\quad])(x \pm [\quad])$$

Now look at the third term in the trinomial. The third term is 1, and the only factors of 1 are $1 \cdot 1$. So, place 1 in the last term of each factor.

$$(x \pm 1)(x \pm 1)$$

You are almost finished, but you still need to determine the signs of the factors. Look at the original trinomial. The sign of the third term is $+1$. You know that $+1 \cdot +1 = +1$ and $-1 \cdot -1 = +1$, but only one will give you the correct answer. Look at the original trinomial again. If the sign in front of the second term is positive, you want $+1 \cdot +1$.

$$(x + 1)(x + 1)$$

Example: $x^2 - 5x + 4$

The factors of x^2 are $x \cdot x$. The factors of 4 are $(1 \cdot 4)$ or $(2 \cdot 2)$. Try $(1 \cdot 4)$ first.

$$(x \pm 1)(x \pm 4)$$

Determine the sign. To get a $+4$, your numbers must be either both positive or both negative. The sign in front of the second term is negative, so they will both be negative.

$$(x - 1)(x - 4)$$

Check using FOIL.

$$(x - 1)(x - 4) = x^2 - 4x - 1x + 4 = x^2 - 5x + 4$$

When the Sign in Front of the Third Term Is Negative

When the sign in front of the third term is negative, you can use similar steps to factor the trinomial. Look carefully at the following examples.

Example: $x^2 + 3x - 4$

The factors for x^2 are $(x \cdot x)$. The factors for 4 are $(1 \cdot 4)$ and $(2 \cdot 2)$. To get a negative number for the third term, one sign has to be positive and one sign has to be negative. Let's try the factors $(1 \cdot 4)$ first.

$$(x + 1)(x - 4)$$

To get -4 for the third term, one factor must be positive and one factor must be negative. You don't know which one is positive and which is negative, so use trial and error until you get the right answer.

$$(x + 1)(x - 4) = x^2 - 4x + 1x - 4 = x^2 - 3x - 4$$

This is not the original trinomial. You have the right numbers, but the signs aren't the same. Try changing the signs in the factors.

$$(x - 1)(x + 4) = x^2 + 4x - 1x - 4 = x^2 + 3x - 4$$

This does check out, so the correct factors for the trinomial are $(x - 1)(x + 4)$.

Factoring Trinomials That Have a Coefficient Other Than One for the First Term

Factoring trinomials that have a coefficient other than 1 for the first term is more complex because it increases the choices of factors. You will use what you have already learned factoring trinomials, but you may need to go through many more steps to determine the factors. Study the following examples.

Example: $2x^2 + 7x + 5$

The factors for $2x^2$ are $(2x \cdot x)$.	$(2x \pm [\quad])(x \pm [\quad])$
The signs for the factors will both be positive.	$(2x + [\quad])(x + [\quad])$
The factors for 5 are $(5 \cdot 1)$.	$(2x + 5)(x + 1)$
Check using FOIL.	$2x^2 + 2x + 5x + 5$
	$= 2x^2 + 7x + 5$

The result is the original trinomial, so the factors of $2x^2 + 7x + 5 = (2x + 5)(x + 1)$.

Example: $6x^2 - 13x + 6$

The factors for $6x^2$ are $(1x \cdot 6x)$ and $(2x \cdot 3x)$. First, let's try $1x$ and $6x$.

$$(x \pm [\quad])(6x \pm [\quad])$$

The signs will both be negative. Remember, the sign in front of the third term is positive, which tells you both signs will be the same. The sign in front of the second term is negative, which tells you both signs will be negative.

	$(x - [\quad])(6x - [\quad])$
The factors for the third term are $(1 \cdot 6)$ and $(2 \cdot 3)$. Try $(1 \cdot 6)$.	$(x - 1)(6x - 6)$
Test using FOIL.	$6x^2 - 6x - 6x + 6$
	$= 6x^2 - 12x + 6$

You can see this isn't correct because the original trinomial is different. So, try interchanging the 1 and 6.	$(x - 6)(6x - 1)$
	$6x^2 - x - 36x + 6$
	$= 6x^2 - 37x + 6$
That didn't work either! Now, try using $(2 \cdot 3)$.	$(x - 2)(6x - 3)$
Test using FOIL.	$6x^2 - 3x - 12x + 6$
	$6x^2 - 15x + 6$
That's not it. Try interchanging the 2 and 3.	$(x - 3)(6x - 2)$
Test using FOIL.	$6x^2 - 2x - 18x + 6$

$$= 6x^2 - 20x + 6$$

It's still not right, but keep trying!

Try using $2x$ and $3x$ for the first term.

$$(2x - 1)(3x - 6)$$

Test using FOIL.

$$6x^2 - 12x - 3x + 6$$
$$= 6x^2 - 15x + 6$$

Interchange the 1 and 6.

$$(2x - 6)(3x - 1)$$

Test using FOIL.

$$6x^2 - 2x - 18x + 6$$
$$= 6x^2 - 20x + 6$$

Try using the factors 2 and 3.

$$(2x - 2)(3x - 3)$$

Test using FOIL.

$$6x^2 - 6x - 6x + 6$$
$$= 6x^2 - 12x + 6$$

Interchange the 2 and 3.

$$(2x - 3)(3x - 2)$$

Test using FOIL.

$$6x^2 - 4x - 9x + 6$$
$$= 6x^2 - 13x + 6$$

Finally! Factoring trinomials with a coefficient other than 1 in front of the first term can be complex, as shown in the previous example. But don't get discouraged. You could have found the correct factors on the first try. You will find that the more experience you have factoring trinomials, the easier it will become.

Factoring Using More Than One Method

Sometimes it may be necessary to use more than one method of factoring on the same expression. Always check for the greatest common factor first.

Example: $4x^2 - 4$
Look for the greatest common factor first. $4(x^2 - 1)$
You aren't finished because $x^2 - 1$ is the difference of two squares. $= 4(x - 1)(x + 1)$

Example: $2x^2 + 8x + 8$
Look for the greatest common factor. $2(x^2 + 4x + 4)$
Factor the trinomial. $2(x + 2)(x + 2)$

Solving Quadratic Equations Using Factoring

How do we solve the equation $x^2 = 4$? To solve a quadratic equation, first make one side of the equation zero.

Example: $x^2 = 4$
Subtract 4 from both sides of the equation to make one side of the equation zero. $x^2 - 4 = 4 - 4$
Simplify. $x^2 - 4 = 0$
The next step is to factor $x^2 - 4$. It can be factored as the difference of two squares. $(x - 2)(x + 2) = 0$
If $ab = 0$, you know that either a or b or both factors have to be zero since a times $b = 0$. This

is called the **zero product property**, and it says that if the product of two numbers is zero, then one or both of the numbers must be zero. You can use this idea to help solve quadratic equations with the factoring method.

Use the zero product property, and set each factor equal to zero.

$$(x - 2) = 0 \text{ and } (x + 2) = 0$$

When you use the zero product property, you get linear equations that you already know how to solve.

Solve the equation.	$x - 2 = 0$
Add 2 to both sides of the equation.	$x - 2 + 2 = 0 + 2$
Simplify.	$x = 2$
Solve the equation.	$x + 2 = 0$
Subtract 2 from both sides of the equation.	$x + 2 - 2 = 0 - 2$
Simplify.	$x = -2$

You got two values for x. The two solutions for x are 2 and −2. Note that unlike linear equations that have at most one solution, quadratic equations can have two solutions.

Before you can factor an expression, the expression must be arranged in descending order. An expression is in descending order when you start with the largest exponent and descend to the smallest, as shown in this example: $2x^2 + 5x + 6 = 0$.

Example: $x^2 - 3x - 4 = 0$

Factor the trinomial $x^2 - 3x - 4$.	$(x - 4)(x + 1) = 0$
Set each factor equal to zero.	$x - 4 = 0 \text{ and } x + 1 = 0$

Solve the equation.	$x - 4 = 0$
Add 4 to both sides of the equation.	$x - 4 + 4 = 0 + 4$
Simplify.	$x = 4$

Solve the equation.	$x + 1 = 0$
Subtract 1 from both sides of the equation.	$x + 1 - 1 = 0 - 1$
Simplify.	$x = -1$

The two solutions for the quadratic equation are 4 and −1.

Example: $2x^2 - 33 = -1$

Add 1 to both sides of the equation.	$2x^2 - 33 + 1 = -1 + 1$
Simplify both sides of the equation.	$2x^2 - 32 = 0$
Take out the common factor.	$2(x^2 - 16) = 0$
Factor the difference of two squares.	$2(x - 4)(x + 4) = 0$
Disregard the 2 and set the other factors equal to zero.	$x - 4 = 0 \text{ and } x + 4 = 0$

Solve the equation.	$x - 4 = 0$
Add 4 to both sides of the equation.	$x - 4 + 4 = 0 + 4$
Simplify both sides of the equation.	$x = 4$

When a Quadratic Equation Is Not Factorable

When you encounter a quadratic that is not factorable, you will need to use the quadratic formula.

What Is the Quadratic Formula?

The **quadratic formula** is a formula that allows you to solve any quadratic equation—no matter how simple or difficult. If the equation is written $ax^2 + bx + c = 0$, then the two solutions for x will be $x = \frac{-b \pm \sqrt{b^2 - 4ac}}{2a}$. It is the $\pm$ in the formula that gives us the two answers: one with $+$ in that spot, and one with $-$. The formula contains a radical, which is one of the reasons you will study radicals in the next two lessons. To use the formula, you substitute the values of a, b, and c into the formula and then carry out the calculations.

Example: $3x^2 - x - 2 = 0$

Determine a, b, and c.	$a = 3, b = -1,$ and $c = -2$
Take the quadratic formula.	$\frac{-b \pm \sqrt{b^2 - 4ac}}{2a}$
Substitute in the values of a, b, and c.	$\frac{-(^-1) \pm \sqrt{(-1)^2 - 4 \cdot 3 \cdot -2}}{2 \cdot 3}$
Simplify.	$\frac{1 \pm \sqrt{1 - ^-24}}{6}$
Simplify more.	$\frac{1 \pm \sqrt{25}}{6}$
Take the square root of 25.	$\frac{1 \pm 5}{6}$
The solutions are 1 and $\frac{-2}{3}$.	$\frac{1 + 5}{6} = \frac{6}{6} = 1$ and $\frac{1 - 5}{6} = \frac{-4}{6} = -\frac{2}{3}$

Solving Quadratic Equations That Have a Radical in the Answer

Some equations will have radicals in their answers. The strategy for solving these equations is the same as the equations you just solved. Take a look at the following example.

Example:	$3m^2 - 3m = 1$
Subtract 1 from both sides of the equation.	$3m^2 - 3m - 1 = 1 - 1$
Simplify.	$3m^2 - 3m - 1 = 0$
Use the quadratic formula with $a = 3$, $b = -3$, and $c = -1$.	$\frac{-b \pm \sqrt{b^2 - 4ac}}{2a}$
Substitute the values for a, b, and c.	$\frac{-(^-3) \pm \sqrt{(-3)^2 - 4 \cdot 3 \cdot -1}}{2 \cdot 3}$
Simplify.	$\frac{3 \pm \sqrt{9 - ^-12}}{6}$
Simplify.	$\frac{3 \pm \sqrt{21}}{6}$

The solution to the equation is $m = \frac{3 \pm \sqrt{21}}{6}$ because one answer is $m = \frac{3 + \sqrt{21}}{6}$ and the other answer is $m = \frac{3 - \sqrt{21}}{6}$.

Try this typical SAT problem. (Hint: Use the quadratic formula to the given quadratic equation.)

Practice

1. Let a be the smallest positive real number for which $4x^2 + ax + a = 0$ has at least one real solution. What is the value of a^3?

On the SAT exam, problems involving quadratic equations require you to solve them using some kind of factoring technique or quadratic formula. Some questions will ask you about some characteristic of the solutions OR to figure out the quadratic that produces a certain solution. Other questions will ask you to find the solution and use it in some additional calculation.

Regardless of the way the question is asked, you should look to solve the quadratic to get a better understanding of the problem.

Practice

2. Consider the equation $25x^2 + 1 = 10x$. If j and k represent the solutions of this equation with $j \leq k$, compute $\sqrt{jk}$. Enter your answer as a fraction. _____

3. Suppose m is a real number. Provide the largest positive, whole-number value of m for which the equation has two complex conjugate solutions. _____

4. Consider the equation $6x^2 + 5x - 6 = 0$. If p and q are the two solutions of this equation and $p \leq q$, which of the following is the value of $\frac{p}{q}$?

a. $-\frac{9}{4}$

b. $\frac{4}{9}$

c. $-\frac{4}{9}$

d. -1

Systems Involving Quadratic Equations

You may find some problems on the SAT that involve quadratic equations in systems. To solve them, you can use the substitution method. This involves rewriting one in terms of the other. Take a look at this example.

Example: Solve $x^2 + y > 4$ and $2x + y < 1$.

Solve the second equation for y.

$$y = 1 - 2x$$

Substitute the expression $1 - 2x$ for y in the first equation and solve for x.

$$x^2 + (1 - 2x) = 4$$
$$x^2 - 2x - 3 = 0$$
$$(x - 3)(x + 1) = 0$$
$$x - 3 = 0 \text{ or } x + 1 = 0$$
$$x = 3 \text{ and } x = -1$$

Substitute the x-values into one of the equations:

$$y = 1 - 2(3) = -5$$
$$y = 1 - 2(-1) = 3$$

The solution set is $(3,-5), (-1,3)$

Now, try solving the following system of quadratic equations.

Practice

5. Solve: $y = x^2 + 4x + 5$ and $y = x^2 + 2x - 1$. _____

6. Consider the system $\begin{cases} y = x^2 - 2x - 15 \\ y = 5x + 3 \end{cases}$

If (x_1, y_1) and (x_2, y_2) are the two solutions of this system, compute $|y_1 + y_2|$. _____

Problems Involving Quadratic Inequalities

A quadratic inequality is one that involves an inequality sign such as $<, >, \leq,$ or $\geq$. When solving these types of quadratics, you actually solve the corresponding equations using the equal sign. The difference is that you need to check your solution to see if it falls within the constraint that is given by the original equation.

Example: Solve $x^2 + x - 6 > 0$.

$$x^2 + x - 6 > 0$$
$$(x + 3)(x - 2) = 0$$
$$x + 3 = 0 \text{ or } x - 2 = 0$$
$$x = -3 \text{ and } x = 2$$

Try these practice problems involving quadratic inequalities.

Practice

7. Solve $x^2 - 3x - 10 \geq 0$. _____

8. Solve $x^2 + 2x - 8 \leq 0$. _____

Answers and Explanations

1. 64. Solve the equation using the quadratic formula:

$$x = \frac{-a \pm \sqrt{a^2 - 4a}}{2(4)}$$

The only way for a quadratic equation to have "at least one real solution" is for the radicand in the expression arising from the quadratic formula to be nonnegative. Here, this means that a must satisfy the inequality $a^2 - 4a \geq 0$. The left side factors as $a(a - 4)$. We want the values of a for which both factors are positive or both are negative. Here, this occurs when $a \leq 0$ or when $a \geq 4$. So, the smallest *positive* real number for which this is true is 4. As such, a^3 for this value of a is $4^3 = 64$.

2. $\frac{1}{5}$. Solve the equation for x as follows:
$$25x^2 + 1 = 10x$$
$$25x^2 - 10x + 1 = 0$$
$$(5x - 1)2 = 0$$
$$5x - 1 = 0$$
$$x = \frac{1}{5}$$

The two solutions, j and k, are actually the same value, namely $\frac{1}{5}$. Hence, $\sqrt{j \cdot k} = \sqrt{\frac{1}{5} \cdot \frac{1}{5}} = \frac{1}{5}$.

3. 4. First, write the quadratic equation in standard form: $2x^2 + mx + 3 = 0$. Then solve for x using the quadratic formula:

$$x = \frac{-m \pm \sqrt{m^2 - 4(2)(3)}}{2(2)} = \frac{-m \pm \sqrt{m^2 - 24}}{4}$$

The only way for a quadratic equation to have two complex conjugate solutions is for the radicand to be negative. Here, this means m must satisfy the inequality $m^2 - 24 < 0$. It's easy to identify possible values for m just by looking at this inequality; for example, m could equal 0, 1, 2, 3, or 4. More precisely, any value of m between $-2\sqrt{6}$ and $2\sqrt{6}$ will make the inequality true. As $2\sqrt{6} \approx 4.899$, the largest positive whole number for which the equation has two complex conjugate solutions is 4.

4. a. Factor the left side of the equation to get $(2x + 3)(3x − 2) = 0$. The two solutions of this equation must be $−\frac{3}{2}$ and $\frac{2}{3}$. Now decide which of these is p and which is q. Since $p \le q$, p must be $−\frac{3}{2}$ and q must be $\frac{2}{3}$. So,

$$\frac{p}{q} = \frac{−\frac{3}{2}}{\frac{2}{3}} = −\frac{3}{2} \div \frac{2}{3} = −\frac{3}{2} \times \frac{3}{2} = −\frac{9}{4}.$$

Choice **b** is incorrect because it assumes both solutions were positive. Choice **c** is the reciprocal of the correct answer. Choice **d** is also incorrect—it looks like you multiplied p and q instead of dividing p by q. Remember that when converting to a multiplication problem, you must multiply p by the reciprocal of q, not by q itself.

5. $(−3,2)$. Substitute the expression $x^2 + 4x + 5$ for y in the first equation and solve for x:

$$y = x^2 + 2x −1$$
$$x^2 + 4x + 5 = x^2 + 2x − 1$$
$$2x = −6$$
$$x = −3$$
$$y = (−3)2 + 4(−3) + 5 = 2$$

The solution is $(−3,2)$.

6. 41. To solve this system, solve both equations for y:

$$\begin{cases} y = x^2 − 2x − 15 \\ y = 5x + 3 \end{cases}$$

Now, equate the two right sides and solve for x:

$$x^2 − 2x − 15 = 5x + 3$$
$$x^2 − 7x − 18 = 0$$
$$(x − 9)(x + 2) = 0$$
$$x = 9, −2$$

Next, substitute each of these into the second equation (for simplicity) to find the corresponding y-coordinates:

$$x_1 = 9 \Rightarrow y_1 = 5 \cdot 9 + 3 = 48$$
$$x_2 = −2 \Rightarrow y_2 = 5 \cdot (−2) + 3 = −7$$

(Note that you could have alternatively identified as −2 and as 9.)

Hence, $|y_1 + y_2| = |48 + (−7)| = |41| = 41$.

7. $x \le −2$ and $x \ge 5$.

$$x^2 − 3x − 10 = 0$$
$$(x − 5)(x + 2) = 0$$
$$x − 5 = 0 \text{ or } x + 2 = 0$$
$$x = 5 \text{ and } x = −2$$

Considering the constraint, we have to plot the numbers on a number line. The solutions $x = 5$ and $x = −2$ are considered "critical values" that help determine the regions that the number line is divided into.

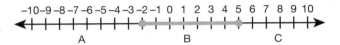

We need to pick numbers in each region A, B, and C.

For region A, test $x = −4$ in the original equation:

$$x^2 − 3x − 10 \ge 0$$
$$(−4)^2 − 3(−4) − 10 \ge 0$$
$$16 + 12 − 10 \ge 0$$
$$18 \ge 0$$

True, so numbers in region A are in the solution.

For region B, test $x = 0$ in the original equation:

$$x^2 − 3x − 10 \ge 0$$
$$(0)^2 − 3(0) − 10 \ge 0$$
$$−10 \ge 0$$

False, so numbers in region B are NOT in the solution.

For region C, test $x = 6$ in the original equation:

$$x^2 − 3x − 10 \ge 0$$
$$(6)^2 − 3(6) − 10 \ge 0$$
$$36 − 18 − 10 \ge 0$$
$$8 \ge 0$$

True, so numbers in region C are in the solution.

Finally, we conclude the solution to the inequality is $x \le −2$ and $x \ge 5$.

8. $-4 \leq x \leq 2.$

$$x^2 + 2x - 8 = 0$$
$$(x + 4)(x - 2) = 0$$
$$x + 4 = 0 \text{ or } x - 2 = 0$$
$$x = -4 \text{ and } x = 2$$

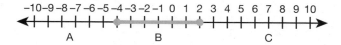

For region A, test $x = -5$ in the original equation:

$$x^2 + 2x - 8 \leq 0$$
$$(-5)^2 + 2(-5) - 8 \leq 0$$
$$25 - 10 - 8 \leq 0$$
$$7 \leq 0$$

False, so numbers in region A are NOT in the solution.

For region B, test $x = 0$ in the original equation:

$$x^2 + 2x - 8 \leq 0$$
$$(0)^2 + 2(0) - 8 \leq 0$$
$$-8 \leq 0$$

True, so numbers in region B are in the solution.

For region C, test $x = 6$ in the original equation:

$$x^2 + 2x - 8 \leq 0$$
$$(6)^2 + 2(6) - 8 \leq 0$$
$$36 + 12 - 8 \leq 0$$
$$40 \leq 0$$

False, so numbers in region C are NOT in the solution.

Finally, we conclude the solution to the inequality is $-4 \leq x \leq 2$.

13 ▶ POLYNOMIAL, RADICAL, AND RATIONAL EXPRESSIONS

Mathematics expresses values that reflect the cosmos, including orderliness, balance, harmony, logic, and abstract beauty.

—DEEPAK CHOPRA

LESSON SUMMARY

This lesson gives you practice on performing polynomial operations. Also covered are radical expressions involving square/cube roots and fractional coefficients. The lesson will walk you through how to solve these types of expressions on the SAT exam.

This lesson is long and covers a lot of material—we recommend you cover it in two to three 20-minute sessions.

What Is a Polynomial?

A **polynomial** is a sum of numbers and positive integer powers of a single variable. For instance, 2, $x + 3$, and $5x^2 + 3$ are polynomials.

Performing Operations with Polynomial Expressions

Operations with polynomial expressions involve combining **like terms** and then performing the operations needed. Two terms are **like terms** if their variable parts are identical. They are **unlike terms** if their variable parts are different.

Addition and Subtraction

Do you know which of the terms are like and unlike in the expression $-3a^2 + 4b - 7a^2 - 9b + c$?

The like terms are $-3a^2$ and $-7a^2$ because each has the same variable part. The terms $+4b$ and $-9b$ are also like terms. The unlike term is c because its variable part is different.

To combine like terms, add the coefficients and write the same variable part. So, the like terms combined would be $-3a^2$ and $-7a^2 = (-3 - 7)a^2 = -10a^2$. For the other like terms, $+4b$ and $-9b = (+4 - 9)b = -5b$. The original expression $-10a^2 - 5b + c$ is in its **simplest form** because it is easiest to use.

To be more organized, write like terms next to each other. The **commutative property** allows for this. It states that $a + b = b + a$. For example, $5 + 3$ is the same as $3 + 5$. (It also works for multiplication, in that $a \times b = b \times a$. For example, $2 \times 4 = 4 \times 2$.)

So, for something like $-3a + 4b - 7a - 9b$, write the like terms together $(-3a - 7a + 4b - 9b)$ to make it more organized and easier to simplify.

Multiplication

Sometimes, you may have to multiply instead of add to combine like terms. For example, to simplify $2y(3 - 5x)$, use the **distributive property**, which says that $a(b + c) = ab + ac$. Using the distributive property results in $+2y(3) + 2y(-5x)$, which is $+6y - 10xy$. Notice how the $2y$ in the original problem becomes $+2y$ in the distributed property. This makes all the signs clear when multiplying the terms.

When using the distributive property with a missing coefficient in front of the parentheses, write it as 1. For instance, $-(x - 4)$ is written as $-1(x - 4)$, which is $-1(x) - 1(-4) = -1x + 4$.

Multiplying Expressions by a Monomial

A polynomial that consists of a single term is called a **monomial**. To multiply a polynomial with one term (monomial) by a polynomial consisting of more than one term, use the distributive property. You multiply the term outside the parentheses by every term inside the parentheses.

> **Examples:** $2(a + b - 3) = 2a + 2b - 6$
> $3x(x^2 + 2x) = 3x^3 + 6x^2$

Multiplying a Binomial by a Binomial

What is a binomial? A **binomial** is a polynomial consisting of two terms. To multiply a binomial by a binomial, you will use a method called "FOIL." This process is called FOIL because you work the problem in this order:

FIRST
OUTER
INNER
LAST

Example: $(x + 2)(x + 3)$

Multiply the **first** terms in each binomial.	$([x] + 2)([x] + 3)$ $= x^2$
Multiply the two **outer** terms in each binomial.	$([x] + 2)(x + [3])$ $= x^2 + 3x$
Multiply the two **inner** terms in each binomial.	$(x + [2])([x] + 3)$ $= x^2 + 3x + 2x$
Multiply the two **last** terms in each binomial.	$(x + [2])(x + [3])$ $= x^2 + 3x + 2x + 6$
Simplify.	$= x^2 + 5x + 6$

Example: $(x + 3)(x - 1)$

Multiply the two **first** terms in each binomial.	$([x] + 3)([x] - 1)$ $= x^2$
Multiply the two **outer** terms in each binomial.	$([x] + 3)(x - [1])$ $= x^2 - 1x$
Multiply the two **inner** terms in each binomial.	$(x + [3])([x] - 1)$ $= x^2 - 1x + 3x$
Multiply the two **last** terms in each binomial.	$(x + [3])(x - [1])$ $= x^2 - 1x + 3x - 3$
Simplify.	$= x^2 + 2x - 3$

Multiplying a Binomial by a Trinomial

A bicycle has two wheels; a tricycle has three wheels. Likewise, a binomial has two terms, and a **trinomial** has three terms. Here's how you would multiply a binomial by a trinomial.

Example: $(x + 2)(x^2 + 2x + 1)$
To work this problem, you need to multiply each term in the first polynomial with each term in the second polynomial.

Multiply x by each term in the second polynomial.	$x(x^2 + 2x + 1)$ $= x^3 + 2x^2 + x$
Multiply 2 by each term in the second polynomial.	$2(x^2 + 2x + 1)$ $= 2x^2 + 4x + 2$
Simplify.	$x^3 + 2x^2 + x$ $+ 2x^2 + 4x + 2$ $= x^3 + 4x^2 + 5x + 2$

SAT TEST-TAKING TIP

When performing operations on polynomials, remember your like terms. In addition and subtraction, you need the same variable and powers in order to combine. So, $5x + 8y$ cannot be combined.

Practice

1. Which of these expressions is equivalent to $(3xy - 2x - y^2) - (2xy - y^2 - 5x - 2)$?
   a. $xy - 7x - 2y^2 - 2$
   b. $5xy - 2y^2 - 7x - 2$
   c. $3x - 2y^2 + 2 + xy$
   d. $xy + 3x + 2$

2. If $(2x - 1)(3x + 2)(2x + 1) = 12x^3 + ax^2 - 3x + b$, what is the value of $a - b$? _____

3. Which of these expressions is equivalent to $-(3z - 2x + xz) + 2(-xz - x + z)$?
   a. $-z(1 + 3x)$
   b. $-z + 3xz$
   c. $-z + 4x - 3xz$
   d. $-2z - 3x - xz$

What Are Radical Expressions?

You have seen how the addition in $x + 5 = 11$ can be undone by subtracting 5 from both sides of the equation. You have also seen how the multiplication in $3x = 21$ can be undone by dividing both sides by 3. Taking the **square root** (also called a **radical**) is the way to undo the exponent from an equation like $x^2 = 25$.

The exponent in 7^2 tells you to square 7. You multiply $7 \cdot 7$ and get $7^2 = 49$.

The **radical sign** $\sqrt{}$ in $\sqrt{36}$ tells you to find the positive number whose square is 36. In other words, $\sqrt{36}$ asks: What number times itself is 36? The answer is $\sqrt{36} = 6$ because $6 \cdot 6 = 36$.

The number inside the radical sign is called the **radicand**. For example, in $\sqrt{9}$, the radicand is 9.

Square Roots of Perfect Squares

The easiest radicands to deal with are perfect squares. Because they appear so often, it is useful to learn to recognize the first few perfect squares: $0^2 = 0$, $1^2 = 1$, $2^2 = 4$, $3^2 = 9$, $4^2 = 16$, $5^2 = 25$, $6^2 = 36$, $7^2 = 49$, $8^2 = 64$, $9^2 = 81$, $10^2 = 100$, $11^2 = 121$, and $12^2 = 144$. It is even easier to recognize when a variable is a perfect square because the exponent is even. For example: $x^{14} = x^7 \cdot x^7$, or $(x^7)^2$, and $a^8 = a^4 \cdot a^4$, or $(a^4)^2$.

Example: $\sqrt{64x^2y^{10}}$

Write as a square. $\sqrt{8xy^5 \cdot 8xy^5}$
Evaluate. $8xy^5$

You could also have split the radical into parts and evaluated them separately:

Example: $\sqrt{64x^2y^{10}}$

Split into perfect squares. $\sqrt{64 \cdot x^2 \cdot y^{10}}$

Write as squares. $\sqrt{8 \cdot 8} \cdot \sqrt{x \cdot x} \cdot \sqrt{y^5 \cdot y^5}$

Evaluate. $8 \cdot x \cdot y^5$
Multiply together. $8xy^5$

If your radical has a coefficient like $3\sqrt{25}$, evaluate the square root before multiplying: $3\sqrt{25} = 3 \cdot 5 = 15$.

When the Radicand Contains a Perfect Square

To determine if a radicand contains any factors that are perfect squares, factor the radicand completely. All the factors must be prime. A number is prime if its only factors are 1 and the number itself. A prime number cannot be factored any further.

For example, here's how you simplify $\sqrt{12}$. The number 12 can be factored into $2 \cdot 6$. This is not completely factored because 6 is not prime. The number 6 can be further factored into $2 \cdot 3$. The number 12 completely factored is $2 \cdot 2 \cdot 3$.

The radical $\sqrt{12}$ can be written as $\sqrt{2 \cdot 2 \cdot 3}$. This can be split up into $\sqrt{2 \cdot 2} \cdot \sqrt{3}$. Since $\sqrt{2 \cdot 2} = 2$, the simplified form of $\sqrt{12}$ is $2\sqrt{3}$.

Example: $\sqrt{18}$
Factor completely. $\sqrt{2 \cdot 3 \cdot 3}$
Separate out the perfect square $3 \cdot 3$. $\sqrt{3 \cdot 3} \cdot \sqrt{2}$
Simplify. $3\sqrt{2}$

Example: $\sqrt{60}$
Factor completely. $\sqrt{6 \cdot 10}$
Neither 6 nor 10 is prime.
Both can be factored further. $\sqrt{2 \cdot 3 \cdot 2 \cdot 5}$
Separate out the perfect square $2 \cdot 2$. $\sqrt{2 \cdot 2} \cdot \sqrt{3 \cdot 5}$
Because $\sqrt{3 \cdot 5}$ contains no perfect squares, it cannot be simplified further. $2\sqrt{15}$

When the Radicand Contains a Fraction

The radicand cannot be a fraction. If you get rid of the denominator in the radicand, then you no longer have a fraction. This process is called **rationalizing the denominator**. Your strategy will be to make the denominator a perfect square. To do that, you multiply the denominator by itself. However, if you multiply the denominator of a fraction by a number, you must multiply the numerator of the fraction by the same number. Take a look at the following examples.

Example: $\sqrt{\frac{1}{2}}$
Make the denominator a perfect square. $\sqrt{\frac{1}{2} \cdot \frac{2}{2}}$
Take out the square roots.
One is a perfect square and so is $2 \cdot 2$. $\frac{1}{2} \; \frac{\sqrt{1 \cdot 2}}{\sqrt{2 \cdot 2}} = \frac{\sqrt{2}}{2}$

When a Radical Is in the Denominator

When you have a radical in the denominator, the expression is not in simplest form. The expression $\frac{2}{\sqrt{3}}$ contains a radical in the denominator. To get rid of the radical in the denominator, rationalize the denominator. In other words, make the denominator a perfect square. To do that, you need to multiply the denominator by itself.

Example: $\frac{2}{\sqrt{3}} \cdot \frac{\sqrt{3}}{\sqrt{3}}$

Simplify. $\qquad \frac{2\sqrt{3}}{\sqrt{9}}$

The number 9 is a perfect square. $\quad \frac{2\sqrt{3}}{3}$

Example: $\frac{\sqrt{6}}{\sqrt{2}}$

Rationalize the denominator. $\quad \frac{\sqrt{6}}{\sqrt{2}} \cdot \frac{\sqrt{2}}{\sqrt{2}}$

Simplify. $\qquad\qquad\qquad\quad \frac{\sqrt{12}}{\sqrt{4}}$

You aren't finished yet because both radicands contain perfect

squares. $\qquad\qquad\qquad\quad \frac{\sqrt{3 \cdot 4}}{\sqrt{4}}$

Take the square root of 4. $\quad \frac{2\sqrt{3}}{2}$

Finished? Not quite. You can

divide 2 into 2, or cancel the 2's. $\quad \sqrt{3}$

Adding and Subtracting Radicals

You can add and subtract radicals if the radicands are the same. For example, you can add $3\sqrt{2}$ and $5\sqrt{2}$ because the radicands are the same. To add or subtract radicals, you add the number in front of the radicals and leave the radicand the same. When you add $3\sqrt{2} + 5\sqrt{2}$, you add the 3 and the 5, but the radicand $\sqrt{2}$ stays the same. The answer is $8\sqrt{2}$.

SAT TEST-TAKING TIP

You can add or subtract radicals only when the radicand is the same. You add radicals by adding the number in front of the radicals and keeping the radicand the same. When you subtract radicals, you subtract the numbers in front of the radicals and keep the radicand the same.

Example: $2\sqrt{5} + 7\sqrt{5}$
Add the numbers in front of
the radicals. $\qquad\qquad\qquad 9\sqrt{5}$

Example: $11\sqrt{5} - 4\sqrt{5}$
Subtract the numbers in front of
the radicals. $\qquad\qquad\qquad 7\sqrt{5}$

Multiplying and Dividing Radicals

To multiply radicals like $4\sqrt{3}$ by $2\sqrt{2}$, you multiply the numbers in front of the radicals: 4 times 2. Then multiply the radicands: 3 times 2. The answer is $8\sqrt{6}$.

Example: $5\sqrt{3} \cdot 2\sqrt{2}$
Multiply the numbers in front of the
radicals. Then multiply the radicands. $\quad 10\sqrt{6}$

Example: $2\sqrt{6} \cdot 3\sqrt{3}$
Multiply the numbers in front of the
radicals. Then multiply the radicands. $\quad 6\sqrt{18}$

Memorize the square roots of perfect squares. This will help you simplify radicals on the SAT exam. When multiplying and dividing radicals, multiply and divide the numbers and/or terms inside the radicals.

Practice

4. Assume that s is not zero. Which of the following expressions is equivalent to $\frac{\sqrt{3s^3} \times \sqrt{27s^5}}{s\sqrt{9s}}$?

   a. $s^2\sqrt{s}$

   b. $3\sqrt{s^7}$

   c. $27s^5\sqrt{s}$

   d. $3s^2\sqrt{s}$

What Are Rational Expressions?

By definition, a rational expression is a fraction in the form of $\frac{P}{Q}$, where P and Q are polynomials. So, a rational expression can also be thought of as a division of polynomials. Most of the time, we look to simplify rational expressions as much as possible. This involves looking for like terms in the numerator and denominator. Remember, like terms occur when the same variable and exponent exist.

For example, in simplifying the rational expression $\frac{4x^2}{4x}$, we can divide the numerator and denominator by $4x$ to reduce the fraction to $\frac{x}{1}$ or x. In this case, we are dividing with exponents.

When dividing like terms, subtract the exponents. For example, when you divide expressions that contain exponents like $\frac{4x^5}{2x^3}$, divide the numbers (4 and 2) and subtract the exponents (5 and 3). The answer for the expression is $\frac{4x^5}{2x^3} = 2x^2$.

Reducing fractions to their lowest terms, like in the above example, is referred to as simplifying.

Let's look at some examples of simplifying rational expressions.

Example
Simplify: $\frac{54x^2}{72x^5}$
In this example, the common term to the numerator and denominator is $18x^2$. So, dividing the top and bottom of the fraction by $18x^2$ yields $\frac{3}{4x^3}$.

Example
Simplify: $\frac{14s^2 + 51s + 40}{12s^2 + 16s - 35}$
In this example, we have two trinomials in the numerator and denominator of the fraction. We need to factor them to see what terms they have in common. Factoring the numerator yields $(2s + 5)(7s + 8)$. Factoring the denominator yields $(2s + 5)(6s - 7)$. So, the original fraction factored is $\frac{(2s+5)(7s+8)}{(2s+5)(6s-7)}$. Since $(2s + 5)$ is common to the numerator and denominator, we can cancel (cross) them out of the top and bottom to get $\frac{(7s+8)}{(6s-7)}$.

Adding and Subtracting Rational Expressions

Rational expressions are simply fractions with variables in them. So, they can be added and subtracted in the same manner. When adding and subtracting rational expressions, it is all about the denominator. If the denominators are like, then simply add the terms in both numerators.

For example, let's look at $\frac{7b-2}{6b^2+5} + \frac{2b}{6b^2+5}$. Since the denominators are like, you need to add $7b - 2 + 2b$ to get $9b - 2$ in the numerator. Then, write that over the same denominator: $\frac{9b-2}{6b^2+5}$.

If the denominators are unlike, then you have to find a least common denominator, or LCD. This process is very similar to finding the LCD in numerical fractions. To find the LCD, factor each denominator. Then choose the greatest power of each unique factor. The product of these will be the LCD.

Example: $\frac{3k}{5} + \frac{2k+1}{5k+9}$

In this case, the denominators are the terms 5 and $(5k + 9)$, which are unlike. (Notice that the 5 in $5k + 9$ is not separated.) So, the only thing to do is multiply them to get an LCD of $(5)(5k + 9)$. In the first fraction, multiply the top and bottom by $(5k + 9)$. In the second fraction, multiply the top and bottom by 5:

$$\frac{(5k+9)3k}{5(5k+9)} + \frac{2k+1(5)}{5k+9(5)}$$

Multiplying the terms in the numerator yields $(5k + 9)(3k) + (2k + 1)(5)$. Combining like terms yields $15k^2 + 27k + 10k + 5$, which results in the final answer:

$$\frac{15k^2 + 37k + 5}{5(5k+9)}$$

Here is another example.

Example: Which of the following is equivalent to $\frac{4x+6}{16x^2+24x+9} - \frac{2}{4x+3}$?

Factor the denominator of the first fraction to get $(4x + 3)^2$. Since the denominators are unlike, make the LCD $(4x + 3)^2$. Combine the rational expressions on the right side using the LCD $(4x + 3)^2$ and simplify:

$$\frac{4x+6}{(4x+3)^2} - \frac{2}{4x+3} = \frac{4x+6}{(4x+3)^2} - \frac{2(4x+3)}{(4x+3)^2}$$
$$= \frac{4x+6-2(4x+3)}{(4x+3)^2}$$
$$= \frac{4x+6-8x-6}{(4x+3)^2}$$
$$= \frac{-4x}{(4x+3)^2}$$
$$= \frac{-4x}{16x^2+24x+9}$$

Multiplying and Dividing Rational Expressions

To multiply rational expressions, first look to reduce the original fractions you are working with and then multiply the numerators and then the denominators. When you are multiplying expressions, you ADD the exponents.

Example
Multiply: $(\frac{1}{x^2})(\frac{1}{x^3})$.

$$\frac{1}{x\cdot x} \cdot \frac{1}{x\cdot x\cdot x} = 1x^{2+3} = \frac{1}{x^5}$$

Note that this can also be written as a negative exponent: x^{-5}.

Example
Multiply: $\frac{4-x}{5x} \times \frac{x^2+5x}{x^2+x-20}$.

Start by simplifying each factorable polynomial in the problem. In the second fraction, the numerator $x^2 + 5x$ simplifies to $x(x + 5)$. The denominator $x^2 + x - 20$ simplifies to $(x + 5)(x - 4)$. The result is $\frac{4-x}{5x} \times \frac{x(x+5)}{(x+5)(x-4)}$.

After the canceling, the only factor left is -1 on the top and 5 on the bottom. $-\frac{1}{5}$ is the final answer.

Notice how when canceling $(x - 4)$ and $(4 - x)$, there is still a factor of -1. This is because $(4 - x) = -1(x - 4)$.

Dividing rational expressions is similar to dividing fractions by reducing them to their lowest terms. To divide rational expressions, invert the second rational fraction and multiply the two fractions, as you did in the previous examples.

Example

Divide: $\dfrac{g+12}{g+22g+120} \div \dfrac{6g}{g-3}$.

In division, it is important to invert (flip) the second fraction before getting started, turning the operation into multiplication:

$$\frac{g+12}{g+22g+120} \div \frac{g-3}{6g}$$

Then, factor the denominator of the first fraction:

$$\frac{g+12}{(g+12)(g+10)} \div \frac{g-3}{6g}$$

Finally, simplify:

$$\frac{g-3}{6g(g+10)}$$

Practice

5. Multiply: $\dfrac{2x^2-13x-15}{2x-3} \times \dfrac{4x-6}{x^2-10x+25}$.

_____

6. Divide: $\dfrac{h^2+7h+12}{h^2+12h+27} \div \dfrac{1}{h+9}$. _____

7. Which of the following is equivalent to $\dfrac{3x^2-2x}{2(1+3x)} \div \dfrac{4x^2-9}{12x^2+4x}$?

a. $\dfrac{-(2x+3)(2x-3)^2}{2(1+3x)}$

b. $\dfrac{-2x^2}{2x+3}$

c. $\dfrac{-x}{3}$

d. $\dfrac{2x+3}{-2x^2}$

Complex Fractions

Complex fractions in rational expressions occur when there is a fraction in the numerator, in the denominator, or in both.

Example

$$\frac{4+\frac{8}{x}}{1-\frac{4}{x^2}}$$

To simplify, first find the LCD for x and x^2, which is x^2.

Next, multiply the top and bottom by x^2:

$$\frac{4+\frac{8}{x}}{1-\frac{4}{x^2}} \times \frac{x^2}{x^2} = \frac{4x^2+8x}{x^2-4}$$

The numerator factors into $4x(x-2)$. The denominator factors into $(x+2)(x-1)$. This yields

$$\frac{4x(x-2)}{(x-2)(x+2)}$$

Cancel like terms on top and bottom:

$$\frac{4x\cancel{(x-2)}}{\cancel{(x-2)}(x+2)}$$

The final answer is $\dfrac{4x}{x+2}$.

SAT TEST-TAKING TIP

Rational expressions on the SAT are usually straightforward in that you have to perform the indicated operation. To complete these problems, you need to know how to simplify by reducing and canceling terms, add, subtract, multiply, and divide. You should also practice working with complex fractions, as these sometimes appear. The best way to practice working with rational expressions is to hone your skills involving factoring, simplifying terms, combining like terms, and working with exponents.

Answers and Explanations

1. d. First, distribute the negative sign to all terms in the second expression. Then combine like terms:

$(3xy - 2x - y^2) - (2xy - y^2 - 5x - 2)$
$= 3xy - 2x - y^2 - 2xy + y^2 + 5x + 2$
$= (3xy - 2xy) + (-2x + 5x) + (-y^2 + y^2) + 2$
$= xy + 3x + 2$

Choice **a** is incorrect because you applied the negative sign to only the first term of the expression $(2xy - y^2 - 5x - 2)$, but you should have applied it to all of the terms. Choice **b** is incorrect because you added the expressions rather than subtracting them. Choice **c** is incorrect because you treated the y^2 terms incorrectly. Remember, when you have a double negative, it becomes a positive. In this case, $-y^2 - (-y^2)^2 = -y^2 + y^2 = 0$, not $2y^2$.

2. 10. First, expand the left side of the equation and arrange the terms in decreasing order according to degree:

$(2x - 1)(3x + 2)(2x + 1)$
$= (2x - 1)(2x + 1)(3x + 2)$
$= (4x^2 - 1)(3x + 2)$
$= 12x^3 + 8x^2 - 3x - 2$

Now, equate corresponding coefficients to find that $a = 8$ and $b = -2$. This means that $a - b = 8 - (-2) = 10$.

3. a. First, distribute the negative to all terms in the first expression and the 2 to all terms in the second one. Then, combine like terms:

$-(3z - 2x + xz) + 2(-xz - x + z)$
$= -3z + 2x - xz - 2xz - 2x + 2z$
$= (-3z + 2z) + (2x - 2x) + (-xz - 2xz)$
$= -z - 3xz$

Finally, factor out $-z$ from the binomial to get $-z(1 + 3x)$. Choice **b** is incorrect because the second term in the expression should have a negative sign in front of it. Choice **c** is incorrect because you treated the x terms incorrectly. When simplifying, you should get $2x$ and $-2x$, which would then cancel. Choice **d** is incorrect because you misapplied the distributive property. Remember, you must distribute such a constant multiple to ALL terms of the quantity.

4. d. Use the rules for combining radicals and the connection between fractional exponents and radicals, as follows:

$$\frac{\sqrt{3s^3} \cdot \sqrt{27s^5}}{s\sqrt{9s}} = \frac{\sqrt{81s^8}}{s\sqrt{9s}}$$
$$= \frac{9s^4}{3s\sqrt{s}}$$
$$= \frac{3s^4}{s^{\frac{3}{2}}}$$
$$= 3s^{\frac{5}{2}}$$
$$= 3s^2\sqrt{s}$$

In choice **a**, the simplification of the constant terms is incorrect. Choice **b** is incorrect because when multiplying powers of s, you need to add the exponents, not multiply them. Choice **c** is incorrect because you multiplied the numerator and the denominator instead of dividing them.

5. $\frac{4x^2 - 26x - 30}{x^2 - 10x + 25}$. Start by simplifying each factorable polynomial in the problem. The numerator $2x^2 - 13x - 15$ simplifies to $(2x - 15)(x + 1)$. The numerator in the second fraction $4x - 6$ simplifies to $2(2x - 3)$. The denominator $x^2 - 10x + 25$ simplifies to $(x - 5)(x - 5)$. Rewriting the problem yields

$$\frac{(2x - 15)(x + 1)}{2x - 3} \times \frac{2(2x - 3)}{(x - 5)(x - 5)}$$

Canceling like terms from the top and bottom yields

$$\frac{(2x - 15)(x + 1)}{\cancel{2x - 3}} \times \frac{2\cancel{(2x - 3)}}{(x - 5)(x - 5)}$$

Thus the final answer is

$$\frac{4x^2 - 26x - 30}{x^2 - 10x + 25}$$

6. $h + 4$. The first step is to invert (flip) the second fraction before getting started:

$$\frac{h^2 + 7h + 12}{h^2 + 12h + 27} \times \frac{h + 9}{1}$$

Then, factor:

$$\frac{(h + 3)(h + 4)}{(h + 3)(h + 9)} \times \frac{h + 9}{1}$$

Simplify:

$$\frac{\cancel{(h + 3)}(h + 4)}{\cancel{(h + 3)}\cancel{(h + 9)}} \times \frac{\cancel{h + 9}}{1}$$

The final answer is $h + 4$.

7. b. First, write the division problem as a multiplication problem. Then, factor all parts and cancel like terms:

$$\frac{3x^2 - 2x}{2(1 + 3x)} \div \frac{4x^2 - 9}{12x^2 + 4x}$$

$$= \frac{3x - 2x^2}{2(1 + 3x)} \cdot \frac{12x^2 + 4x}{4x^2 - 9}$$

$$= \frac{-x\cancel{(2 - 3x)}}{\cancel{2}\cancel{(1 + 3x)}} \cdot \frac{\cancel{4}^2 x \cancel{(3x + 1)}}{\cancel{(2x - 3)}(2x + 3)}$$

$$= \frac{-2x^2}{2x + 3}$$

Choice **a** is incorrect because you did not convert the division problem to a multiplication problem before simplifying. Rather, you just multiplied the two rational expressions. Choice **c** is incorrect because once you correctly factored and canceled like terms, you incorrectly canceled a common term in the top and bottom. Note:

$$\frac{-2x^2}{2x + 3} \neq \frac{-2\cancel{x}^{2x}}{2\cancel{x} + 3} = -\frac{x}{3}$$

Choice **d** is incorrect because when dividing, you do convert the problem initially to a multiplication problem by flipping the divisor, but you do not do that again once you have the final answer.

14 ▶ RADICAL AND RATIONAL FUNCTIONS IN ONE VARIABLE

Math is a language.

—Josiah Willard Gibbs

LESSON SUMMARY

This lesson presents radical and rational functions. These types of functions often contain solutions that do not satisfy the function. These extraneous solutions are mathematically sound but can cause the original function to be undefined.

Radical functions are functions that contain a root. The most common radical functions are the square root function $f(x) = \sqrt{x}$ and cube root function $f(x) = \sqrt{x} \; g(x) = \sqrt[3]{x}$.

Solving Radical Functions

The process of **squaring** or **cubing** a function is used to eliminate radicals from either side of an equation. If the radical is a square root, then squaring would eliminate the radical. If the radical is a cube root, then cubing would eliminate the radical. Like other algebraic equations, a radical equation may have no solutions.

An **extraneous solution** can occur when the solution process results in a value that satisfies the original equation but creates an invalid equation by placing a negative value under the radical. An extraneous solution can also occur when a solution results in a value that is irrelevant in the context of the original equation.

Example: What is the solution to $\sqrt{x} = 2$?

Square both sides to clear the radical sign:

$$(\sqrt{x})^2 = (2)^2$$
$$x = 4$$

Example: Solve the radical equation $\sqrt{3x} - 5 = 3$.

First, isolate the radical expression by adding 5 to both sides of the equation:

$$\sqrt{3x} - 5 = 3 \text{ Original equation}$$
$$\sqrt{3x} = 8 \text{ Add 5 to both sides}$$

Because there is a square root on the left side of the equation, raise both sides to the power of 2 to eliminate the radical expression. In other words, square both sides:

$$\sqrt{3x} = 8$$
$$(\sqrt{3x})^2 = 8^2 \text{ Square both sides}$$
$$3x = 64 \text{ Simplify}$$

Solve the resulting equation by dividing both sides by 3:

$$x = \frac{64}{3}$$

The solution appears to be $x = \frac{64}{3}$. However, confirm that this is not an extraneous solution by verifying the solution. Substitute the potential solution into the original equation and check the result:

$$\sqrt{3x} - 5 = 3 \qquad \text{Original equation}$$
$$\sqrt{3\left(\frac{64}{3}\right)} - 5 = 3 \qquad \text{Substitute } \frac{64}{3} \text{ for } x$$
$$\sqrt{64} - 5 = 3 \qquad \text{Simplify}$$
$$8 - 5 = 3$$

The solution satisfies the original equation and is therefore valid.

Practice

1. Solve the radical equation $2\sqrt{x + 2} = \sqrt{x + 10}$.

   _____

2. Solve $x - 1 = \sqrt{x + 5}$. _____

3. Solve $\sqrt[3]{2x - 1} = 3$. _____

SAT TEST-TAKING TIP

Some of the most common mistakes made in solving radical equations are

- not isolating the radical before squaring both sides.
- squaring or cubing the entire side in an equation, not the individual terms.
- not checking for all extraneous solutions.

Keep in mind: no matter what the question is, solve the radical equation first. Knowing the solution will always allow you to eliminate choices and lead you to the correct answer. So, the key is to practice the skill of solving radical equations quickly and accurately each time you encounter them.

Try these SAT-style problems for more practice solving radical equations.

Practice

4. What is the largest x-value that is a solution of the equation $\sqrt{2x(x - 7)} = 4$? _____

5. Which of the following is the solution set for the equation $x - 2\sqrt{x} = 3$?
   a. $\{1,3\}$
   b. $\{1,9\}$
   c. $\{9\}$
   d. θ

Rational Functions

A rational function is an equation that contains fractions with variables in them. For instance, in the equation $\frac{1}{x} = \frac{3}{9}$, you can cross multiply to get $3x = 9$, which is $x = 3$.

In some rational functions, you may have more than one fraction containing variables.

Example
Solve for h:

$$\frac{1}{h} = \frac{9}{5h} - 6$$

First, find the LCD of h and $5h$, which is $5h$. Multiply both sides of the equation by $5h$:

$$5h(\tfrac{1}{h}) = (\tfrac{9}{5h} - 6)5h$$

The result is $5 = 9 - 30h$.
Solving this equation for h yields $-4 = -30h$, with a final answer of $h = \frac{2}{15}$.

Example
Solve for x:

$$\frac{1}{x} + \frac{7x + 12}{x^2 + 3x} = \frac{5x - 10}{x^2 + 3x}$$

First, factor $x^2 + 3x$ in the denominators on the left and right sides of the equation.

$$\frac{1}{x} + \frac{7x + 12}{x(x + 3)} = \frac{5(x - 2)}{x(x + 3)}$$

Then, find the LCD of x and $(x + 3)$, which is $x(x + 3)$. Multiply the left and right sides of the equation by the LCD:

$$x(x + 3)(\tfrac{1}{x} + \tfrac{7x + 12}{x(x+3)}) = (\tfrac{5(x-2)}{x(x+3)})x(x + 3)$$

Canceling like terms on the top and bottom yields

$$x + 3 + 7x + 12 = 5(x - 2)$$
$$8x + 15 = 5x - 10$$
$$3x + 15 = -10$$
$$3x = -25$$

The final answer is $x = -\frac{25}{3}$.

Solving Rational Functions on the SAT Exam

Rational functions on the SAT exam may come in the form of word problems that require you to set up and solve a rational function to answer the question. Even when the equation is given, you will need to use the LCD to clear fractions and solve for the variable in the rational function. While some questions are word problems with rational functions, other questions ask you about the solution of the rational function. By knowing how to find and use the LCD to clear fractions, you can answer these questions with no difficulty.

Practice
6. Identify the real numbers A and B that make the following equation true:

$$\frac{\frac{1}{2x + 1}}{2x^2 + 1} = (x + A) + \frac{B}{2x + 1}$$

a. $A = \frac{1}{2}, B = 0$

b. $A = \frac{1}{2}, B = \frac{3}{2}$

c. $A = 0, B = 0$

d. $A = -\frac{1}{2}, B = \frac{3}{2}$

7. Which of the following is the smallest value of x that satisfies the equation $\frac{1}{3-x} = \frac{2x}{3+x}$?

a. $\frac{1}{2}$

b. $\frac{3}{2}$

c. 1

d. $-\frac{3}{2}$

Answers and Explanations

1. $\frac{2}{3}$. First, isolate the radical expressions. The equation contains two distinct radical expressions. Raise both sides of the equation to a power to eliminate the radicals, and then simplify the result. Then, square both sides of the equation to solve algebraically.

$2\sqrt{x+2} = \sqrt{x+10}$	Original equation
$(2\sqrt{x+2})^2 = (\sqrt{x+10})^2$	Square both sides
$4(x+2) = x+10$	Simplify
$4x+8 = x+10$	
$3x+8 = 10$	
$3x = 2$	
$x = \frac{2}{3}$	

The solution appears to be $x = \frac{2}{3}$. You can verify the solution by substituting into the original equation to check the result:

$2\sqrt{x+2} = \sqrt{x+10}$	Original equation
$2\sqrt{\left(\frac{2}{3}\right)+2} = \sqrt{\left(\frac{2}{3}\right)+10}$	Substitute $\frac{2}{3}$ for x
$2\sqrt{2\frac{2}{3}} = \sqrt{10\frac{2}{3}}$	Simplify
$2\sqrt{\frac{8}{3}} = \sqrt{\frac{32}{3}}$	
$2\sqrt{\frac{4 \cdot 2}{3}} = \sqrt{\frac{16 \cdot 2}{3}}$	Factor the perfect squares inside the radicals
$4\sqrt{\frac{2}{3}} = 4\sqrt{\frac{2}{3}}$	Simplify

Since the first solution satisfies the original equation, the solution is valid.

2. 4. First, raise both sides of the equation to a power of 2 to eliminate the radicals, and then simplify the result:

$x - 1 = \sqrt{x + 5}$	Original equation
$(x - 1)^2 = (\sqrt{x + 5})^2$	Square both sides
$(x - 1)(x - 1) = x + 5$	Perform FOIL multiplication on the left side
$x^2 - 1x - 1x + 1 = x + 5$	Isolate variables and numbers on one side to form a quadratic in standard form $ax^2 + bx + c = 0$

$x^2 - 2x - x + 1 - 5 = 0$
$x^2 - 3x - 4 = 0$

Then, solve the resulting quadratic equation by factoring and solve for x:

$(x - 4)(x + 1) = 0$	Factor the left side
$(x - 4) = 0, (x + 1) = 0$	Set each factor to 0
$x = 4$ and $x = -1$	Solve for x

Finally, verify the solution(s). Substitute the potential solution into the original equation, and check the result:

$(4) - 1 = \sqrt{(4) + 5}$
$3 = 3$
$(-1) - 1 = \sqrt{(-1) + 5}$
$-2 \neq 2$

The value of -1 does not work in the original equation, so it is an extraneous solution. The value of 4 does, so it is a valid solution.

3. 14. Raise both sides of the equation to a power of 3 to eliminate the radicals, and then simplify the result:

$(\sqrt[3]{2x - 1})^3 = (3)^3$	Cube each side of the original radical equation
$2x - 1 = 27$	
$2x = 28$	Isolate the variable on one side and number on the other side
$x = 14$	Solve for x

Verify the solution in the original equation.

$\sqrt[3]{2(14) - 1} = 3$	Substitute the x value into the original equation
$\sqrt[3]{27} = 3$	Simplify
$3 = 3$	The value of 2 checks in the original equation, so it is a valid solution

4. 8. Solve the equation as follows:

$$\sqrt{2x(x - 7)} = 4$$
$$2x(x - 7) = 16$$
$$2x^2 - 14x = 16$$
$$2x^2 - 14x - 16 = 0$$
$$2(x^2 - 7x - 8) = 0$$
$$2(x - 8)(x + 1) = 0$$
$$x = -1, 8$$

Both of these values actually satisfy the equation (meaning that neither is extraneous), so the *largest* x-value that satisfies the equation is 8.

5. c. First isolate the radical term on one side of the equation, and then square both sides. Then solve the resulting quadratic equation.

$$x - 2\sqrt{x} = 3$$
$$x - 3 = 2\sqrt{x}$$
$$(x-3)^2 = (2\sqrt{x})^2$$
$$x^2 - 6x + 9 = 4x$$
$$x^2 - 10x + 9 = 0$$
$$(x-9)(x-1) = 0$$
$$x = 1, 9$$

If you substitute both of these values back into the original equation, you will see that $x = 9$ checks out, but $x = 1$ is an extraneous root. So, the solution set is just $\{9\}$. Choice **a** is incorrect because instead of isolating the radical term on one side, you squared both sides directly and in so doing squared the binomial incorrectly. Note that $(a-b)^2$ does not equal $a^2 - b^2$. Choice **b** is incorrect because $x = 1$ is an extraneous solution and does not belong in the solution set. Choice **d** is incorrect because there is one solution of this equation, namely $x = 9$.

6. d. First, rewrite the left side of the equation and then use long division, like so:

$$\require{enclose}
\begin{array}{r}
x - \frac{1}{2} + \frac{\frac{3}{2}}{2x+1} \\
2x+1 \enclose{longdiv}{2x^2 + 0x + 1} \\
\underline{-(2x^2 + x)} \\
-x + 1 \\
\underline{-(-x - \frac{1}{2})} \\
\frac{3}{2}
\end{array}$$

Identifying $A = -\frac{1}{2}$, $B = \frac{3}{2}$ in the result yields the correct answer. Choice **a** is incorrect because when using long division, you forgot to multiply the constant term of the divisor by $-\frac{1}{2}$. Remember to distribute the constant when multiplying by a polynomial. Choice **b** is incorrect because the sign of A should be negative. The given form is $x + A$. Note that $x + (-\frac{1}{2}) = x - \frac{1}{2}$. Choice **c** is incorrect because you likely tried to cancel $2x$ in the top and bottom of the complex fraction on the left side of the equation but you are only allowed to cancel like *factors* in this situation. You can't cancel like *terms*.

7. c. First, multiply both sides by the least common denominator of the two fractions in the equation, namely $(3 - x)(3 + x)$, and solve the quadratic equation that arises:

$$\frac{1}{3-x} = \frac{2x}{3+x}$$
$$3 + x = 2x(3 - x)$$
$$3 + x = 6x - 2x^2$$
$$2x^2 - 5x + 3 = 0$$
$$(2x - 3)(x - 1) = 0$$
$$x = \frac{3}{2}, 1$$

Both of these values of x actually satisfy the original equation (that is, neither one is extraneous), so the smallest value of x that satisfies the equation is 1. Choice **a** is incorrect because you simply equated the numerators and solved for x. But the denominators are different, and so you must first multiply both sides of the equation by the least common denominator and *then* solve for x. Choice **b** is incorrect because this is actually the largest value of x that satisfies this equation. Choice **d** is incorrect because after clearing the fractions, you factored the resulting quadratic expression incorrectly. Specifically, $2x^2 - 5x + 3 = (2x - 3)(x - 1)$.

15 ▶ FACTORABLE POLYNOMIALS AND NON-LINEAR FUNCTIONS

Pure mathematics is, in its way, the poetry of logical ideas.
—ALBERT EINSTEIN

LESSON SUMMARY

In this lesson, you'll practice methods for factoring trinomials, or polynomials with three terms. By factoring trinomials, you can find solutions or zeros. This lesson will teach you how to handle SAT problems that involve finding the zeros and interpreting what they mean.

P olynomial functions are equations that have degrees greater than 2, in the standard form $f(x) = ax^n + bx^n + \ldots + c = 0$. Some polynomials are named by their highest degree, such as cubic (or third-degree) and quartic (or fourth-degree). For polynomials over degree 4, it is customary to refer to a polynomial as a **higher-order degree** polynomial. A typical polynomial curve will cross the x-axis at its zeros. The zeros are the values that make the equation equal to 0. They are also considered the solutions to the polynomial.

Factoring Polynomials

In this lesson, you must utilize your knowledge of factoring (as discussed in Lessons 12 and 13) to solve the questions we'll cover. The following table summarizes the different types of factoring you may need to use.

FACTORING METHOD	FACTORING EXAMPLES
GCF (greatest common factor)	$3x^4 + 9x$ factors to $3x(x^3 + 3)$
FOIL (first-outer-inner-last)	$x^4 + 4x^2 + 3$ factors to $(x^2 + 3)(x^2 + 1)$
Difference of squares	$x^6 - 9$ factors to $(x^3 - 3)(x^3 + 3)$

Example: Given the quadratic function $f(x) = 3x^2 - 2x - 5$, find the zeros.

$f(x) = 3x^2 - 2x - 5$ Write the original function

$f(x) = (3x - 5)(x + 1)$ Factor the quadratic into two binomials

Solve each binomial for x to find the zeros of the function:

$(3x - 5) = 0$ $(x + 1) = 0$

$3x = 5$ $x = -1$

$x = \frac{5}{3}$

The zeros of the function are $x = \frac{5}{3}$ and $x = -1$.

Example: Show $f(x) = x^3 - x^2 - 2x$ has zeros at $x = 0, 2,$ and -1.

$f(x) = (0)^3 - (0)^2 - 2(0) = 0$

$f(x) = (2)^3 - (2)^2 - 2(2) = 0$

$f(x) = (-1)^3 - (-1)^2 - 2(-1) = 0$

SAT TEST-TAKING TIP

Refresh your memory of various factoring techniques. When solving polynomials for zeros, you will need to factor to obtain them. Also, remember that zeros are values that make the given equation equal to 0.

Practice

1. How many distinct real zeros does the polynomial $p(x)$ have?
   a. 0
   b. 1
   c. 3
   d. 5

2. Suppose $p(x) = 2x^3 - x^2 - 13x - 6$. If 3 and -2 are both x-intercepts of $p(x)$, which of the following must be true?
   a. $(x + 3)$ is a factor of $p(x)$.
   b. The remainder when $p(x)$ is divided by $(2x + 1)$ is 0.
   c. $p(-2)$ is a positive number.
   d. $p(x) = a(x - 3)(x + 2)^2$ for some real number a.

3. Suppose that $p(x)$ is a fifth-degree polynomial for which $p(3) = p(-1) = 0$, $x + 6$ is one of its factors, and $\frac{p(x)}{x^2 + 4} = 0$. Which of the following could be the equation of such a polynomial?
   a. $p(x) = (x + 3)(x - 1)(x + 6)(x^2 + 4)$
   b. $p(x) = (x - 3)(x + 1)(x + 6)(x^2 + 4)$
   c. $p(x) = (x - 3)(x - 2)(x + 1)(x + 2)(x + 6)$
   d. $p(x) = (x - 1)^2(x - 3)(x + 6)(x^2 + 4)$

Non-Linear Functions and Their Graphs

The following table summarizes the standard form of non-linear functions and their graphs. For each function, note the overall shape of the graph and where each graph crosses the x-axis. These points represent the zeros or solutions for the functions.

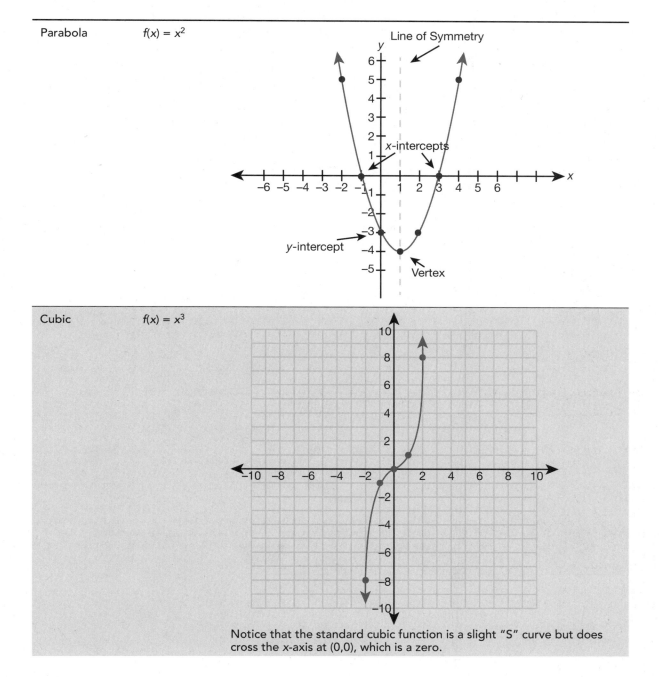

Parabola $f(x) = x^2$

Cubic $f(x) = x^3$

Notice that the standard cubic function is a slight "S" curve but does cross the x-axis at (0,0), which is a zero.

Quartic $f(x) = x^4$

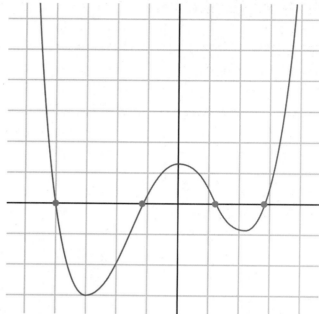

Note: Not all quartic functions have 4 zeros. In some quartic functions, there are 0, 2, or 4 zeros that are real numbers.

Hyperbola $f(x) = \frac{1}{x}$

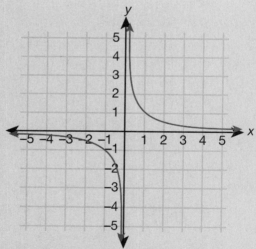

Notice that the curves come very close to the x- and y-axes but never touch them. In this case, the x- and y-axes are called **asymptotes**. Since the hyperbola never crosses the x-axis, there are no zeros. In other words, there are no values that make $\frac{1}{x} = 0$.

SAT TEST-TAKING TIP

You should memorize the standard forms and graphs of non-linear functions from the table given on the preceding two pages. Most questions on the SAT exam regarding these functions ask you to identify a graph or an equation belonging to a non-linear function. Also make a note of some language used to describe key features or characteristics of graphs.

Intercepts	Points at which the curve crosses an axis. So, a y-intercept is the point where a curve crosses the y-axis.
Reflection	A graph that is flipped over an axis.
Symmetry	A mirror image of a graph over an axis.

Example

The following is the graph of a fourth-degree polynomial $p(x)$.

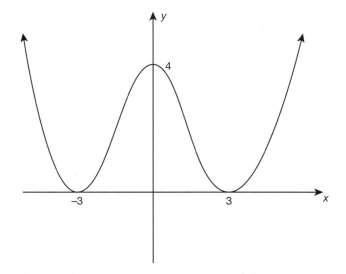

Which of the following is true?
a. The equation for $p(x)$ is $p(x) = (x^2 - 9)(x^2 + 9)$.
b. The maximum value of the function $y = -p(x)$ is 0.
c. $\frac{p(x)}{x^2 + 9} = 0$
d. $p(4) = 0$

The graph of the polynomial $y = -p(x)$ is the reflection of $p(x)$ over the x-axis. Since the minimum value of $p(x)$ is 0, it follows then that the maximum value of $y = -p(x)$ is 0 (choice **b**).

Practice

4. The following is the graph of a third-degree polynomial $p(x)$.

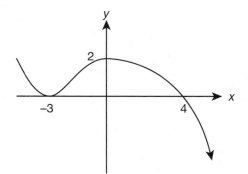

Which of the following is NOT true?
a. The graph of p has two x-intercepts.
b. The remainder when $p(x)$ is divided by $(x + 3)$ is 0.
c. $p(0)$ is a positive number.
d. $(x - 4)^2$ is a factor of $p(x)$.

5. The following is the graph of a fourth-degree polynomial $p(x)$.

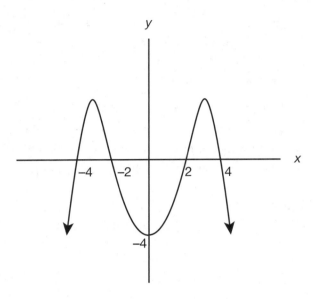

Which of the following can be its equation?

a. $p(x) = -4(x^2 + 16)(x^2 + 4)$

b. $p(x) = -4(x^2 - 16)(x^2 - 4)$

c. $p(x) = -\frac{1}{16}(x^2 + 16)(x^2 + 4)$

d. $p(x) = -\frac{1}{16}(x^2 - 16)(x^2 - 4)$

Answers and Explanations

1. c. Notice that $p(x)$ can be factored as $p(x) = x(x^2 - 4)(x^2 + 1) = x(x - 2)(x + 2)(x^2 + 1)$. Each linear factor gives another real zero, so $p(x)$ has three distinct real zeros.

2. b. We know that since 3 and -2 are zeros, $(x - 3)$ and $(x + 2)$ are both factors of $p(x)$. As such, for the statement to be true, we must show that $\frac{p(x)}{(x - 3)(x + 2)} = 2x + 1$. Equivalently, we can show that $p(x) = (2x + 1)(x - 3)(x + 2)$. Multiplying out the right side, we see that

$$(2x + 1)(x - 3)(x + 2) = (2x + 1)(x^2 - x - 6)$$
$$= 2x^3 - x^2 - 13x - 6$$
$$= p(x)$$

3. b. First, since $p(3) = p(-1) = 0$, it follows that $x - 3$ and $x + 1$ are factors of $p(x)$. The condition $\frac{p(x)}{x^2 + 4} = 0$ implies that $x^2 + 4$ is a factor of $p(x)$. Since we are also given that $x + 6$ is a factor, and the product of all of these factors produces a polynomial of degree 5, this equation could describe the given polynomial.

4. d. The graph of the polynomial is not tangent to the x-axis at $x = 4$, but it is tangent at $x = -3$. So, the power of $(x - 4)$ must be 1 and the power of $(x - (-3))$ must be 2. Choice **a** is incorrect because the graph crosses the x-axis at two distinct places, so it has two x-intercepts. Choice **b** is incorrect because this is a true statement. In fact, $(x + 3)^2$ is a factor of $p(x)$ because the graph is tangent to the x-axis at $x = -3$. Choice **c** is incorrect because $p(0) = 2$, which is positive. So this statement is true.

5. d. First, observe that $x^2 - 16 = (x - 4)(x + 4)$ and $x^2 - 4 = (x - 2)(x + 2)$. So, the zeros of this function are -4, -2, 2, and 4, exactly where the graph crosses the x-axis. Also, observe that $p(0) = 4$, as needed. Choice **a** is incorrect because for this equation, $p(0)$ does not equal -4, as shown, and its two factors are never zero, so that it couldn't cross the x-axis at -4, -2, 2, or 4. Choice **b** is incorrect because for this equation, $p(0)$ does not equal -4, although the factors are both correct. Choice **c** is incorrect because its two factors are never zero, so it couldn't cross the x-axis at -4, -2, 2, or 4. Note that $x^2 + 16 \neq x^2 - 16$, the latter of which factors as $(x - 4)(x + 4)$.

16 ▶ TRANSFORMATIONS AND COMPOSITIONS OF FUNCTIONS

Math is like going to the gym for your brain. It sharpens your mind.

—DANICA McKELLAR

LESSON SUMMARY

This lesson covers transforming functions in the coordinate plane. Using function notation allows you to flip, shift, and invert a function. In this lesson, you'll also learn how to compose functions using function notation.

What would you do with your smartphone to capture the different views of the city skyline? You could rotate the smartphone 90 degrees counterclockwise (or clockwise). The size and shape of the smartphone would not change; only its orientation would (from portrait/vertical to landscape/horizontal).

When an object is moved, we refer to the original object as the *preimage* and the "new" object after it has been moved as the *image*. The process of changing or mapping the original object (preimage) to the new object (image) is called a **transformation**. So, just think of a transformation as the "instructions" needed to change a preimage to an image.

Types of Transformations

In this lesson, we'll explore three types of isometric transformations that we can perform on an object while preserving its original size, shape, and angle. Since an object does not change during the transformation, we can also refer to the actual movement of the object as a **rigid motion**.

Rotations

Remember the picture-taking example? In it, you positioned the camera to take a portrait and a landscape picture. The smartphone had to be rotated from its original position 90 degrees counterclockwise to take a landscape picture from a portrait one. A graph (image) can rotate clockwise or counterclockwise by any angle between 0 to 360 degrees.

Translations

We can also shift an object to another location. Think of when you walk down the street from one place to the other. If you are the object, your body is shifting from one place to the other by a certain number of steps. This is called a translation. A graph can translate or shift by a given number of units up, down, left, or right. To translate a graph up or down by C units, add (up) them to or subtract (down) them from the original function. So, if $f(x) = x^2$, then

$g(x) = x^2 + C$ will move the graph up C units.
$g(x) = x^2 - C$ will move the graph down C units.
$g(x + C) = (x + C)^2$ will move the graph left C units.
$g(x - C) = (x - C)^2$ will move the graph right C units.

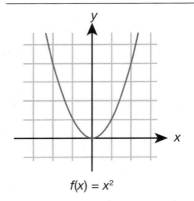

$$f(x) = x^2$$

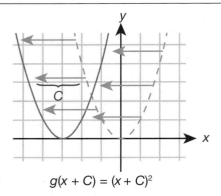

$$g(x + C) = (x + C)^2$$

An example of a translation in which the original $f(x)$ has been shifted left C units

Reflections

When you look in a mirror, what do you see? Another you, right? Your preimage has been reflected into the mirror, and the mirror shows you an image after the reflection. Your reflected image is the exact opposite of your original image. So, your left eye is now your right eye in the mirror, and so on. A graph (image) can reflect or appear over the x-axis, over the y-axis, or over the line $y = x$ (diagonal). So, if the original function is $f(x) = x^2$:

> $g(x) = -(x^2)$ will reflect the graph about the x-axis.
>
> $g(x) = (-x^2)$ will reflect the graph about the y-axis.

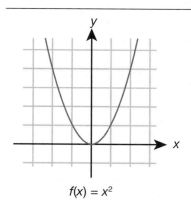

$f(x) = x^2$

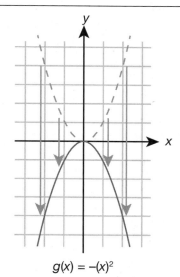

$g(x) = -(x)^2$

An example of a reflection about the x-axis of the original graph $f(x)$

Stretches

Take a deep breath and watch your chest get larger. This expansion is called a stretch. When you exhale your breath and your chest gets smaller again, this is called a shrinking. A graph (image) can stretch or shrink by a given number of units. We can stretch a function by multiplying by a constant. So, if the original function is $f(x) = x^2$, then

$g(x) = Cx^2$ will stretch the graph by C units.
$g(x) = (Cx)^2$ will shrink the graph by C units.

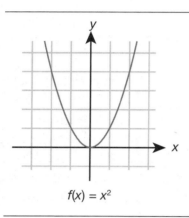

$f(x) = x^2$

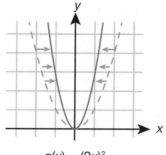

$g(x) = (2x)^2$

An example of a shrink in which the original graph shrinks by 2 units

Practice

1. Which transformation of the parent function $f(x) = x^2$ represents the equation $g(x) = (x + 2)^2 - 5$?

   a. Shift 2 units left; shift 5 units down.
   b. Shift 5 units right; shift 2 units down.
   c. Shift 2 units left; shift 5 units up.
   d. Shift 5 units right; shift 2 units up.

2. The graph of $f(x)$ is shown here. If the graph of $f(x)$ is reflected about the x-axis and then translated up 4 units to create $f'(x)$, what is the y-intercept of $f'(x)$? _____

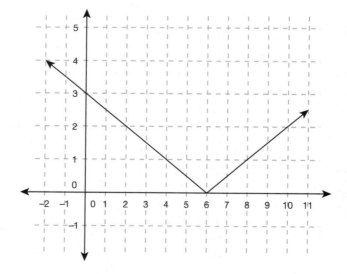

3. The graph of $f(x)$ has been reduced by one-half and then reflected about the y-axis to form the graph $f'(x)$. What is the equation for the graph of $f'(x)$? _____

What Are Compositions?

Suppose there are two functions, $f(x)$ and $g(x)$. We could combine $f(x)$ and $g(x)$ by adding, subtracting, multiplying, or dividing them. To compose the two functions means to write one in terms of the other. In other words, f compose g means $f(g(x))$ or that the function $g(x)$ becomes the input for the function $f(x)$.

   Example
   $f(x) = 3x$ and $g(x) = x + 1$. To find $f(g(3))$:

   Step 1: Find $g(3) = (3) + 1 = 4$
   Step 2: Find $f(g(3)) = f(4) = 3(4) = 12$

   So, f compose g of 3 would be 12.

Now you may wonder if f compose g is the same as g compose f. Let's find out using the same example.

   Again, $f(x) = 3x$ and $g(x) = x + 1$. To find $g(f(3))$:

   Step 1: Find $f(3) = 3(3) = 9$
   Step 2: Find $g(f(x)) = g(f(3)) = g(9) = (9) + 1$
   $= 10$

So, g compose f would be 10, which is NOT the same as f compose g.

Example

x	−1	0	1	2	3
f(x)	3	2	1	0	−1
g(x)	16	9	4	1	0

Consider the functions f and g whose values are in the table above. What is the value of $f(g(3))$?

From the table, the value of $g(3)$ is 0. So, $f(g(3))$ $= f(0)$, which is 2.

Problems Involving Compositions on the SAT Exam

Problems involving compositions with functions will be fairly straightforward on the SAT exam. There are usually a variety of functions to compose such as linear with a rational or quadratic with a rational. Also, you may be asked to find an expression involving the composite of two functions.

> ### SAT TEST-TAKING TIP
>
> When finding composites, always be sure to evaluate the innermost function first and then work your way outward. This is by far the easiest way to approach these problems.

Practice

4. If $f(x) = 25x^2 + 10x$ and $g(x) = \frac{1}{x-1}$, find $f(g(6))$.

5. If $a(x) = x^2$ and $b(x) = 2x + 5$, find $b(a(x))$.

6. If $f(x) = x^2$ and $g(x) = x + 3$, find $f(g(x)) - 9x$.

7. What is $u(w(2))$ when $u(x) = x^2 + 3x + 2$ and $w(x) = \frac{1}{x-1}$?

Answers and Explanations

1. **a.** In the equation, the +2 means that the function has been shifted to the left 2 units. The −5 means that the function has been shifted down 5 units.

2. **(0,1).** The formula to find the points of the transformation is $(x,y) \rightarrow (x, -y + 4)$. For the point $(0,3)$, the point on the transformation would be $(x, -y + 4)$, which is $(0, (-3) + 4)$, or $(0,1)$.

3. $f'(x) = f(\frac{1}{2}x) - 2$. $f(\frac{1}{2}x)$ will shrink the original $f(x)$ by one-half. $f(-x)$ will reflect the graph about the y-axis. So, $f'(x) = f(-\frac{1}{2}x) - 2$ will shrink the original $f(x)$ by one-half and reflect it about the y-axis.

4. **3.**

$$g(6) = \frac{1}{(6) - 1} = \frac{1}{5}$$
$$f(g(6)) = f(\tfrac{1}{5}) = 25(\tfrac{1}{5})^2 + 10(\tfrac{1}{5})$$
$$= 25(\tfrac{1}{25}) + 10(\tfrac{1}{5})$$
$$= 1 + 2 = 3$$

5. $2x^2 + 5$.

$$a(x) = x^2$$
$$b(a(x)) = 2(x^2) + 5$$
$$= 2x^2 + 5$$

6. $x^2 - 3x + 9$.

$$f(g(x)) = (x + 3)^2$$
$$= x^2 + 6x + 9$$
$$f(g(x)) - 9x = x^2 + 6x + 9 - 9x$$
$$= x^2 - 3x + 9$$

7. **6.**

$$w(2) = \frac{1}{(2) - 1} = 1$$
$$u(1) = (1)^2 + 3(1) + 2$$
$$= 1 + 3 + 2$$
$$= 6$$

17 ▶ OPERATIONS WITH COMPLEX NUMBERS

I have hardly ever known a mathematician who was able to reason.

—STEPHEN HAWKING (quoting Plato)

LESSON SUMMARY

In this lesson, you'll learn about complex numbers and how to add, subtract, multiply, and divide with them. Complex numbers contain a real part and an imaginary part but can be manipulated like binomials.

What do you get when you take the square root of a negative number? If you answered "an imaginary number," you are correct. As you may know from using the quadratic formula, sometimes you may arrive at a negative number under the square root. Not to worry, complex numbers come to your rescue.

What Are Complex Numbers?

A complex number is a number in the form $a + bi$, where a represents a real number and bi represents an imaginary number. The variable i represents the special quantity $\sqrt{-1}$. Using complex numbers expands the number base that is possible. Complex numbers $a + bi$ contain

- real numbers (0, 1, 2.5, .355555, etc.)
- imaginary numbers ($3 + 4i$, $-6 + 7i$)
- pure imaginary numbers ($4i$, $7i$)

Working with i

By defining i, we get several important quantities immediately by just using properties of multiplication. For instance

$$i = \sqrt{-1}$$
$$i^2 = (\sqrt{-1})^2 = -1$$
$$i^3 = (i^2)(i) = -1i = -i$$
$$i^4 = (i^2)^2 = (-1)^2 = 1$$
$$i^5 = (i^3)(i^2) = (-i)(-1) = i$$
$$i^6 = (i^3)^2 = (-i)(-i) = i^2 = -1$$
$$i^7 = (i^5)(i^2) = (i)(-1) = -i$$
$$i^8 = (i^4)^2 = (1)^2 = 1$$

How would you solve i^{60}? As long as you have the value of a few powers of i, you have all you need. You just need to factor the powers into powers of i that you already know.

$$i^{60} = (i^4)^{15} = (1)^{15} = 1$$
$$i^{29} = (i^{28})(i) = ((i^4)^7(i) = (1)^7(i) = i$$

Try these problems on your own.

Practice

1. Which of the following is equivalent to i^{18}?
   a. -1
   b. i
   c. 1
   d. $-i$

2. What is the sum of i^{22} and i^{23}? _____

What about Square Roots?

Now that we have i as the square root of a negative number, we can use this notation: $\sqrt{-n} = (\sqrt{-1})(\sqrt{n}) = i(\sqrt{n})$, where n is any real number.

So, for example, $\sqrt{-3} = (\sqrt{-1})(\sqrt{3}) = i(\sqrt{3})$.

Adding Complex Numbers

To add two complex numbers, $a + bi$ and $c + di$, simply add the real parts and the imaginary parts and rewrite the variable i.

So, to add $(5 + 9i) + (-2 + 4i)$:

1. Add the real parts: $5 - 2 = 3$
2. Add the imaginary parts: $(9 + 4) = 13$
3. Rewrite the answer using i: $3 + 13i$

You can write this as $(5 + 9i) + (-2 + 4i) = (5 - 2) + (9 + 13)i = 3 + 13i$.

Practice

3. Two complex numbers are represented by $w = -2 + 5i$ and $z = 1 - 3i$. What is $w + z$?

   _____

Subtracting Complex Numbers

To subtract two complex numbers, change the sign of the second complex number.

For instance, to subtract $(8 + 5i) - (3 - 2i)$:
1. Subtract the real parts: $8 - 3 = 5$
2. Subtract the imaginary parts: $(5 - (-2)) = 5 + 2 = 7$
3. Rewrite the answer using i: $5 + 7i$

You can write this problem as $(8 + 5i) - (3 - 2i) = (8 - 3) - (5 - (-2))i = 5 + 7i$.

Multiplying Complex Numbers

Since complex numbers have a real part and an imaginary part, we can multiply them like binomials using the FOIL method.

Let's look at $(a + bi)(c + di)$:

$F = (a)(c) = ac$
$O = (a)(di) = adi$
$I = (bi)(c) = bci$
$L = (bi)(di) = (bd)i^2 = -bd$

The final answer would be $ac + adi + bci - bd = ac + (ad + bc)i - bd$.

Note: To multiply a number by a complex number, just use the distributive property. So, for example, $8(2 - 1i)$ would be $(8)(2) + (8)(-1)i = 16 - 8i$.

Example
$$7i(5 - 6i) = (7i)(5) + (7i)(-6i)$$
$$= 35i - 42i^2$$
$$= 35i - 42(-1)$$
$$= 35i + 42 \text{ or } 42 + 35i$$

Practice
4. In the equation $-2i(3 - 5i) = a + bi$, what is the value of b?
   a. -10
   b. -6
   c. 0
   d. 6

Dividing Complex Numbers

When dividing complex numbers, the goal is to clear the denominator by multiplying the quotient by the conjugate of the denominator.

COMPLEX CONJUGATES

If you have two of the same complex numbers with opposite signs, each member of the pair is called a **conjugate** of the other. Conjugates are important because they help us quickly perform arithmetic operations on complex numbers. For instance, $(4 - 2i)$ and $(4 + 2i)$ are conjugates. $(-9 + 2i)(9 - 2i)$ are NOT conjugates, because the real parts are different. $(5 + 5i)(5 - 4i)$ are NOT conjugates because the imaginary parts are different.

For instance, to divide $\frac{5 + 2i}{3 - 6i}$, we need to multiply the denominator by the conjugate of $3 - 6i$.

By definition, the conjugate contains the same real and imaginary parts with the opposite sign. So, the conjugate of $3 - 6i$ is $3 + 6i$.

Multiply the numerator and denominator by the conjugate:

$$\left(\frac{5 + 2i}{3 - 6i}\right)\left(\frac{3 + 6i}{3 + 6i}\right)$$

FOILing the numerator yields $(5 + 2i)(3 + 6i)$:

$$(5)(3) = 15$$
$$(5)(+6i) = +30i$$
$$(+2i)(3) = +6i$$
$$(+2i)(+6i) = +12i^2 = +12(-1) = -12$$

So, the numerator is $15 + 30i + 6i - 12 = 15 + 36i - 12$ $= 3 + 36i$.

FOILing the denominator yields $(3 - 6i)(3 + 6i)$:

$$(3)(3) = 9$$
$$(3)(+6i) = +18i$$
$$(-6i)(3) = -18i$$
$$(-6i)(+6i) = -36i^2 = -36(-1) = 36$$

So, the denominator is $9 + 36 = 45$. The result is $\frac{3 + 36i}{45}$.

Practice

5. Consider the quotient $\frac{8 - 4i}{-2 + 2i}$. What is the value of b if the final expression is in the form $a + bi$?

_____

Handling Complex Number Problems on the SAT Exam

Complex numbers on the SAT exam can be a bit tricky depending on the way that the question is asked, but there is one certainty. The principles that you have learned in this lesson will always apply, so master them. Specifically, you will need to know:

- powers of i (for example, i, i^2, i^3, i^4, i^5)
- how to add, subtract, multiply, and divide complex numbers
- using conjugates to divide complex numbers

Try out some more practice problems to drive home the skills you've learned here.

Practice

6. For $i = \sqrt{-1}$, which of the following equals $(5 - 3i)^2$?
   a. $-14i$
   b. $34 - 30i$
   c. $16 - 30i$
   d. $25 - 21i$

7. For $i = \sqrt{-1}$, which of the following equals $3i + (1 - 8i)(1 + 8i)$?
   a. $65 + 3i$
   b. $-63 + 3i$
   c. $68i$
   d. $1 - 13i$

8. For $i = \sqrt{-1}$, which answer is equivalent to $\frac{3 - 5i}{10i}$?
   a. $-\frac{4}{5} + 0i$
   b. $-\frac{1}{2} + \frac{3}{10}i$
   c. $1 + 0i$
   d. $-\frac{1}{2} - \frac{3}{10}i$

Answers and Explanations

1. a. $i^{18} = (i^2)^9 = (-1)^9$, which is -1.

2. $-1 - i$. First, find i^{22}. We have that $i^{22} = (i^2)^{11} = (-1)^{11} = -1$. Then, find i^{23}. We have that $i^{23} = (i^{22})(i) = -1i$, or $-i$. The final answer is $-1 - i$.

3. $-1 + 2i$.
$$w + z = (-2 + 5i) + (1 - 3i)$$
$$= (-2 + 1) + (5 - 3)^i$$
$$= -1 + 2i$$

4. b.
$$-2i(3 - 5i) = (-2i)(3) + (-2i)(-5i)$$
$$= -6i + 10i^2$$
$$= -6i + 10(-1)$$
$$= -6i - 10 \text{ or } -10 - 6i$$
Therefore, $b = -6$.

5. -1. Multiply $\frac{8-4i}{-2+2i}$ by the conjugate of $-2 + 2i$, which is $-2 - 2i$. This yields $(\frac{8-4i}{-2+2i})(\frac{-2-2i}{-2-2i})$.
FOILing the numerator yields $(8 - 4i)(-2 - 2i)$:
$$(8)(-2) = -16$$
$$(8)(-2i) = -16i$$
$$(-4i)(-2) = +8i$$
$$(-4i)(-2i) = +8i^2 = 8(-1) = -8$$
So, the numerator is $-16 - 16i + 8i - 8 = -24 - 8i$.
FOILing the denominator yields $(-2 + 2i)(-2 - 2i)$:
$$(-2)(-2) = 4$$
$$(-2)(-2i) = +4i$$
$$(+2i)(-2) = -4i$$
$$(+2i)(-2i) = -4i^2 = -4(-1) = 4$$
So, the denominator is $4 + 4 = 8$.
The result is $\frac{-24 - 8i}{8}$. Notice that you can simplify by dividing both terms in the numerator by 8. The final complex number is $-3 - 1i$. So, this means $b = -1$.

6. c. Write $(5 - 3i)^2$ as $(5 - 3i)(5 - 3i)$, FOIL the product, and simplify using the fact that $i^2 = -1$. Then, add like terms:
$$(5 - 3i)(5 - 3i) = 25 - 15i - 15i + 9i^2$$
$$= 25 - 30i - 9$$
$$= 16 - 30i$$

7. a. FOIL the product, simplify using the fact that $i^2 = -1$, and then add like terms:
$$3i + (1 - 8i)(1 + 8i)$$
$$= 3i + (1^2 + 8i - 8i - (8i)^2)$$
$$= 3i + 1 + 64$$
$$= 3i + 65$$
$$= 65 + 3i$$

8. d. First multiply top and bottom by i and then simplify, as follows:
$$\frac{3-5i}{10i} = \frac{3-5i}{10i} \cdot \frac{i}{i} = \frac{3i - 5i^2}{10i^2} = \frac{3i+5}{-10}$$
$$= \frac{3i}{-10} + \frac{5}{-10} = -\frac{1}{2} - \frac{3}{10}i$$

18 ▶

USING TRIGONOMETRY TO SOLVE PROBLEMS INVOLVING LINES, ANGLES, AND RIGHT TRIANGLES

Geometry existed before creation.

—PLATO

LESSON SUMMARY

This lesson delves into geometry, with properties of lines, angles, and right triangles. You'll learn how to use trigonometric ratios and the Pythagorean theorem in problems.

This is a longer lesson you will likely want to break into three 20-minute sessions to fully absorb all of the concepts presented. A good place to stop for the day is after each practice set.

ngles, lines, and shapes are the basic building blocks of geometry. They are representative of the physical world and thus make it easier to observe and study things in the real world.

Working with Angles

Many of us use the term *angle* in everyday conversations. For example, we talk about camera angles, angles for pool shots and golf shots, and angles for furniture placement. In geometry, an *angle* is formed by two rays with a common endpoint. The symbol used to indicate an angle is ∠. The two rays are the sides of the angle. The common endpoint is the vertex of the angle. In the following figure, the sides are $\overrightarrow{RD}$ and $\overrightarrow{RY}$, and the vertex is R.

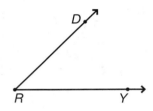

Naming Angles

People call you different names at different times. These different names don't change who you are—just the way others refer to you. For example, you may be called your given name at work, but your friends might call you by a nickname. Confusion can sometimes arise when these names are different.

Just like you, an angle can be named in different ways. The different ways an angle can be named may be confusing if you do not understand the logic behind the different methods of naming.

If three letters are used to name an angle, then the middle letter always names the vertex. If the angle does not share the vertex point with another angle, then you can name the angle with only the letter of the vertex. If a number is written inside the angle that is not the angle measurement, then you can name the

angle by that number. You can name the following angle any one of these names: ∠WET, ∠TEW, ∠E, or ∠1.

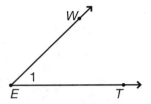

Right Angles

Angles that make a square corner are called *right angles*. In drawings, the following symbol is used to indicate a right angle:

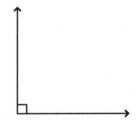

Straight Angles

Opposite rays are two rays with the same endpoint that extend in opposite directions and form a line. They form a *straight angle*. In the following figure, $\overrightarrow{HD}$ and $\overrightarrow{HS}$ are opposite rays that form the straight angle *DHS*.

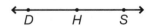

Classifying Angles

Angles are often classified by their measures. The degree is the most commonly used unit for measuring angles. One full turn, or a circle, equals 360°.

Acute Angles

An *acute angle* has a measure between 0° and 90°. Here are two examples of acute angles:

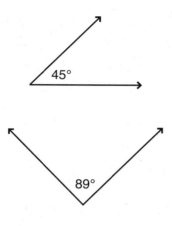

Obtuse Angles

An *obtuse angle* has a measure between 90° and 180°. Here are two examples of obtuse angles:

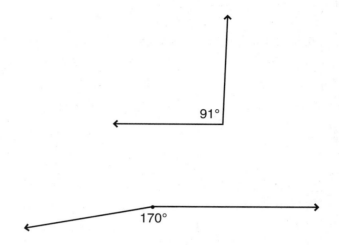

Right Angles

A *right angle* has a 90° measure. The corner of a piece of paper will fit exactly into a right angle. Here are two examples of right angles:

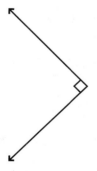

Straight Angles

A *straight angle* has a 180° measure. ∠*ABC* is an example of a straight angle:

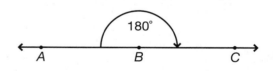

Supplementary Angles

When two angles sum to 180°, they are called *supplementary angles*. When two angles share a side, they are called *adjacent angles*. Supplementary angles can be adjacent, such as ∠BAD and ∠DAN, although sometimes supplementary angles are not adjacent, like ∠TEN and ∠KAI.

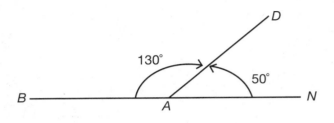

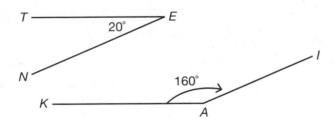

Working with Lines

Both intersecting and nonintersecting lines surround you, but you probably don't pay much attention to them most of the time. Let's look at two different types of intersecting lines: transversals and perpendicular lines. We'll also look at nonintersecting lines: parallel and skew lines.

Intersecting Lines

On a piece of scratch paper, draw two straight lines that cross. Can you make these straight lines cross at more than one point? No, you can't, because intersecting lines cross at only one point (unless they are the same line). The point where they cross is called the *point of intersection*. They actually share this point because it is on both lines. Two special types of

intersecting lines are called *transversals* and *perpendicular lines*.

Transversals

A *transversal* is a line that intersects two or more other lines, each at a different point. In the following figure, line *t* is a transversal; line *s* is not.

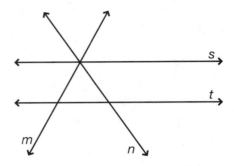

The prefix *trans* means *across*. In the previous figure, you can see that line *t* cuts across the two lines *m* and *n*. Line *m* is a transversal for lines *s* and *t*. Also, line *n* is a transversal across lines *s* and *t*. Line *s* crosses lines *m* and *n* at the same point (their point of intersection); therefore, line *s* is not a transversal. A transversal can cut across parallel as well as intersecting lines, as shown here:

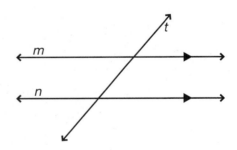

Perpendicular Lines

Perpendicular lines are another type of intersecting line. Everyday examples of perpendicular lines include the horizontal and vertical lines of a plaid fabric and the lines formed by panes in a window. Perpendicular lines meet to form right angles. Right angles always measure 90°. In the following figure, lines *x* and *y* are perpendicular:

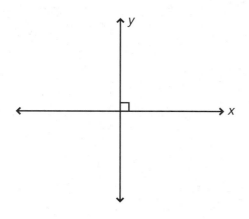

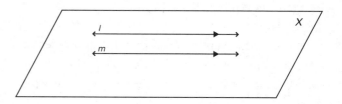

Lines *l* and *m* are coplanar lines.
Lines *l* and *m* do not intersect.
Lines *l* and *m* are parallel.

The symbol "⊥" means perpendicular. You could write $x \perp y$ to show these lines are perpendicular. Also, the symbol that makes a square in the corner where lines *x* and *y* meet indicates a right angle. In geometry, you shouldn't assume anything without being told. Never assume a pair of lines are perpendicular without one of these symbols. A transversal *can* be perpendicular to a pair of lines, but it does not *have* to be. In the following figure, line *t* is perpendicular to both line *l* and line *m*.

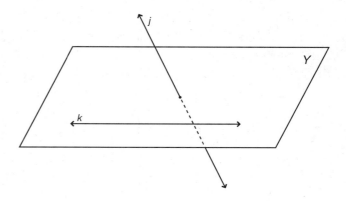

Lines *j* and *k* are noncoplanar lines.
Lines *j* and *k* do not intersect.
Lines *j* and *k* are skew.

The symbol "||" means parallel. So you can abbreviate the sentence, "Lines *l* and *m* are parallel," by writing "*l* || *m*." Do not assume a pair of lines are parallel unless it is indicated. Arrowheads on the lines in a figure indicate that the lines are parallel. Sometimes, double arrowheads are necessary to differentiate two sets of parallel lines, as shown in the following figure:

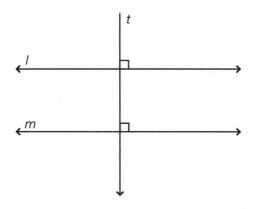

Nonintersecting Lines

There are two types of nonintersecting lines: parallel and skew. Coplanar lines that do not intersect are called *parallel*. Noncoplanar lines that do not intersect are called *skew*.

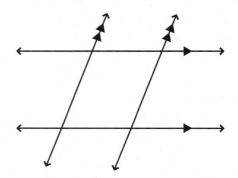

Everyday examples of parallel lines include rows of crops on a farm and railroad tracks. An example of skew lines is the vapor trails of a northbound jet and a westbound jet flying at different altitudes. One jet would pass over the other, but their paths would not cross.

Angles Formed by Parallel Lines and a Transversal

If a pair of parallel lines are cut by a transversal, then eight angles are formed. In the following figure, line l is parallel to line m, and line t is a transversal forming angles 1–8. Angles 3, 4, 5, and 6 are inside the parallel lines and are called *interior* angles. Angles 1, 2, 7, and 8 are outside the parallel lines and are called *exterior* angles.

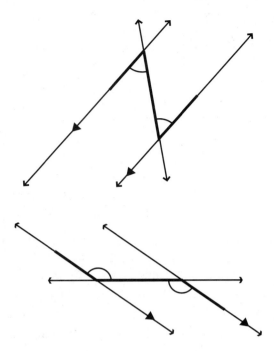

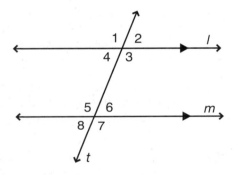

Same-Side Interior Angles

Same-side interior angles are interior angles on the same side of the transversal. To spot same-side interior angles, look for a U-shaped figure in various positions, as shown in the following examples:

Alternate Interior Angles

Alternate interior angles are interior angles on opposite sides of the transversal. In the previous figure, angles 3 and 5 and angles 4 and 6 are examples of alternate interior angles. To spot alternate interior angles, look for a Z-shaped figure, as shown in the following figures:

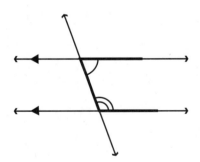

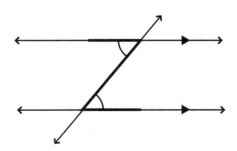

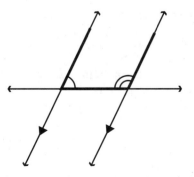

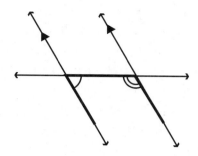

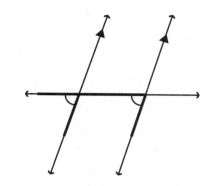

Corresponding Angles

Corresponding angles are so named because they appear to be in corresponding positions in relation to the two parallel lines. Examples of corresponding angles in the following figure are angles 1 and 5, 4 and 8, 2 and 6, and 3 and 7.

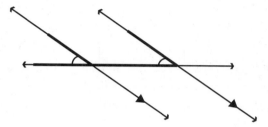

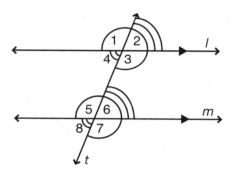

Angles Formed by Nonparallel Lines and a Transversal

Even when lines cut by a transversal are not parallel, you still use the same terms to describe angles, such as corresponding, alternate interior, and same-side interior angles. For example, look at the following figure:

To spot corresponding angles, look for an F-shaped figure in various positions, as shown in these examples:

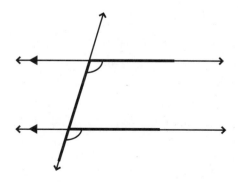

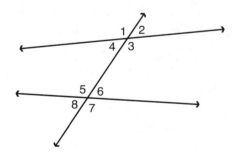

∠1 and ∠5 are corresponding angles.
∠3 and ∠5 are alternate interior angles.
∠4 and ∠5 are same-side interior angles.

Postulates and Theorems

As mentioned previously, *postulates* are statements of fact that we accept without proof. *Theorems* are statements of fact that can be proven. You will apply both types of facts to problems in this book. Some geometry books teach formal proofs of theorems. Although you will not go through that process in this book, you will still use both postulates and theorems for applications. There are some important facts you need to know about the special pairs of angles formed by two parallel lines and a transversal. If you noticed that some of those pairs of angles appear to have equal measure, then you are on the right track. The term used for two angles with equal measure is *congruent*.

An important fact you should remember is that a pair of angles whose sum is 180° is called *supplementary*.

> *Postulate:* If two parallel lines are cut by a transversal, then corresponding angles are congruent.
>
> *Theorem:* If two parallel lines are cut by a transversal, then alternate interior angles are congruent.
>
> *Theorem:* If two parallel lines are cut by a transversal, then same-side interior angles are supplementary.

Pairs of Angles

When two angles come together to form a 90° angle, the angle can be very useful for solving a variety of problems. Angles measuring 90° are essential in construction and sewing, just to name two areas.

Pairs of angles whose measures add up to 90° are called *complementary* angles. If you know the measurement of one angle, then you can find the measurement of the other.

When two angles come together to form a 180° angle, or a straight line, the applications are endless. These pairs of angles are called *supplementary* angles. You can find the measurement of one angle if the measurement of the other is given.

When two lines intersect, two pairs of *vertical* angles are always formed. You can see pairs of intersecting lines in fabric patterns, at construction sites, and on road maps. If you know the measurement of one of these angles, you can find the measurements of the other three angles.

Complementary Angles

Two angles are complementary angles if and only if the sum of their measures is 90°. Each angle is a complement of the other. To be complementary, a pair of angles do not need to be adjacent.

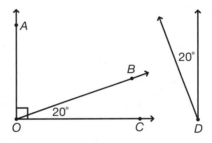

In the previous figure, $\angle AOB$ and $\angle BOC$ are a pair of complementary angles. $\angle AOB$ and $\angle D$ are also a pair of complementary angles. $\angle AOB$ is a complement of $\angle BOC$ and $\angle D$.

Supplementary Angles

Two angles are supplementary angles if and only if the sum of their measures is 180°. Each angle is a supplement of the other. Similar to complementary angles, supplementary angles do not need to be adjacent.

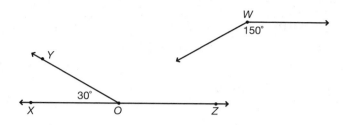

In this figure, ∠XOY and ∠YOZ are supplementary angles. ∠XOY and ∠W are also supplementary angles. ∠XOY is a supplement of ∠YOZ and ∠W.

Vertical Angles

Vertical angles are two angles whose sides form two pairs of opposite rays. When two lines intersect, they form two pairs of vertical angles.

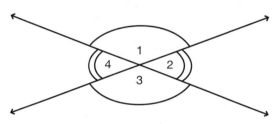

In the previous figure, the two pairs of vertical angles are the obtuse pair, ∠1 and ∠3, as well as the acute pair, ∠2 and ∠4. Notice that ∠1 and ∠2 are supplementary angles and that ∠2 and ∠3 are also supplementary. Since ∠1 and ∠3 are both supplements to ∠2, it can be determined that ∠1 ≅ ∠3. Looking at the figure, notice that the pair of acute vertical angles, ∠2 and ∠4, are also congruent by the same reasoning. The following is one of the most useful theorems in geometry:

> *Vertical Angles Theorem:* Vertical angles are congruent.

Practice

1. An angle with measure 90° is called a(n) _____ angle.

2. An angle with measure 180° is called a(n) _____ angle.

3. An angle with a measure between 0° and 90° is called a(n) _____ angle.

4. An angle with a measure between 90° and 180° is called a(n) _____ angle.

5. Two adjacent right angles combine to make a(n) _____ angle.

6. A straight angle minus an acute angle would result in a(n) _____ angle.

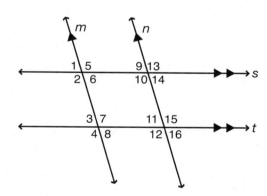

Identify two terms that describe the two angles given in each question below.

7. ∠2 and ∠10
   a. _____ b. _____

8. ∠6 and ∠7
   a. _____ b. _____

9. ∠13 and ∠15
   a. _____ b. _____

10. ∠11 and ∠14
   a. _____ b. _____

11. List all angles that are congruent to ∠1.

12. List all angles that are supplementary to ∠11.

Use the following figure to answer practice problems 13–16.

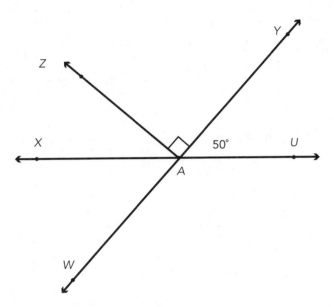

13. List the supplementary angles of ∠WAU. ____

14. List the names of the complementary angle(s) of ∠WAX. ____

15. List two different pairs of vertical angles shown in the figure. ____

16. What is the measure of ∠ZAX? ____

Types of Triangles

One of the first important skills to master with triangles is learning how to identify and classify them. Triangles can be classified by their sides or by their angles. Each type of triangle has special properties

that you will apply to solve increasingly complex geometry problems as you move through this book.

Classification by Sides

You can classify triangles by the lengths of their sides. When classifying triangles by side length, every triangle will fall into one of three categories: *equilateral*, *isosceles*, or *scalene*. *Equilateral* triangles have three congruent sides, *isosceles* triangles have two congruent sides, and *scalene* triangles have no congruent sides.

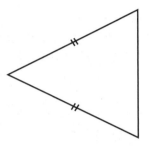

Isosceles
two ≅ sides

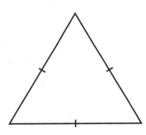

Equilateral
three ≅ sides

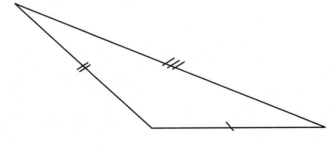

Scalene
no congruent sides

To show that two or more sides of a triangle have the same measurement, a hatch mark is made through the congruent sides. Sometimes, two hatch marks are made on each congruent side, and sometimes, three hatch marks are made on each congruent side. You can match up the number of hatch marks to find which sides are congruent. If a triangle has different numbers of hatch marks on each side, it means none of the sides are congruent. You'll see these hatch marks in most geometry books. The symbol for congruent is ≅.

Isosceles Triangles

Isosceles triangles are important geometric figures to understand. Isosceles triangles have exactly two congruent sides. The parts of isosceles triangles have special names. The two congruent sides of an isosceles triangle are called the *legs*. The angle formed by the two congruent sides is called the *vertex angle*. The other two angles are called the *base angles*. And finally, the side opposite the vertex angle is called the *base*.

Example:

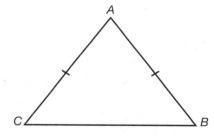

legs: $\overline{AC}$ and $\overline{AB}$ base angles: $\angle B$ and $\angle C$
vertex angle: $\angle A$ base: $\overline{BC}$

Classification by Angles

You can also classify triangles by the measurements of their angles. Here are four examples of special triangles. They are called **acute**, **equiangular**, **right**, and **obtuse**.

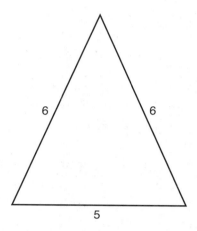

Acute
three acute angles

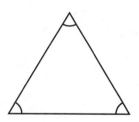

Equiangular
three ≅ angles

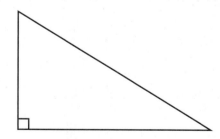

Right
one right angle

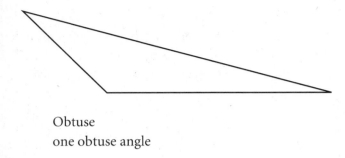

Obtuse
one obtuse angle

To show that two or more angles of a triangle have the same measurement, a small curve is made in the congruent angles. You can also use two small curves to show that angles are congruent.

Equilateral and Equiangular Triangles

Did you notice that the **equilateral** triangle, which has three congruent sides, looks very similar to the **equiangular** triangle, which has three congruent angles? Any triangle that is equilateral is also guaranteed to be equiangular, and vice versa! So, when you are given a triangle that has three congruent angles, you can also draw the conclusion that it has three congruent sides. The following figure illustrates this:

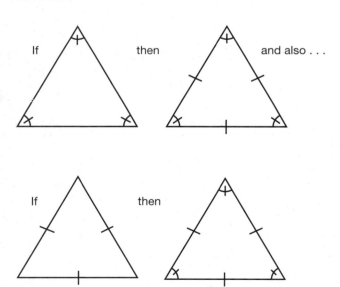

Congruent Triangles

When you buy floor tiles, you get tiles that are all the same shape and size. One tile will fit right on top of another. In geometry, you would say one tile is congruent to another tile. Similarly, in the following figure, $\triangle ABC$ and $\triangle XYZ$ are **congruent**. They have the same size and shape.

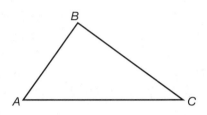

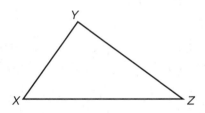

Imagine sliding one triangle over to fit on top of the other triangle. You would put point A on point X, point B on point Y, and point C on point Z. When the vertices are matched in this way, $\angle A$ and $\angle X$ are called **corresponding angles**, and $\overline{AB}$ and $\overline{XY}$ are called **corresponding sides**.

Corresponding angles and corresponding sides are often referred to as corresponding parts of the triangles. In other words, you could say Corresponding Parts of Congruent Triangles are Congruent. This statement is often referred to by the initials CPCTC.

When $\triangle ABC$ is congruent to $\triangle XYZ$, you write $\triangle ABC \cong \triangle XYZ$. This means that all of the following are true:

$$\angle A \cong \angle X \qquad \angle B \cong \angle Y \qquad \angle C \cong \angle Z$$
$$\overline{AB} \cong \overline{XY} \qquad \overline{BC} \cong \overline{YZ} \qquad \overline{AC} \cong \overline{XZ}$$

Suppose instead of writing $\triangle ABC \cong \triangle XYZ$, you started to write $\triangle CAB \cong$ _____. Since you started with C to name the first triangle, you must start with the corresponding letter, Z, to name the second triangle. Corresponding parts are named in the same order. If you name the first triangle $\triangle CAB$, then the second triangle must be named $\triangle ZXY$. In other words, $\triangle CAB \cong \triangle ZXY$.

Example: Name the corresponding angles and corresponding sides.

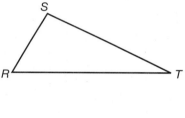

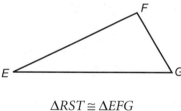

$$\triangle RST \cong \triangle EFG$$

Corresponding angles: $\angle R$ and $\angle E$; $\angle S$ and $\angle F$; $\angle T$ and $\angle G$
Corresponding sides: $\overline{RS}$ and $\overline{EF}$; $\overline{ST}$ and $\overline{FG}$; $\overline{RT}$ and $\overline{EG}$

Side-Side-Side (SSS) Postulate

If you have three sticks that make a triangle and a friend has identical sticks, would it be possible for each of you to make different-looking triangles? No, it is impossible to do this. A postulate of geometry states this same idea. It is called the **side-side-side postulate**.

> *Side-Side-Side Postulate:* If three sides of one triangle are congruent to three sides of another triangle, then the two triangles are congruent.

Take a look at the following triangles to see this postulate in action:

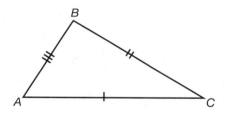

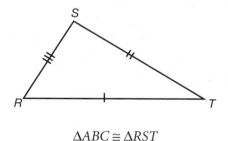

$$\triangle ABC \cong \triangle RST$$

The hatch marks on the triangles show which sides are congruent to which in the two triangles. For example, $\overline{AC}$ and $\overline{RT}$ both have one hatch mark, which shows that these two segments are congruent. $\overline{BC}$ is congruent to $\overline{ST}$, as shown by the two hatch marks, and $\overline{AB}$ and $\overline{RS}$ are congruent as shown by the three hatch marks.

Since the markings indicate that the three pairs of sides are congruent, you can conclude that the three pairs of angles are also congruent. From the definition of congruent triangles, it follows that all six parts of $\triangle ABC$ are congruent to the corresponding parts of $\triangle RST$.

Side-Angle-Side (SAS) Postulate

If you put two sticks together at a certain angle, there is only one way to finish forming a triangle. Would it be possible for a friend to form a different-looking triangle if he or she started with the same two lengths and the same angle? No, it would be impossible. Another postulate of geometry states this same idea; it is called the **side-angle-side postulate**.

> *Side-Angle-Side Postulate:* If two sides and the included angle of one triangle are congruent to the corresponding two sides and included angle of another triangle, then the triangles are congruent.

Look at the following two triangles to see an example of this postulate:

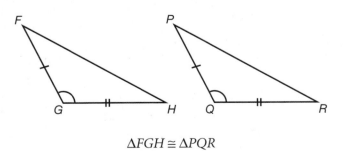

$$\triangle FGH \cong \triangle PQR$$

Angle-Side-Angle (ASA) Postulate

There is one more postulate used to determine two congruent triangles. **Angle-side-angle** involves two angles and a side between them. The side is called an included side.

> *Angle-Side-Angle Postulate:* If two angles and the included side of one triangle are congruent to the corresponding two angles and included side of another triangle, then the triangles are congruent.

Take a look at the following two triangles:

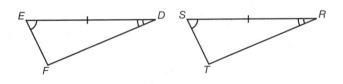

$$\triangle DEF \cong \triangle RST$$

The Pythagorean Theorem

The Pythagorean theorem uncovers a special and important relationship between the lengths of the sides of right triangles. As you move forward in geometry, you will see that right triangles are also used to solve problems involving other shapes such as trapezoids, rhombuses, and parallelograms.

Parts of a Right Triangle

In a right triangle, the sides that meet to form the right angle are called the **legs**. The side opposite the right angle is called the **hypotenuse**. The hypotenuse is always the longest of the three sides. It is important that you can correctly identify the sides of a right triangle, regardless of what position the triangle is in.

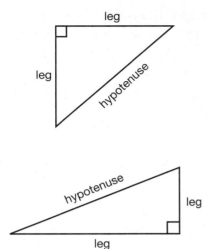

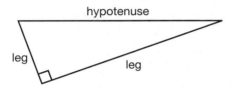

Pythagorean Theorem: In a right triangle, the sum of the squares of the lengths of the legs is equal to the square of the length of the hypotenuse.

$$a^2 + b^2 = c^2$$

The Pythagorean Theorem

The Pythagorean theorem is one of the most famous theorems in mathematics. The Greek mathematician Pythagoras (circa 585–500 B.C.) is given credit for originating it. Evidence shows that it was used by the Egyptians and Babylonians for hundreds of years before Pythagoras.

The Pythagorean theorem can be used to solve many real-life problems. Any unknown length can be found if you can make it a part of a right triangle. You need to know only two of the sides of a right triangle to find the third unknown side. A common mistake is always adding the squares of the two known lengths. You add the squares of the legs only when you are looking for the hypotenuse. If you know the hypotenuse and one of the legs, then you subtract the square of the leg from the square of the hypotenuse. Another common mistake is forgetting to take the square root as your final step. You need to remember that important last calculation.

Examples: Find each missing length.

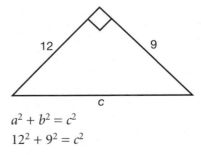

$$a^2 + b^2 = c^2$$
$$12^2 + 9^2 = c^2$$

$144 + 81 = c^2$

$225 = c^2$

$\sqrt{225} = \sqrt{c^2}$

$15 = c$

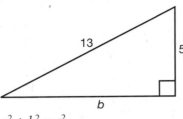

$a^2 + b^2 = c^2$

$5^2 + b^2 = 13^2$

$25 + b^2 = 169$

$b^2 = 144$

$\sqrt{b^2} = \sqrt{144}$

$b = 12$

Converse of the Pythagorean Theorem

Another practical use of the Pythagorean theorem involves determining whether a triangle is a right triangle or not. This involves using the converse of the Pythagorean theorem.

> *Converse of the Pythagorean Theorem:* If the square of the length of the longest side of a triangle is equal to the sum of the squares of the lengths of the two shorter sides, then the triangle is a right triangle.

Examples: Determine whether the following are right triangles. Note that c represents the length of the longest side in each triangle.

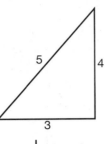

c^2	$a^2 + b^2$
5^2	$3^2 + 4^2$
25	$9 + 16$

Since $25 = 9 + 16$, the three sides with lengths of 5, 3, and 4 make a right triangle.

Here is another example:

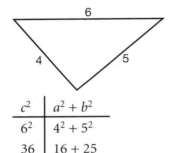

c^2	$a^2 + b^2$
6^2	$4^2 + 5^2$
36	$16 + 25$

Since $36 \neq 16 + 25$, the three sides with lengths of 6, 4, and 5 do not make a right triangle.

Acute and Obtuse Triangles

If you have determined that a triangle is not a right triangle, then you can determine whether it is an acute or obtuse triangle by using one of the following theorems:

> *Theorem:* If the square of the length of the longest side is greater than the sum of the squares of the lengths of the other two shorter sides, then the triangle is obtuse.
>
>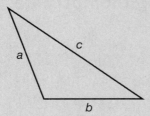
>
> $$c^2 > a^2 + b^2$$
>
> *Theorem:* If the square of the length of the longest side is less than the sum of the squares of the lengths of the other two shorter sides, then the triangle is acute.
>
>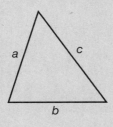
>
> $$c^2 < a^2 + b^2$$

Let's take a look at a couple of examples to see these theorems in action.

Example: In $\triangle ABC$, the lengths of the sides are $c = 24, a = 15, b = 20$.

c^2	$a^2 + b^2$
24^2	$15^2 + 20^2$
576	225 + 400
576	625

Since $576 < 625$, this is an acute triangle.

Example: In $\triangle ABC$, the lengths of the sides are $c = 9, a = 5, b = 7$.

c^2	$a^2 + b^2$
9^2	$5^2 + 7^2$
81	25 + 49
81	74

Since $81 > 74$, this is an obtuse triangle.

Practice
Classify each triangle shown or described as acute, right, obtuse, or equiangular.

17.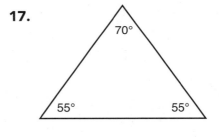

18.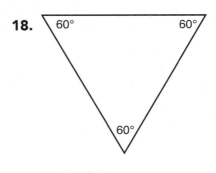

19.

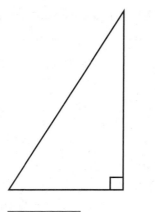

_____

20.

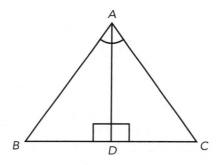

_____

Use the following figure to answer practice problems 21–25.

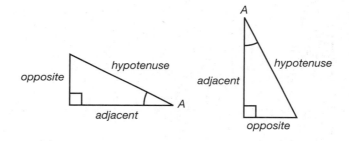

21. ∠BDA corresponds to _____.

22. $\overline{DC}$ corresponds to _____.

23. Is ∠ACD ≅ ∠DBA?

24. Is ∠BAD ≅ ∠CAD?

25. Is ∠B ≅ ∠C?

The lengths of three sides of a triangle are given. Determine whether the triangles are right triangles.

26. 25, 24, 7 _____

27. 5, 7, 9 _____

28. 15, 36, 39 _____

29. 9, 40, 41 _____

Trigonometry Basics

Recall that the hypotenuse is the side of the triangle across from the right angle. The other two sides of the triangle are called legs. These two legs have special names in relation to a given angle: adjacent leg and opposite leg. The word **adjacent** means beside, so the adjacent leg is the leg beside the angle. The opposite leg is across from the angle. You can see in the following figure how the legs are named depending on which acute angle is selected.

Using Trigonometric Ratios

Sine, **cosine**, and **tangent** are the names of the three principal ratios between the different pairs of sides of a right triangle. These ratios are abbreviated *sin*, *cos*, and *tan*, respectively. Sine, cosine, and tangent ratios for the acute angle A in a right triangle are as follows:

$$\sin A = \frac{opposite\ leg}{hypotenuse}$$

$$\cos A = \frac{adjacent\ leg}{hypotenuse}$$

$$\tan A = \frac{opposite\ leg}{adjacent\ leg}$$

Hint: A pneumonic that is commonly used to remember these ratios is *SOHCAHTOA*:

SOH stands for: <u>S</u>in A equals <u>O</u>pposite over <u>H</u>ypotenuse

CAH stands for: <u>C</u>os A equals <u>A</u>djacent over <u>H</u>ypotenuse

TOA stands for: <u>T</u>an A equals <u>O</u>pposite over <u>A</u>djacent

Example: Express each ratio as a decimal to the nearest thousandth.

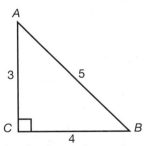

1. sin A, cos A, tan A
2. sin B, cos B, tan B

1. $\sin A = \frac{opp}{hyp} = \frac{4}{5} = 0.800$

$\cos A = \frac{adj}{hyp} = \frac{3}{5} = 0.600$

$\tan A = \frac{opp}{adj} = \frac{4}{3} ≈ 1.3\overline{3}$

2. $\sin B = \frac{opp}{hyp} = \frac{3}{5} = 0.600$

$\cos B = \frac{adj}{hyp} = \frac{4}{5} = 0.800$

$\tan B = \frac{opp}{adj} = \frac{3}{4} = 0.750$

Finding the Measure of an Acute Angle

The trigonometric ratio used to find the measure of an acute angle of a right triangle depends on which side lengths are known.

Example: Find $m\angle A$.

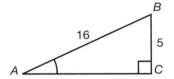

Solution: The sin A involves the two lengths known.

$$\sin A = \frac{opp}{hyp} = \frac{5}{16} ≈ 0.313$$

Note that the ≈ symbol is used in the previous solution because the decimal 0.313 has been rounded to the nearest thousandths place. Using the sin column of a trigonometric table, you'll find:

sin A ≈ 0.313
sin 18° = 0.309 } difference 0.004
sin 19° = 0.326 } difference 0.013

Since 0.313 is closer to 0.309, $m\angle A ≈ 18°$ to the nearest degree.

A scientific calculator typically has a button that reads sin⁻¹, which means *inverse sine*, and can be used to find an angle measure when the sine is known.

Calculator tip: Some calculators require that you type in 0.313 first, then hit the sin⁻¹ button, in order for the angle measurement to appear. With other calculators, you will have to select sin⁻¹ first, then type 0.313, and when you hit *enter* you should see a number that rounds to 18.2. (Sometimes the second key needs to be used to access the sin⁻¹ function.) Try these two methods now to make sure you know how to use your calculator!

Example: Find $m\angle C$.

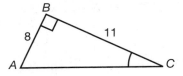

Solution: The tan C involves the two lengths known.

$$\tan C = \frac{opp}{adj} = \frac{8}{11} \approx 0.727$$

Using the tan column, you'll find:

$$\tan 36 = 0.727$$

Therefore, $m\angle C = 36°$.

Again, the $\tan^{-1}$ button on a scientific calculator can be used to find an angle measure when its tangent is known.

Finding the Measure of a Side

When you are given one angle and one side length of a right triangle, you can solve for the other missing side lengths using trigonometry. The trigonometric ratio used to find the length of a side of a right triangle depends on which side length and angle are known.

Example: Find the value of x to the nearest tenth.

(a)

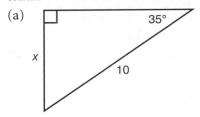

Solution: $\sin 35 = \dfrac{\text{opposite}}{\text{hypotenuse}} = \dfrac{x}{10}$

$$0.574 = \frac{x}{10}$$
$$x = 10(0.574)$$
$$x \approx 5.7$$

(b)

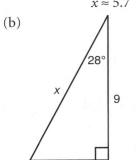

Solution: $\cos 28 = \dfrac{\text{adjacent}}{\text{hypotenuse}} = \dfrac{9}{x}$

$$0.883 = \frac{9}{x}$$
$$x = \frac{9}{0.883}$$
$$x \approx 10.2$$

Trigonometry Problems on the SAT Exam

SAT problems on this topic run the gamut in that you are required to know about lines, angles, and the properties of right triangles. The most common types of problems utilize the trigonometric ratios and the Pythagorean theorem.

SAT TEST-TAKING TIP

First, memorize SOHCAHTOA and the most common trigonometric ratios: sine, cosine, and tangent.

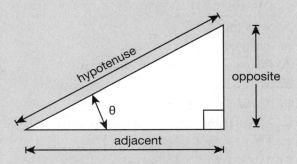

sin θ	opposite / hypotenuse
cos θ	adjacent / hypotenuse
tan θ	opposite / adjacent

Always remember that the hypotenuse of a triangle is the longest side and is opposite the right angle.

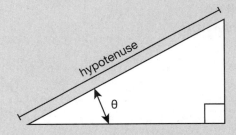

Remember these facts about triangles:

- Congruent means *same* and similar means *proportional*.
- All of the angles in a triangle must add up to 180 degrees.
- The sum of any two sides of a triangle will always be greater than the third side.

Try these practice problems. Then, study the reasoning used to answer each question.

Practice

30. Consider the following right triangle:

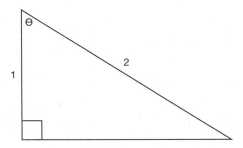

What is the value of 2θ in degrees? _____

31. In a circus tent, two cables will be fastened from the top of a trapeze platform to the floor, as shown in the following diagram:

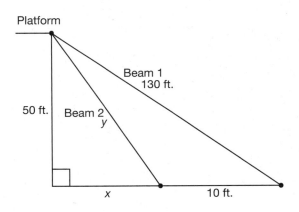

What is the approximate length, *y*, of Beam 2?
a. 160.0 feet
b. 129.6 feet
c. 120.8 feet
d. 110.0 feet

32. Consider the following diagram:

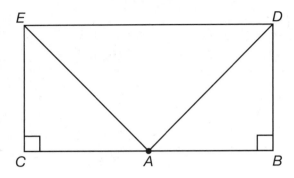

Suppose that triangles *ABD* and *ACE* are isosceles right triangles, such that the length of *DB* is 1 inch and the length of *EC* is 2 inches. What is the length of *ED*?

a. $\sqrt{5}$ inches

b. 10 inches

c. 5 inches

d. $\sqrt{10}$ inches

33. The triangle *KLM* shown here is isosceles:

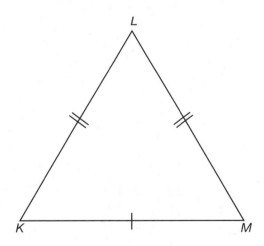

If the length of *KL* is strictly between 3 feet and 3.5 feet, to the nearest foot, what is the largest possible value of the length of *KM*?

_____

Answers and Explanations

1. **Right**
2. **Straight**
3. **Acute**
4. **Obtuse**
5. **Straight**
6. **Obtuse**
7. **Corresponding angles; congruent**
8. **Same-side interior angles; congruent**
9. **Corresponding angles; congruent**
10. **Alternate interior angles; congruent**
11. **3, 6, 8, 9, 11, 14, and 16**
12. **2, 4, 5, 7, 10, 12, 13, and 15**
13. **$\angle XAW$ and $\angle YAU$**
14. **$\angle XAZ$ and $\angle ZAX$**
15. **$\angle XAY$ and $\angle WAU$; $\angle XAW$ and $\angle YAU$**
16. **40°**
17. **Acute**
18. **Equiangular and acute**
19. **Right**
20. **Obtuse**
21. **$\angle CDA$**
22. **$\overline{DB}$**
23. **No, $\angle ACD \cong \angle ABD$**
24. **Yes**
25. **Yes**
26. **Yes**
27. **No**
28. **Yes**
29. **Yes**
30. **120°.** Observe that $\cos \theta = \frac{1}{2}$, so $\theta = 60°$. This means that $2\theta = 120°$.

31. c. First, apply the Pythagorean theorem on the larger right triangle with side lengths 50, $x + 10$, and 130, and find x:

$$(x + 10)^2 + 50^2 = 130^2$$
$$(x + 10)^2 = 130^2 - 50^2$$
$$(x + 10)^2 = 14{,}420$$
$$(x + 10)^2 = 120^2$$
$$x + 10 = 120$$
$$x = 110$$

Next, apply the Pythagorean theorem to the smaller right triangle with side lengths 50, x, and y and find y:

$$50^2 + x^2 = y^2$$
$$50^2 + 110^2 = y^2$$
$$14{,}600 = y^2$$
$$y = \sqrt{14{,}600} \approx 120.8$$

Beam 2 is approximately 120.8 feet long. Choice **a** is incorrect because although you correctly found the value of x first, you did not square the lengths of the sides when applying the Pythagorean theorem to find y. Choice **b** is incorrect because you used the Pythagorean theorem on a *non-right* triangle with side lengths of y, 10, and 130. You must first apply the Pythagorean theorem on the larger right triangle with side lengths of 50, $x + 10$, and 130 to find x and then on the smaller right triangle with side lengths of 50, x, and y to find y. Choice **d** is the value of x, not y. This is how far away from the base of the platform that Beam 2 is affixed to the ground, not the length of Beam 2.

32. d. First, find the lengths of AD and AE using the Pythagorean theorem. Since triangle ABD is isosceles, we know that AB and BD both have a length of 1 inch. So, using the Pythagorean theorem, we see that AD has a length of $\sqrt{2}$ inches. Similarly, since triangle ACE is isosceles, we know that AC and EC both have a length of 2 inches. Using the Pythagorean theorem again, we see that AE has a length of $2\sqrt{2}$ inches. Next, note that the measures of angles CAE and BAD are both 45° because triangles ABD and ACE are isosceles right triangles. As such, triangle EAD is a right triangle with hypotenuse ED, since the three angles of a triangle must add up to 180 degrees and two of the three angles are 45 degrees. Finally, the Pythagorean theorem tells us that $AE^2 + AD^2 = ED^2$, so $ED^2 = (2\sqrt{2})^2 + (\sqrt{2})^2 = 10$, which means ED has length of $\sqrt{10}$ inches. Choices **a** and **c** are incorrect because you used the Pythagorean theorem directly on a non-right triangle with sides 1 and 2 inches, but the Pythagorean theorem applies only to right triangles. Choice **b** is incorrect because you forgot to take the square root in the final step when finding the length of ED.

33. 5 feet. This problem involves the use of the triangle law. The sum of the lengths of any two sides must be strictly larger than the length of the third side. For this triangle, we know that $KL = LM$. So, $3 < KL < 3.5$ and $3 < LM < 3.5$, so that $6 < KL + LM < 7$. As such, the length of the third side KM must be less than 6. In addition to this restriction, we must have $KM + KL > 3.5$ and $KM + LM > 3.5$. Since KL and KM both must be larger than 3, we must have $KM > 0.5$. That means $0.5 < KM < 6$. Any real number in this range is a possible length for KM. This inequality does not include 6; therefore, to the nearest foot, the largest possible length for KM is 5 feet.

19 ▶ VOLUME PROBLEMS

It is not enough to have a good mind. The main thing is to use it well.

—RENÉ DESCARTES

LESSON SUMMARY
Geometry is essentially the study of shapes in the physical world and properties of them. This nineteenth lesson will teach you about volume of basic geometric shapes. It covers essential volume formulas and how to use them to solve volume problems.

When you are interested in finding out how much a refrigerator holds or the amount of storage space in a closet, you are looking for the volume of a prism. Volume is expressed in cubic units. Just like an ice tray is filled with cubes of ice, volume tells you how many cubic units will fit into a space.

Do you remember that since area is measured in squares, it is written with an exponent of 2 after the unit of measurement, such as 8 cm^2? Since volume is a three-dimensional measurement of cubic space, an exponent of 3 is similarly used after the unit of measurement. For example, if a box has a volume of 84 cm^3, that means it can hold 84 cubes that are each 1 cm wide by 1 cm deep by 1 cm tall. The way 84 cm^3 is said is "84 cubic centimeters."

Volume of Prisms

Prisms can have bases in the shape of any polygon. A prism with a rectangle for its bases is called a **rectangular prism**. A prism with triangles for its bases is referred to as a **triangular prism**. A prism with hexagons as its bases is called a **hexagonal prism**, and so on. Prisms can be right or oblique. A right prism is a prism with its bases perpendicular to its sides, meaning they form right angles. Bases of oblique prisms do not form right angles with their sides. An example of an oblique prism would be a skyscraper that is leaning over. In this lesson, you will concentrate on the volume of right prisms, so when we refer to prisms, you can assume we mean a right prism.

> *Theorem:* To find the volume (V) of a rectangular prism, multiply the length (l), width (w), and height (h) together.
> $$V = lwh$$

The volume of a rectangular prism could also be calculated in another way. The area of the base of a rectangular prism is the length (l) times the width (w). The volume of a rectangular prism can be calculated by multiplying the area of the base (B) times the height (h) of the prism. This approach of multiplying the area of the base by the height can also be applied to other solid prisms where the base is not a rectangle. When the base is a triangle, trapezoid, or other polygon, use the area formula for that shape, and then multiply by the height (h) of the figure.

> *Theorem:* To find the volume (V) of any prism, multiply the area of a base (B) by the height (h).
> $$V = Bh$$

Example: Find the volume of each prism.

1.

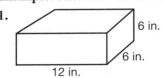

$V = lwh$
$V = (12)(6)(6)$
$V = 432$ in.^{3}

2.

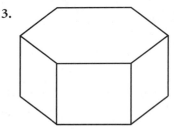

First, find the area of a base. The formula for finding the area of any triangle is $A = \frac{1}{2}bh$.

$A = \frac{1}{2}(3)(4)$
$A = \frac{1}{2}(12)$
$A = 6$ in.^{2}

The area, A, becomes the base, B, in the volume formula $V = Bh$.

$V = Bh$
$V = (6)(8)$
$V = 48$ in.^{3}

3.

$B = 30$ ft.^{2} $V = Bh$
$h = 5$ ft. $V = (30)(5)$
     $V = 150$ ft.^{3}

4. Prism: $B = 42$ m^2, $V = Bh$
     $h = 10$ m $V = (42)(10)$
     $V = 420$ m^3

Volume of a Cube

Recall that the edges (e) of a cube all have the same measurement; therefore, if you replace the length (l), width (w), and height (h) with the measurement of the edge of the cube, then you will have the formula for the volume of the cube, $V = e^3$.

> *Theorem:* The volume of a cube is determined by cubing the length of the edge.
> $$V = e^3$$

Example: Find the volume of the cube.

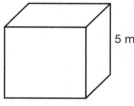

5 m

$V = e^3$
$V = (5)^3$
$V = 125 \text{ m}^3$

Volume of a Pyramid

A polyhedron is a three-dimensional figure whose surfaces are all polygons. A regular pyramid is a polyhedron with a base that is a regular polygon and a vertex point that lies directly over the center of the base.

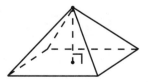

If you have a pyramid and a rectangular prism with the same length, width, and height, you would find that it would take three of the pyramids to fill the prism. In other words, one-third of the volume of the prism is the volume of the pyramid.

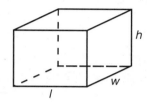 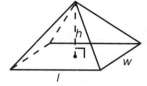

$V = lwh$ or $V = Bh$ $\qquad$ $V = \frac{1}{3}lwh$ or $V = \frac{1}{3}Bh$

Examples: Find the volume of each pyramid.

(a)

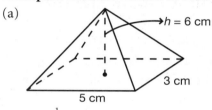

→$h = 6$ cm

3 cm

5 cm

$V = \frac{1}{3}lwh$
$V = \frac{1}{3}(5)(3)(6)$
$V = 30 \text{ cm}^3$

(b)

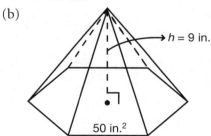

→$h = 9$ in.

50 in.²

$V = \frac{1}{3}Bh$
$V = \frac{1}{3}(50)(9)$
$V = 150 \text{ in.}^3$

(c) Regular pyramid: $B = 36 \text{ ft.}^2$, $h = 8$ ft.

Solution: $V = \frac{1}{3}Bh$
$$V = \frac{1}{3}(36)(8)$$
$$V = 96 \text{ ft.}^3$$

Practice

1. A doctor's office purchases a pair of cubed glass containers that are 9 inches across in which to store bandages. If the amount of bandages in one container takes up $\frac{1}{6}$ of the total volume, how much volume is left in both containers? _____

2. You have 10 blankets that each take up 686 cubic inches of space. How many blankets could you pack into an 18-inch moving box?

_____

Volume of a Cylinder

Similar to finding the volume of a prism, you can find the volume of a cylinder by finding the product of the area of the base and the height of the figure. Of course, the base of a cylinder is a circle, so you need to find the area of a circle times the height.

> *Theorem:* The volume (*V*) of a cylinder is the product of the area of the base (*B*) and the height (*h*).
> $$V = Bh \text{ or } V = \pi r^2 h$$

Example: Find the volume of each cylinder. Use 3.14 for π.

1. 3 cm

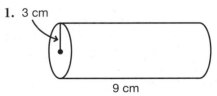

9 cm

$V = \pi r^2 h$
$V \approx (3.14)(3)2(9)$
$V \approx (3.14)(9)(9)$
$V \approx 254.34 \text{ cm}^3$

2.

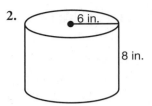

6 in.

8 in.

$V = \pi r^2 h$
$V \approx (3.14)(6)^2(8)$
$V \approx (3.14)(36)(8)$
$V \approx 904.32 \text{ in.}^3$

Volume of a Cone

A cone relates to a cylinder in the same way that a pyramid relates to a prism. If you have a cone and a cylinder with the same radius and height, it would take three of the cones to fill the cylinder. In other words, the cone holds one-third the amount of the cylinder.

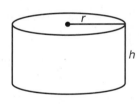

$V = Bh \text{ or } V = \pi r^2 h$ $V = \frac{1}{3}Bh \text{ or } V = \frac{1}{3}\pi r^2 h$

Example: Find the volume of the cone. Use 3.14 for π.

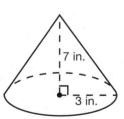

7 in.

3 in.

$V = \frac{1}{3}\pi r^2 h$
$V \approx \frac{1}{3}(3.14)(3)^2(7)$
$V \approx 65.94 \text{ in.}^3$

Volume of a Sphere

If you were filling balloons with helium, it would be important for you to know the volume of a sphere. To find the volume of a sphere, picture the sphere filled with numerous pyramids. The height of each pyramid represents the radius (r) of the sphere. The sum of the areas of all the bases represents the surface area of the sphere.

Volume of each pyramid $= \frac{1}{3}Bh$

Sum of the volumes $= n \times \frac{1}{3}Br$ Substitute r for h of n pyramids

$= \frac{1}{3}(nB)r$ Substitute nB with the SA of a sphere

$= \frac{1}{3}(4\pi r^2)r$

$= \frac{4}{3}\pi r^3$

Theorem: The volume (V) of a sphere is determined by the product of $\frac{4}{3}\pi$ and the cube of the radius.

$$V = \frac{4}{3}\pi r^3$$

Example: Find the volume of the sphere. Use 3.14 for π.

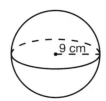

9 cm

$V = \frac{4}{3}\pi r^3$

$V \approx \frac{4}{3}(3.14)(9)^3$

$V \approx 3,052.08$ cm^3

Practice

3. What is the volume of a cylinder with a height of 18 yards and diameter of 15 yards?

_____

4. How much water will completely fill the cylindrical tank shown in the picture? _____

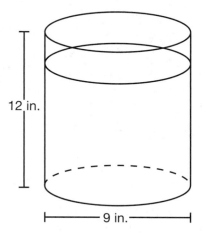

12 in.

9 in.

5. What is the volume of a beach ball if its width is 24 inches wide?
   a. 375.69 in.^{3}
   b. 904.78 in.^{3}
   c. 7,238.23 in.^{3}
   d. 57,905.84 in.^{3}

SAT TEST-TAKING TIP

Often the volume problems on the SAT exam require you to use the volume of an object as a starting point. The best way to study for volume problems on the SAT is to first memorize the volume formulas in relation the image of the shape. Then practice to become fluent in using the formulas to find the volume of a shape.

Also, most volume problems will involve diagrams, so label the diagram to make sure not to misuse the values in the volume formulas. Finally, use your calculator for volume calculations. This will help you to complete these problems more efficiently.

Here is a table of volume formulas that you should study before you take your SAT exam.

Figure	Formulas for Volume (V)
Rectangular Prism	$V = lwh = \text{length} \times \text{width} \times \text{height}$
Prisms	$V = Bh = \text{area of base} \times \text{height}$
Right Circular Cylinder	$V = Bh = \text{area of base} \times \text{height}$
Right Pyramid	$V = \frac{1}{3}Bh = \frac{1}{3} \times \text{area of base} \times \text{height}$
Right Circular Cone	$V = \frac{1}{3}Bh = \frac{1}{3} \times \text{area of base} \times \text{height}$
Sphere	$V = \frac{4}{3}\pi r^3 = \frac{4}{3} \times \pi \times \text{cube of radius}$

Practice

6. The clerk at a party supply store uses a helium machine to blow up spherical balloons. The machine adds air to a balloon at the rate of 8π cubic inches per second. If it takes her 12 seconds to fill the balloon, what is the radius of the balloon when it is filled? Round your answer to the nearest tenth. _____

7. The volume of a conical-shaped ice cream cake treat is to be 8 cubic inches and the height of it is to be three times the base radius. What is the diameter of the base of such a conical treat?

_____

8. The following figure shows a cylindrical pipe whose base has a circumference of 6π inches. If the surface area of the pipe is 300 square inches, what is the volume of the pipe?

(Note: The surface area A of a right circular cylinder with radius r and length h is $A = 2\pi r^2 + 2\pi rh$.)

Answers and Explanations

1. 1,215 cubic inches. The total volume of one container is $9^3 = 729$ cu. in. The bandages in one container take up $\frac{1}{6}(729) = 121.5$ cu. in. So, there is $729 - 121.5 = 607.5$ cu. in. of remaining volume. Since there are two containers, multiply 607.5 times 2 to get 1,215 cu. in.

2. 8. The total volume of the moving box is $18^3 = 5,832$ cu. in. Since each blanket takes 686 cu. in., the box would hold $\frac{5,832}{686} = 8.5$, or 8 blankets.

3. 3,179.25 yd³. The radius is $\frac{1}{2}$ of the diameter, or 7.5 yds. The volume would be $(3.14)(7.5^2)(18)$, which yields 3,179.25 yd³.

4. 763 in³. The volume would be $V = (3.14)(4.5^2)(12)$, which yields 763.02, or 763 in³.

5. c. If the width of the beach ball is 24, the radius is 12 inches. The volume is $V = (\frac{4}{3})(r^3)$, which yields $V = \frac{4}{3}(3.14)(12^3) = 7,238.23$.

6. 4.3 inches. First we must determine how much air is in the balloon once it is filled. Multiply 12 seconds $\times 8\pi$ cubic inches per second to get that the volume of the balloon is 108π cubic inches. The volume of a sphere with radius r is $V = \frac{4}{3}\pi r^3$. Here, $V = 108\pi$. Solve for r:

$$108\pi = \frac{4}{3}\pi r^3$$
$$r^3 = \frac{108\pi}{\frac{4}{3}\pi} = 81$$
$$r = \sqrt[3]{81} \approx 4.3$$

So, the radius is approximately 4.3 inches.

7. 4 inches. The volume of a right circular cone with height h and radius r is $V = \frac{1}{3}\pi r^2 h$. Here, $V = 8\pi$ and $h = 3r$. Substituting those expressions into the volume formula yields $8\pi = \frac{1}{3}\pi r^2(3r) = \pi r^3$. Solving this equation for r yields $r = 2$ inches; therefore, the diameter of the base is 4 inches.

8. **423π cubic inches.** First, find the length h and
base radius r of the pipe shown. Notice that the
circumference of the base is given as $2\pi r = 6\pi$,
so that $r = 3$ inches. Next, use the surface area
formula to find the length h:

$$A = 2\pi r^2 + 2\pi rh$$
$$300\pi = 2\pi(3)^2 + 2\pi(3)h$$
$$300\pi = 18\pi + 6\pi h$$
$$282\pi = 6\pi h$$
$$h = 47$$

So, the length is $h = 47$ inches. The volume of
the pipe shown, therefore, is $V = \pi r^2 h = \pi(3)^2 \cdot$
$(47) = 423\pi$ cubic inches.

LESSON
20  CIRCLES, SECTOR
AREA, AND
ARC LENGTH

*I have only to touch mathematics, and I forget everything
else on earth.*

—SONYA KOVALEVSKY

LESSON SUMMARY

In this lesson, you will focus on the circle, define its parts, and use formulas to find measures for them. It covers the process for calculating the area of a sector and the arc length. You will also learn how to visualize circles from word problems and how to solve them using knowledge of circles.

What if you were a baker and needed to decorate around a circular cake? You would need to measure the distance around the cake, right? A tape measure might get a little messy. Also, this method doesn't quite work when the object you are measuring is really big. Imagine if you had to measure a water tank instead of a cake. Luckily, there are proven geometric formulas that you can use because the top of the cake is a circle. But first you will need to learn more about the circle and its various parts.

Parts of a Circle

Radius

The radius of a circle *G* is a line segment that has its endpoints at the center of the circle and on the edge of the circle. Multiple radius lines in a circle are called radii. For instance, the radii of the circle *G* below are *GJ* and *GH*.

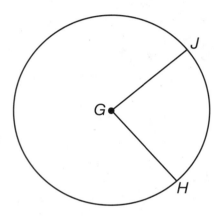

Diameter

Two radii positioned in a collinear way form the diameter of the circle. In other words, the diameter of a circle is twice a radius line. The diameter of circle *C* below is the line *DE*, which is the combination of radii *CD* and *CE*. The diameter of a circle will reach from one end of the circle edge to the other end of the edge and go through the center point of the circle.

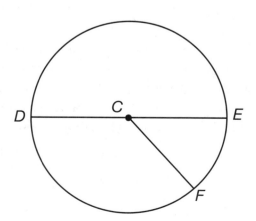

Chord

Sometimes you might see SAT problems involving the chord of a circle. The chord of a circle is a line segment that extends from one end of the circle to the other.

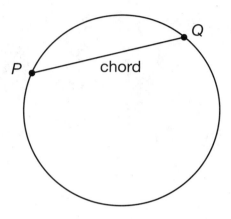

Circumference

The circumference of a circle tells you how much distance is covered around the circle. The distance around any circle to the width or diameter of the circle will be equal to the number pi, or π.

The most commonly used numbers for π are $\frac{22}{7}$ and 3.14. These are not the true values of π, only rounded approximations. You may have a π key on your calculator. This key will give you an approximation for π that varies according to how many digits your calculator displays.

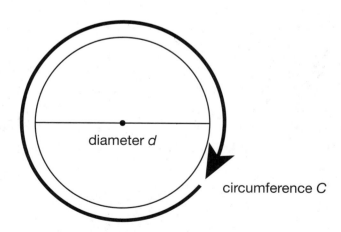

The circumference (C) of a circle divided by its diameter (d) = π, or 3.14. If $\frac{C}{d}$ = 3.14, then the circumference can be found by calculating $C = 3.14d$, or πd.

Example: Parking spaces surround a circular sports arena that is 79 feet wide. If a patron drives around the whole stadium looking for a parking space, how many feet would he have to drive to cover the whole arena?

The circumference C, of the arena, would be $\pi \times 79$, which is $3.14 \times 79 = 248.19$ feet.

Example: Justin is building a circular patio for his backyard. The design contains an outer circle of reddish stones and an inner circle of beige-colored stones. The radius of the outer circle is 5 feet and the radius of the inner circle is 3 feet. Find the circumference of both circles.

For the outer circle:
radius = 5 feet
diameter = 10 feet

$$C = \pi d$$
$$C = \pi 10$$
$$C = (3.14)(10)$$
$$C = 31.40 \text{ feet}$$

For the inner circle:
radius = 3 feet
diameter = 6 feet

$$C = \pi d$$
$$C = \pi 6$$
$$C = (3.14)(6)$$
$$C = 18.84 \text{ feet}$$

Arc Length

So far, you've learned that the distance around a circle is the circumference. What happens if the distance of the circle is not all the way around the circle? What if the distance in the question is just a portion of the entire distance?

An **arc** is a portion of the circumference or distance around a circle. In the picture below, arc AC is a portion of the distance around the entire circle B. It is denoted by writing the capital letters that make up the sides of the arc with a curved line on top, like $\overparen{AC}$.

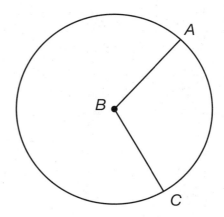

To better understand how arcs work, consider the following example.

Example: Think of a slice in a pie that is 8 inches wide. The measure of the arc would be the degree portion of the entire pie the arc takes up. When working with arcs, we need to know how much of a portion of the circumference of the circle the arc represents. This is usually given in degrees or radians. In this case, the arc is $\frac{1}{4}$ of the entire pie. If the pie is 360 degrees around, then the slice would be $\frac{1}{4}(360)$, or 90 degrees.

The length of the arc would be the length of the crust of the slice. Since the pie slice is $\frac{1}{4}$ of the entire pie, the length of the slice as an arc would be $\frac{1}{4}$ of the circumference of the circle. The circumference of the circle can be found by calculating $C = \pi d$, which is $C = (3.14)(8) = 25.12$ inches. Taking $\frac{1}{4}$ of this, we get the length of the arc by calculating $\frac{1}{4}(25.12) = 6.28$ inches.

Sometimes, you will be given the degrees in radians, which is just another type of measurement. To find degrees given radians, use the formula degrees = radians $\times \frac{180°}{\pi}$. For example:

2π radians = $(2\pi)(\frac{180°}{\pi})$ = 360 degrees

$\frac{3\pi}{2}$ radians is $(\frac{3\pi}{2})(\frac{180°}{\pi})$ = 270 degrees

$\frac{\pi}{2}$ radians is $(\frac{\pi}{2})(\frac{180°}{\pi})$ = 90 degrees

To find radians given degrees, use the following formula: radians = degrees $\times \frac{\pi}{180°}$. For example:

45 degrees = $(45)(\frac{\pi}{180°})$ = $\frac{\pi}{4}$

90 degrees = $(90)(\frac{\pi}{180°})$ = $\frac{\pi}{2}$

180 degrees = $(180)(\frac{\pi}{180°})$ = π

Calculating Arc Length

To calculate the arc length of a circle, use the following formula:

Arc length = $\frac{\text{measure of the central angle}}{360} \times \pi \times 2r$

Example: Estimate the arc length AB in the diagram below.

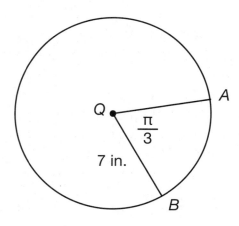

First, convert radians to degrees to use the arc length formula:

$\frac{\pi}{3}$ radians = $(\frac{\pi}{3})(\frac{180}{\pi})$ = 60 degrees

Arc length of AB = $(\frac{60}{360})2\pi(7)$

= $(0.166...)(6.28)(7)$

= approximately 7.32 cm

Example: Find the length of the arc CD.

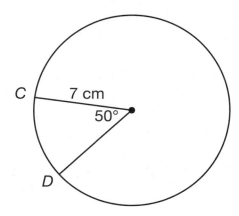

The length of the arc can be found by calculating the following:

Arc length = $\frac{\text{measure of the central angle}}{360} \times \pi \times 2r$

= $\frac{50}{360} \times \pi \times 2(7)$

= $\frac{50}{360} \times \pi \times 14$

= approximately 6.11 cm

Chord Length

If you are given the radius and an angle, you can calculate the chord length by using the sine trigonometric function. The formula is chord length = $2r\sin(\frac{c}{2})$, where r is the radius and c is the "central" angle or angle of origin for the circle.

For instance, consider the circle Q with angle 120 degrees and radius of 10 feet:

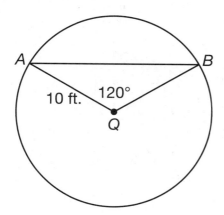

Chord AB can be found by calculating the following:

$$AB = 2r \sin \left(\frac{c}{2}\right)$$

$$= 2(10) \sin \left(\frac{120}{2}\right)$$

$$= 20 \sin (60)$$

You can use your calculator to then find $\sin(60)$:

$$= 20 \sin (60)$$

$$= 20 (0.86)$$

$$= \text{approximately } 17.2$$

So, the chord AB of the circle would be approximately 17.2 feet.

Sectors

So far, you've learned about the radius, diameter, circumference, and arc of a circle. Remember the cake example? While the arc is the angle measure of the cake slice, the sector is the actual slice. This is the easiest way to remember these parts.

Calculating the Area of a Sector

The formula for measuring the area of a sector of a circle is area $= \pi r^2\left(\frac{\pi}{360}\right)$, where r is the radius and c is the "central" angle or angle of origin.

Example: Find the area of the following sector.

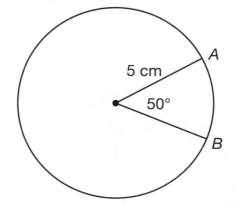

The area of the sector represented in the diagram would be $\pi r^2\left(\frac{c}{360}\right)$:

$$= \pi r^2\left(\frac{50}{360}\right)$$

$$= \pi(5)\left(\frac{c}{360}\right)$$

$$= (3.14)(25)(0.138)$$

$$= 78.5(0.138)$$

$$= 10.83 \text{ cm}$$

You will need to study the parts of the circle and the formulas for circumference, diameter, arc length, and chord length to solve SAT circle problems. Be sure to read the problems carefully to understand what is being asked.

SAT TEST-TAKING TIP

Remember that many answers will be estimated because you are using π, so be prepared to look for rounded answers in multiple-choice questions.

Practice

1. The clock face shows 5:00 P.M. Line segment *YZ* measures 7.6 inches, and angle *Z* is 135 degrees. What is the length of the arc *XY*?

2. The length of the arc shown is 6π in.

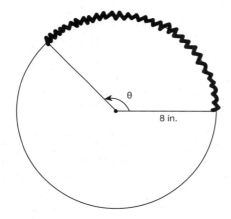

What is the value of sin θ?

a. $\frac{1}{2}$

b. $\frac{\sqrt{2}}{2}$

c. $-\frac{\sqrt{2}}{2}$

d. $-\frac{1}{2}$

3. The radius of the outer circle is three times the radius *r* of the inner circle. What is the area of the shaded region in terms of *r*?

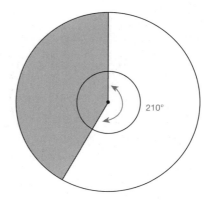

a. $\frac{14\pi}{3} r^2$

b. $\frac{10\pi}{3} r^2$

c. $8\pi r^2$

d. $\frac{25\pi}{54} r^2$

4. The length of the arc shown is $\frac{8\pi}{3}$ cm.

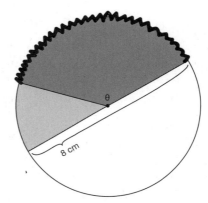

What is the value of cos θ?

a. $\frac{\sqrt{3}}{2}$

b. $-\frac{1}{2}$

c. $\frac{1}{2}$

d. $-\frac{\sqrt{3}}{2}$

Answers and Explanations

1. **17.9 inches.**

$$\text{Arc length} = \frac{\text{measure of the central angle}}{360} \times \pi \times 2r$$
$$= \frac{135}{360}(3.14)(2)(7.6)$$
$$= (0.375)(3.14)(2)(7.6)$$
$$= 17.89$$
$$= \text{approximately 17.9 inches}$$

2. **b.** First, note that the radius of the circle shown is $r = 8$ in. Using the arc length formula $s = r\theta$ with $s = 6\pi$ in. and $r = 8$ in., we see that $6\pi = 8\theta$, so that $\theta = \frac{3\pi}{4}$. So, $\cos\left(\frac{3\pi}{4}\right) = \frac{\sqrt{2}}{2}$. Choice **a** is incorrect because the central angle giving rise to this arc is $\frac{3\pi}{4}$ and sine of $\frac{3\pi}{4}$ is not $\frac{1}{2}$. Rather, this is the value of sine of $\frac{5\pi}{6}$. Choice **c** is incorrect because this value should be positive. The central angle giving rise to this arc is $\frac{3\pi}{4}$, which has terminal side in the second quadrant. Here, values of sine are positive. Choice **d** is incorrect because the central angle for this arc is $\frac{3\pi}{4}$, which is in quadrant II. The sines of such values are positive, not negative.

3. **b.** The central angle of the shaded region is 150°. The radius of the outer circle is $3r$, and the radius of the inner circle is r. This means that the area of the entire sector formed with this central angle with the outer circle is $\frac{150}{360}\pi(3r)^2$ and the area of the sector formed with this central angle with the inner circle is $\frac{150}{360}\pi(r)^2$. The area of the shaded region is the difference of these two areas:

$$\frac{150}{360}\pi(3r)^2 - \frac{150}{360}\pi(r)^2 = \frac{150}{360}\pi[9r^2 - r^2] = \frac{10\pi}{3}r^2$$

Choice **a** is incorrect because it is the area of the unshaded region. Choice **c** is incorrect because this is the area of the entire ring between the two circles. You need to multiply by $\frac{150}{360}$ to get only the shaded region. Choice **d** is incorrect because it looks like you misinterpreted the relationship between the radii. The outer radius is 3 times the inner radius r. So, the outer radius is $3r$, not $\frac{1}{3}r$.

4. **b.** First, note that the radius of the circle shown is $r = 4$ cm. Using the arc length formula $s = r\theta$ with $s = \frac{8\pi}{3}$ cm and $r = 4$ cm, we see that $\frac{8\pi}{3} = 4\theta$, so that $\theta = \frac{2\pi}{3}$. That means $\cos\frac{2\pi}{3} = -\frac{1}{2}$. Choice **a** is incorrect because the central angle giving rise to this arc is $\frac{2\pi}{3}$, and cosine of $\frac{2\pi}{3}$ is not $\frac{\sqrt{3}}{2}$. It's the value of the sine of $\frac{2\pi}{3}$. Choice **c** is incorrect because this value should be negative. The central angle giving rise to this arc is $\frac{2\pi}{3}$, which has terminal side in the second quadrant. Here, values of cosine are negative. Choice **d** is incorrect because this would be the cosine of angles $\frac{5\pi}{6}$ or $\frac{7\pi}{6}$, but the central angle giving rise to this arc is $\frac{2\pi}{3}$.

POSTTEST

Lesson 1: Solving Linear Equations and Inequalities in One Variable

1. Solve: $11x - 3 = -3(-x + 3)$.
   a. $\frac{7}{10}$
   b. $-\frac{3}{4}$
   c. $-\frac{5}{8}$
   d. $-\frac{1}{2}$

2. Solve: $\frac{x}{2} + 9 < x + 11$.
   a. $x > -4$
   b. $x < 4$
   c. $x > -6$
   d. $x < 6$

Lesson 2: Problem-Solving with Linear Functions

3. Susan and Jayne have part-time jobs selling tickets at the theater. This week, Jayne's paycheck was twice the amount of Susan's paycheck. They both were paid $7.50 an hour, and Jayne's paycheck was $60. What formula would you use to figure out how many hours Susan worked this week?
   a. $\$7.50x = \$30$
   b. $\$7.50x = \$60$
   c. $\$15x = \$30$
   d. $\$15x = \$60$

Lesson 3: Solving Systems of Linear Equations and Inequalities in Two Variables

4. Solve the following system of equations using any method:

$$3x + 7y = 4$$
$$6x + 2y = -4$$

a. (5,9)
b. (2,4)
c. (−1,1)
d. (0,2)

Lesson 4: Understanding Equations and Their Graphs

5. Which is true about the following graph?

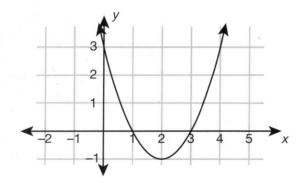

a. The maximum point is at (2,−1).
b. There are no y-intercepts.
c. (1,0) is an x-intercept.
d. The parabola is concave down.

Lesson 5: Ratios, Proportions, and Scale

6. Shezzy's pulse rate is 19 beats every 15 seconds. What is his rate in beats per minute?
a. 60
b. 76
c. 85
d. 94

Lesson 6: Percent Problems

7. Six and one-half feet of thread are used to make one pair of jeans. If 1 foot 11 inches of that thread is used in decorative stitching on the pockets, approximately what percentage of the thread is used for decorating the pockets?
a. 18%
b. 20%
c. 29%
d. 32%

Lesson 7: Unit Conversions

8. Ellie is studying for her physics final by doing a problem set for each chapter that the class covered. If each problem set is 12 problems, and on average Ellie spends 15 minutes on each problem, how long will it take her to review 8 chapters?
a. 6.4 hours
b. 22.5 hours
c. 24 hours
d. 1,440 hours

Lesson 8: Analyzing Graphs and Scatter Plots

9. What type of correlation is shown by the following scatter plot?

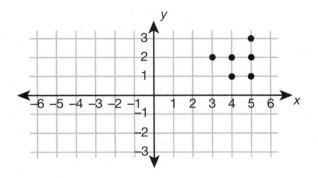

a. No correlation
b. Positively correlated
c. Negatively correlated
d. Not enough information is given

Lesson 9: Using Two-Way Tables to Analyze Data

10. A group of people are contacted and asked to donate to a local charity. The table shows how the group donated: by phone or by e-mail. How many donations were received by those contacted through e-mail?

	Donated	Not Donated	Total
Phone	32	38	70
E-mail	30	120	150
Total	62	158	220

a. 30
b. 62
c. 70
d. 120

Lesson 10: Making Conclusions with Statistical Measures

11. Given the following group of numbers—8, 2, 9, 4, 2, 7, 8, 0, 4, 1—which of the following is/are true?

    I. The mean is 5.
    II. The median is 4.
    III. The sum of the modes is 14.

a. II only
b. II and III
c. I and III
d. I, II, and III

Lesson 11: Problem-Solving with Quadratic and Exponential Functions

12. Mr. Ingram wants to add a garage to his home. The dimensions of his home are 50 ft. by 20 ft. When securing his building permit, he found that his home with the garage cannot be more than 1,400 square ft. How long can he extend the side of his house that is 50 ft. long so that his remodeling project will follow code?

a. 20 ft.
b. 24 ft.
c. 30 ft.
d. 32 ft.

Lesson 12: Solving Quadratic Equations, Systems Involving Quadratic Equations, and Inequalities

13. Solve using the quadratic formula:
$2x^2 + 5x + 3 = 0$
a. $-2, 3$
b. $-4, -5$
c. $-\frac{3}{2}, -1$
d. $\frac{1}{2}, -3$

Lesson 13: Polynomial, Radical, and Rational Expressions

14. Simplify: $\frac{x^2 - 5x - 14}{2x - 14}$.
a. $\frac{2x + 7}{3}$
b. $x + 2$
c. 1
d. $\frac{x + 2}{2}$

15. Multiply: $\frac{1 + 3m}{4 - m} \cdot \frac{m - 4}{3m^2 - 5m - 2}$.
a. $-\frac{4}{5}$
b. $\frac{5m}{m - 3}$
c. $\frac{m}{m - 5}$
d. $-\frac{1}{5}$

Lesson 14: Radical and Rational Functions in One Variable

16. Which of the following is the solution set for the equation $2 + \sqrt{x} = x$?
a. $\{2,3\}$
b. $\{4,1\}$
c. $\{-2\}$
d. θ

17. Solve: $\frac{x}{2} = \frac{3}{x - 5}$.
a. $x = 6$ or -5
b. $x = -1$ or -5
c. $x = 6$ or -1
d. $x = 6$ or -2

Lesson 15: Factorable Polynomials and Non-Linear Functions

18. How many distinct real zeros does the polynomial $p(x) = x(x^4 - 5x^3 - 4x^2)$ have?
a. 0
b. 1
c. 3
d. 5

Lesson 16: Transformations and Compositions of Functions

19. If $f(x) = x^2$, which transformation represents the equation $g(x) = (x + 5)^2 + 1$?
a. Shift 1 unit right; shift 5 units down.
b. Shift 5 units left; shift 1 unit up.
c. Shift 1 unit left; shift 5 units up.
d. Shift 5 units right; shift 1 unit up.

20. Which two functions satisfy the equation $f(g(x)) - g(f(x)) = 0$?
a. $f(x) = x - 8, g(x) = -x + 8$
b. $f(x) = \frac{1}{x^2}, g(x) = x^2$
c. $f(x) = 2x + 1, g(x) = 3x + 1$
d. $f(x) = \frac{2}{5x}, g(x) = \frac{5}{2x}$

Lesson 17: Operations with Complex Numbers

21. For $i = \sqrt{-1}$, which of the following equals $(2i + 3)^2$?

a. $5 + 2i$

b. $4 - 10i$

c. $10 - 5i$

d. $12 + 2i$

Lesson 18: Using Trigonometry to Solve Problems Involving Lines, Angles, and Right Triangles

22. What is the measure of $\angle AXB$?

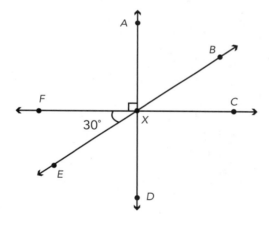

a. 30°

b. 60°

c. 90°

d. 180°

23. What is the sin B for this figure?

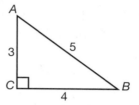

a. $\frac{4}{3}$

b. $\frac{3}{4}$

c. $\frac{3}{5}$

d. $\frac{4}{5}$

Lesson 19: Volume Problems

24. Which formula is correct in computing 50% of the volume of this shape?

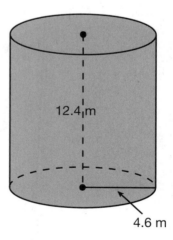

12.4 m

4.6 m

a. $V = \frac{1}{2}\pi(4.6)^2$

b. $V = \frac{1}{2}\pi(9.2)^2(12.4)$

c. $V = \frac{1}{2}\pi(9.2)^2$

d. $V = \frac{1}{2}\pi(4.6)^2(12.4)$

Lesson 20: Circles, Sector Area, and Arc Length

25. What is the measure of the arc represented by the numbers 7 and 4?

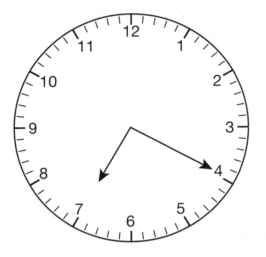

a. 90°
b. 60°
c. 80°
d. 120°

Answer Key

1. **b.** Lesson 1
2. **a.** Lesson 1
3. **a.** Lesson 2
4. **c.** Lesson 3
5. **c.** Lesson 4
6. **b.** Lesson 5
7. **c.** Lesson 6
8. **d.** Lesson 7
9. **a.** Lesson 8
10. **a.** Lesson 9
11. **b.** Lesson 10
12. **a.** Lesson 11
13. **c.** Lesson 12
14. **d.** Lesson 13
15. **b.** Lesson 13
16. **b.** Lesson 14
17. **c.** Lesson 14
18. **c.** Lesson 15
19. **b.** Lesson 16
20. **b.** Lesson 16
21. **a.** Lesson 17
22. **b.** Lesson 18
23. **c.** Lesson 18
24. **d.** Lesson 19
25. **a.** Lesson 20

REVIEW OF NUMBERS

If I were again beginning my studies, I would follow the advice of Plato and start with mathematics.

—GALILEO GALILEI

LESSON SUMMARY

For this review of numbers, you will refresh your knowledge of integers, working with fractions and decimals. The math topics covered in this appendix exist in the preceding lessons and are essential to successfully working through problems on the SAT. The purpose of this review is to fill in the gaps in your knowledge and perhaps present you with shortcuts and tips for dealing with various types of numbers and their operations.

Working with Integers

Positive and Negative Numbers

Positive and negative numbers, also called signed numbers, can be visualized as points along the number line:

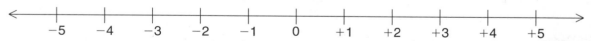

Numbers to the left of 0 are *negative* and those to the right are *positive*. Zero is neither negative nor positive. If a number is written without a sign, it is assumed to be *positive*. On the negative side of the number line, numbers further to the left are actually smaller. For example, –5 is *less than* –2. You come into contact with negative numbers more often than you might think; for example, very cold temperatures are recorded as negative numbers.

As you move to the right along the number line, the numbers get larger. Mathematically, to indicate that one number, say 4, is *greater than* another number, say –2, the *greater than* sign ">" is used:

$$4 > -2$$

Conversely, to say that –2 is *less than* 4, we use the *less than* sign, "<":

$$-2 < 4$$

Adding and Subtracting Integers

You can add and subtract integers, but first, you need to know the rules for determining the sign of an answer. Of course, a calculator can determine the sign of your answer when you are working with integers. However, it is important that you know how to determine the sign of your answer without the use of a calculator. Knowing how to determine the sign of your answer is a basic algebra skill and is *absolutely necessary* to progress to more advanced algebra topics.

The Sign Rules for Adding Integers

When the signs of the numbers are the same, **add** the numbers and keep the same sign for your answer.

> **Examples:** $-3 + -5 = -8$
> $4 + 3 = 7$

Negative integers can be written as (–4), (⁻4), –4, and ⁻4. The negative sign may be raised, or it may remain on the level of the number. The way the integers are represented does not change the results of the

problem. Positive integers, on the other hand, are usually not written with the + sign, as a non-zero integer with no sign is understood to be positive.

If the signs of the numbers are different (one is positive and one is negative), then treat both of them as positive for a moment. Subtract the smaller one from the larger one, and then affix the sign of the larger one to the result.

Example: $4 + {}^-7 = -3$

The answer is negative because 7 is bigger than 4 when we ignore signs.

SAT TEST-TAKING TIP

If there is no sign in front of a non-zero number, the number is positive.

The Sign Rules for Subtracting Integers

All subtraction problems can be converted to addition problems because subtracting is the same as adding the opposite. Once you have converted the subtraction problem to an addition problem, use the **Sign Rules for Adding Integers**.

For example, 2 – 5 can also be written as 2 – ⁺5. Subtraction is the same as adding the opposite, so 2 – ⁺5 can be rewritten as 2 + ⁻5. Because the problem has been rewritten as an addition problem, you can use the **Sign Rules for Adding Integers**. The rule says that if the signs are different, you should subtract the numbers and take the sign of the larger number. Therefore, 2 + ⁻5 = –3. See the following examples.

> **Examples:** $7 - 3 = 7 - {}^+3 = 7 + {}^-3 = 4$
> $6 - {}^-8 = 6 + {}^+8 = 14$
> $-5 - {}^-11 = -5 + {}^+11 = 6$

Shortcuts and Tips

Here are some tips that can shorten your work and save you time!

Tip #1: You may have discovered that $(-\ ^-)$ turns into $(+)$. Whenever you have a problem with two negative signs side by side, change both signs to positive. Then work the problem.

Example: $4 - {}^-8 \; = \; 4 + {}^+8 \; = \; 4 + 8 \; = \; 12$

Tip #2: Subtracting two positive integers is the same as adding integers with opposite signs. You will find that the most frequently used notation is $5 - 9$ rather than $5 + {}^-9$.

Example: $3 - 5 = 3 + {}^-5 = -2$ so $3 - 5 = -2$

Tip #3: When adding more than two numbers, add all the positive numbers, add all the negative numbers, then add the resulting positive and negative numbers to obtain the answer.

Example: $2 + 3 + 5 - 7 \; = \; 10 - 7 \; = \; 3$
$-2 + 5 + 7 + {}^-6 \; = \; 12 + {}^-8 \; = \; 4$
$5 - 7 + 6 - 9 \; = \; 11 + {}^-16 \; = \; -5$

Multiplying and Dividing Integers

When you are multiplying or dividing integers, if the signs are the same, the answer will be positive. If the signs are different, the answer will be negative. The dot $(\cdot)$ indicates multiplication in the following examples.

Examples: $2 \cdot 5 = 10$
$-2 \cdot {}^-5 = 10$
$-2 \cdot 5 = -10$
$10 \sqrt{\ }{}^-2 = -5$
$-10 \sqrt{\ } 2 = -5$
$-10 \sqrt{\ }{}^-2 = 5$

Simplifying Expressions

What does it mean when you are asked to **simplify** an expression? Numbers can be named in many different ways. For example: $\frac{1}{2}$, 0.5, 50%, and $\frac{3}{6}$ all represent the same number. When you are told to simplify an expression, you want to get the simplest name possible. For example, because $\frac{3}{6}$ can be reduced, $\frac{1}{2}$ is the simplest name of the number.

Mathematical expressions, like numbers, can be named in different ways. For example, here are three ways to write the same expression:

1. $x + {}^-3$
2. $x + (-3)$ *When you have two signs side by side, parentheses can be used to keep the signs separate.*
3. $x - 3$ *Remember that Lesson 1 showed that subtracting a positive 3 is the same as adding the opposite of a positive 3.*

The operation of multiplication can be denoted in many ways. In Lesson 1, we used the dot (·) to indicate multiplication. A graphics calculator will display an asterisk when it shows multiplication. You are probably familiar with this notation (2 × 3) to show multiplication. However, in algebra, we rarely use the × to indicate multiplication since it may be unclear whether the × is a variable or a multiplication sign. To avoid confusion over the use of the ×, we express multiplication in other ways. Another way to indicate multiplication is the use of parentheses (2)(3); also, when you see an expression such as $3ab$, it is telling you to multiply 3 by a by b.

Order of Operations

In order to simplify an expression that contains several different operations (such as addition, subtraction, multiplication, and division), it is important to perform them in the right order. This is called the **order of operations**.

For example, suppose you were asked to simplify the following expression:

$$3 + 4 \cdot 2 + 5$$

At first glance, you might think it is easy: $3 + 4 = 7$ and $2 + 5 = 7$, then $7 \cdot 7 = 49$. Another person might say $3 + 4 = 7$ and $7 \cdot 2 = 14$ and $14 + 5 = 19$. Actually, both of these answers are wrong! To eliminate the possibility of getting several answers for the same problem, there is a specific order you must follow. Here are the steps in the order of operations:

1. Perform the operations inside grouping symbols such as (   ), {   }, and [   ]. The division bar can also act as a grouping symbol. The division bar or fraction bar tells you to perform the steps in the numerator and the denominator before you divide.
2. Evaluate exponents (powers) such as 3^2.
3. Do all multiplication and division *in order from left to right.*
4. Do all addition and subtraction *in order from left to right.*

Here are the steps for correctly simplifying $3 + 4 \cdot 2 + 5$:

Multiply $4 \cdot 2$.	$3 + 4 \cdot 2 + 5$
Add the numbers in order from left to right.	$3 + \mathbf{8} + 5$
The correct answer is 16.	$= 16$

Let's try some more examples.

Example: $3 + 4 \div 2 \cdot 3 + 5$
You need to do division and multiplication first *in order from left to right.* The division comes first, so first you divide and then you multiply.

Divide $4 \div 2$.	$3 + \mathbf{4 \div 2} \cdot 3 + 5$
Multiply $2 \cdot 3$.	$3 + \mathbf{2 \cdot 3} + 5$
Add the numbers in order from left to right.	$3 + \mathbf{6} + 5$
	$= 14$

Example: $7 + 3(6 - 2) - 6$
You need to perform the operation inside the (   ) first. Here, the parentheses indicate multiplication. The notation $3(6 - 2)$ means $3 \cdot (6 - 2)$.

Subtract $6 - 2$.	$7 + 3(\mathbf{6 - 2}) - 6$
Multiply $3 \cdot 4$.	$7 + \mathbf{3(4)} - 6$
Add and subtract the numbers in order from left to right.	$7 + \mathbf{12} - 6$
	$\mathbf{19} - 6$
	$= 13$

Example: $3 + 2^3 + 3(15 \div 3) - 2 + 1$
The expression contains parentheses (   ), so you do what's inside the (   ) first. Your next step is to simplify the exponent.

Divide $15 \div 3$.	$3 + 2^3 + 3(\mathbf{15 \div 3}) - 2 + 1$
Simplify the exponent 23.	$3 + \mathbf{2^3} + 3(5) - 2 + 1$
Multiply $3 \cdot 5$.	$3 + 8 + \mathbf{3(5)} - 2 + 1$

Add and subtract in order from left to right.

$$3 + 8 + 15 - 2 + 1$$
$$= 11 + 15 - 2 + 1$$
$$= 26 - 2 + 1$$
$$= 24 + 1$$
$$= 25$$

SAT TEST-TAKING TIP

A **mnemonic** is a memory aid. In order to remember that the order of operations is **P**arentheses, **E**xponents, **M**ultiplication and **D**ivision, then **A**ddition and **S**ubtraction, you can use the mnemonic sentence: "**P**lease **e**xcuse **m**y **d**ear **A**unt **S**ally." Or, you can create your own sentence.

Working with Multiple Grouping Symbols

What would you do if you had grouping symbols inside grouping symbols? To simplify the expression, $2\{4 + 3[10 - 4(2)] + 1\}$, start from the inside and work to the outside. Your first step is to multiply $4(2)$.

Subtract $10 - 8$.	$2\{4 + 3[10 - 8] + 1\}$
Multiply $3 \cdot 2$.	$2\{4 + 3[2] + 1\}$
Add $4 + 6 + 1$.	$2\{4 + 6 + 1\}$
Multiply $2 \cdot 11$.	$2\{11\}$
	$= 22$

Try this problem:

$$2\{12 \div 2[10 - 2(2)] + 3\}$$

If you got 8, you are correct!

Evaluating Algebraic Expressions

What is the difference between simplifying an expression and evaluating an expression? In algebra, letters called **variables** are often used to represent numbers. When you are asked to *evaluate* an algebraic expression, you substitute a number in place of a variable (letter) and then simplify the expression. Study these examples.

Example: Evaluate the expression $2b + a$ when $a = 2$ and $b = 4$.
Substitute 2 for the variable a and 4 for the variable b. When the expression is written as $2b$, it means 2 times b.

	$2b + a$
Multiply $2 \cdot 4$.	$2(4) + 2$
	$8 + 2$
	$= 10$

Example: Evaluate the expression $a^2 + 2b + c$ when $a = 2$, $b = 3$, and $c = 7$.
Substitute 2 for a, 3 for b, and 7 for c.

	$a^2 + 2b + c$
Find the value of 2^2.	$(2)^2 + 2(3) + 7$
Multiply $2 \cdot 3$.	$4 + 2(3) + 7$
Add the numbers.	$4 + 6 + 7$
	$= 17$

Using the Distributive Property to Combine Like Terms

How do you simplify an expression like $2(x + y) + 3(x + 2y)$? According to the order of operations that you learned previously, you would have to do the grouping symbols first. However, you know you can't add x to y because they are not like terms. What you need to do is use the **distributive property**. The distributive property tells you to multiply the number and/or variable(s) outside the parentheses by every term inside the parentheses. You would work the problem like this:

> In 123 BCE, the king of Pompeii wanted a method to ensure that all of the guests at his parties would get the same amount of food. His solution was to line up the guests and have servants pass out pieces of food to each of them in turn. With this decision, he can be credited with early use of the distributive property.

Multiply 2 by x and 2 by y. Then multiply 3 by x and 3 by $2y$. If there is no number in front of the variable, it is understood to be 1, so 2 times x means 2 times $1x$. To multiply, you multiply the numbers and the variable stays the same. When you multiply 3 by $2y$, you multiply 3 by 2 and the variable, y, stays the same, so you would get $6y$. After you have multiplied, you can then combine like terms.

Example:
Multiply $2(x + y)$ and $3(x + 2y)$.
Combine like terms.

$2(x + y) + 3(x + 2y)$
$2x + 2y + 3x + 6y$
$= 5x + 8y$

SAT TEST-TAKING TIP

If there is no number (coefficient) in front of a variable, it is understood to be 1.

Here are two more examples using the distributive property.

Example: $2(x + y) + 3(x - y)$
Multiply 2 by x and 2 by y. Then multiply 3 by x and 3 by $(-y)$. When you multiply 3 by $(-y)$, this is the same as $3(-1y)$. The 1 is understood to be in front of the y even though you don't see it. In this example, you can see how the parentheses are used to indicate multiplication.
Use the distributive property. $2(x + y) + 3(x - y)$
Combine like terms. $2x + 2y + 3x - 3y$
$= 5x - y$

Example: $2(2x + y) - 3(x + 2y)$
Use the distributive property to get rid of the parentheses. The subtraction sign in front of the 3 is the same as multiplying $(-3)(x)$ and $(-3)(2y)$.
Use the distributive property. $2(2x + y) - 3(x + 2y)$
Combine like terms. $4x + 2y - 3x - 6y$
$= x - 4y$

Working with Fractions

What Is a Fraction?
A fraction is a part of a whole.
- **A minute is a fraction of an hour.** It is 1 of the 60 equal parts of an hour, or $\frac{1}{60}$ (one-*sixtieth*) of an hour.
- **The weekend days are a fraction of a week.** The weekend days are 2 of the 7 equal parts of the week, or $\frac{2}{7}$ (two-*sevenths*) of the week.
- **Coins are fractions of a dollar.** A nickel is $\frac{1}{20}$ (one-*twentieth*) of a dollar, because there are 20 nickels in one dollar. A dime is $\frac{1}{10}$ (one-*tenth*) of a dollar, because there are 10 dimes in a dollar.
- **Measurements are expressed in fractions.** There are four quarts in a gallon. One quart is $\frac{1}{4}$ of a gallon. Three quarts are $\frac{3}{4}$ of a gallon.

It is important to know what "0" means in a fraction! $\frac{0}{5} = 0$, because there are zero of five parts. But $\frac{5}{0}$ is undefined, because it is impossible to have five parts of zero. Zero is never allowed to be the denominator of a fraction!

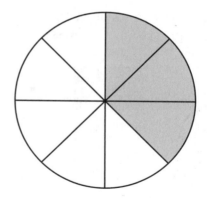

The two numbers that compose a fraction are called the:

$$\frac{\text{numerator}}{\text{denominator}}$$

For example, in the fraction $\frac{3}{8}$, the numerator is 3, and the denominator is 8. An easy way to remember which is which is to associate the word **denominator** with the word **down**. The numerator indicates the number of parts you are considering, and the denominator indicates the number of equal parts that constitute the whole. You can represent any fraction graphically by shading the number of parts being considered (numerator) out of the whole (denominator).

> **Example:** Let's say that a pizza was cut into 8 equal slices, and you ate 3 of them. The fraction $\frac{3}{8}$ tells you what portion of the pizza you ate. The following pizza shows this: It's divided into 8 equal slices, and 3 of the 8 slices (the ones you ate) are shaded. Since the *whole* pizza was cut into 8 equal slices, 8 is the *denominator*. The part you ate was 3 slices, making 3 the *numerator*.

If you have difficulty conceptualizing a particular fraction, think in terms of *pizza fractions*. Just picture yourself eating the top number of slices from a pizza that's cut into the bottom number of slices. This may sound silly, but many people relate much better to visual images than to abstract ideas. Incidentally, this little trick comes in handy when comparing fractions to determine which one is bigger and when adding fractions.

Sometimes the *whole* isn't a *single* object like a pizza, but rather a *group* of objects. However, the shading idea works the same way. Four out of the following five triangles are shaded. Thus, $\frac{4}{5}$ of the triangles are shaded.

The same approach can be applied to other less geometric scenarios. For instance, suppose you have a $5 bill and want to buy cookies, at a local bakery, that cost 50 cents each (tax already included). How many can you buy?

We can visualize the *whole* "$5" in 50-cent parts as follows:

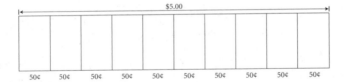

Since the whole $5 can be broken into 10, 50-cent parts, we conclude that you could buy 10 cookies.

A related question is: "What fraction of your $5 would be spent if you bought 4 cookies?" This can be visualized by shading 4 of the 10 parts, as follows:

The fraction of the $5 is $\frac{4}{10}$.

Continuing with this scenario, observe that the total cost for 4 cookies is $2. So, you might quite reasonably ask, "Can we also just describe this as '2 out of 5 dollars,' so that the cost for 4 cookies resembles $\frac{2}{5}$ of the money?" The answer is yes! We could, instead, divide the *whole* $5 into 5, $1 *parts*, illustrated as follows:

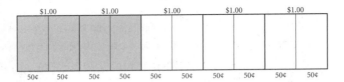

Note that "4, 50-cent parts, out of 10" is equivalent to "2, $1 parts, out of 5." Using fractions, this is equivalent to saying $\frac{4}{10} = \frac{2}{5}$. The fraction on the right-hand side of the equals sign is *reduced*. We elaborated on *reducing fractions* earlier.

Three Kinds of Fractions

There are three kinds of fractions, each explained here.

Proper Fractions

In a proper fraction, the top number is less than the bottom number. Some examples are:

$$\frac{1}{2}, \frac{2}{3}, \frac{4}{9}, \frac{8}{13}$$

The value of a proper fraction is less than 1.

Example: Suppose you eat 3 slices of a pizza that's cut into 8 slices. Each slice is $\frac{1}{8}$ of the pizza. You've eaten $\frac{3}{8}$ of the pizza.

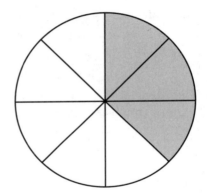

Improper Fractions

In an *improper fraction*, the top number is greater than or equal to the bottom number:

$$\frac{3}{2}, \frac{5}{3}, \frac{14}{9}, \frac{12}{12}$$

The value of an improper fraction is greater than or equal to 1.

- When the top and bottom numbers are the same, the value of the fraction is 1. For example, all of these fractions are equal to 1: $\frac{2}{2}, \frac{3}{3}, \frac{4}{4}, \frac{5}{5}$, etc.

■ Any whole number can be written as an improper fraction by writing that number as the top number of a fraction whose bottom number is 1, for example, $\frac{4}{1} = 4$.

Example: Suppose you're very hungry and eat all 8 slices of that pizza. You could say you ate $\frac{8}{8}$ of the pizza, or 1 entire pizza. If you were still hungry and then ate 1 slice of your best friend's pizza, which was also cut into 8 slices, you'd have eaten $\frac{9}{8}$ of a pizza. However, you would probably use a mixed number, rather than an improper fraction, to tell someone how much pizza you ate.

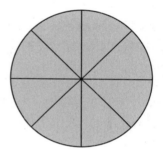

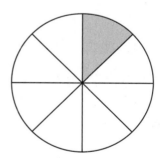

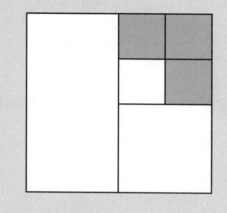
Mixed Numbers

When a proper fraction is written to the right of a whole number, the whole number and fraction together constitute a mixed number:

$$3\frac{1}{2}, 4\frac{2}{3}, 12\frac{3}{4}, 24\frac{2}{5}$$

The value of a mixed number is greater than 1: It is the sum of the whole number and a proper fraction.

It is convenient to clearly separate how many wholes from the remaining proper portion of a fraction when dealing with improper fractions.

Example: Remember those 9 slices you ate? You could also say that you ate $1\frac{1}{8}$ pizzas because you ate one entire pizza and one out of eight slices of your best friend's pizza.

Changing Improper Fractions into Mixed or Whole Numbers

It is more intuitive to add or subtract fractions as mixed numbers than as improper fractions. To change an improper fraction into a mixed number or a whole number, follow these steps:

1. Divide the bottom number into the top number.
2. If there is a remainder, change it into a fraction by writing it as the top number over the bottom number of the improper fraction. Write it next to the whole number.

Example: Change $\frac{13}{2}$ into a mixed number.

1. Divide the bottom number (2) into the top number (13) to get the whole number portion (6) of the mixed number:

$$\begin{array}{r} 6 \\ 2\overline{)13} \\ \underline{12} \\ 1 \end{array}$$

2. Write the remainder of the division (1) over the original bottom number (2): $\frac{1}{2}$

3. Write the two numbers together: $6\frac{1}{2}$

4. Check: Change the mixed number back into an improper fraction (see steps in next section). If you get the original improper fraction, your answer is correct.

⚠ **CAUTION**

It is important to realize that $6\frac{1}{2}$ does *not* mean "6 times $\frac{1}{2}$."

Example: Change $\frac{12}{4}$ into a mixed number.

1. Divide the bottom number (4) into the top number (12) to get the whole number portion (3) of the mixed number:

$$\begin{array}{r} 3 \\ 4\overline{)12} \\ \underline{12} \\ 0 \end{array}$$

2. Since the remainder of the division is zero, you're done. The improper fraction $\frac{12}{4}$ is actually a whole number: 3

3. Check: Multiply 3 by the original bottom number (4) to make sure you get the original top number (12) as the answer.

Changing Mixed Numbers into Improper Fractions

Unlike with addition and subtraction, fractions are easier to multiply and divide as improper fractions than as mixed numbers. To change a mixed number into an improper fraction:

1. Multiply the whole number by the bottom number.
2. Add the top number to the product from step 1.
3. Write the total as the top number of a fraction over the original bottom number.

Example: Change $2\frac{3}{4}$ into an improper fraction.

1. Multiply the whole number (2) by the bottom number (4): $2 \times 4 = 8$

2. Add the result (8) to the top number (3): $8 + 3 = 11$

3. Put the total (11) over the bottom number (4): $\frac{11}{4}$

4. Check: Reverse the process by changing the improper fraction into a mixed number. Since you get back $2\frac{3}{4}$, your answer is right.

Example: Change $3\frac{5}{8}$ into an improper fraction.

1. Multiply the whole number (3) by the bottom number (8): $3 \times 8 = 24$
2. Add the result (24) to the top number (5): $24 + 5 = 29$
3. Put the total (29) over the bottom number (8): $\frac{29}{8}$
4. Check: Change the improper fraction into a mixed number. Since you get back $3\frac{5}{8}$, your answer is right.

Reducing a Fraction

Reducing a fraction means writing it in *lowest terms*. For instance, 50¢ is $\frac{50}{100}$ of a dollar, or $\frac{1}{2}$ of a dollar. In fact, if you have 50¢ in your pocket, you say that you have *half* a dollar. We say that the fraction $\frac{50}{100}$ reduces to $\frac{1}{2}$. Reducing a fraction does not change its value. **When you do arithmetic with fractions, always reduce your answer to lowest terms.** To reduce a fraction:

1. Find a whole number that divides *evenly* into the top number and the bottom number.
2. Divide that number into both the top and bottom numbers and replace them with the resulting quotients (the division answers).
3. Repeat the process until you can't find a number that divides evenly into both the top and bottom numbers.

It's faster to reduce when you find the *largest* number that divides evenly into both the top and bottom numbers of the fraction.

Example: Reduce $\frac{8}{24}$ to lowest terms.

Two steps:
1. Divide by 4: $\frac{8 \div 4}{24 \div 4} = \frac{2}{6}$
2. Divide by 2: $\frac{2 \div 2}{6 \div 2} = \frac{1}{3}$

One step:
1. Divide by 8: $\frac{8 \div 8}{24 \div 8} = \frac{1}{3}$

Reducing Shortcut

When the top and bottom numbers both end in zeros, cross out the same number of zeros in both numbers to begin the reducing process. (Crossing out zeros is the same as dividing by 10, 100, 1,000, etc., depending on the number of zeros you cross out.) For example, $\frac{300}{4,000}$ reduces to $\frac{3}{40}$ when you cross out two zeros in both numbers:

$$\frac{3\cancel{0}\cancel{0}}{4,0\cancel{0}\cancel{0}} = \frac{3}{40}$$

Operations with Fractions

Adding Fractions

If you have to add two fractions that have the same bottom numbers, just add the top numbers together and write the total over the bottom number.

Example: $\frac{2}{8} + \frac{4}{8} = \frac{2+4}{8} = \frac{6}{8}$, which can be reduced to $\frac{3}{4}$.

You can visualize the addition of fractions using the same "pizza slice" examples.

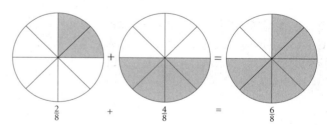

$$\frac{2}{8} \quad + \quad \frac{4}{8} \quad = \quad \frac{6}{8}$$

Both pizzas are divided into the same number of equally sized pieces, so you can interpret the sum as the total number of slices from a single pizza.

Example

$\frac{5}{11} + \frac{20}{11} = \frac{25}{11}$, which can be written equivalently as $2\frac{3}{11}$.

⚠ CAUTION

Do NOT add the bottom numbers. Specifically, $\frac{2}{9} + \frac{4}{9} \neq \frac{2+4}{9+9}$!

Finding the Least Common Denominator

To add fractions with different bottom numbers, raise some or all the fractions to higher terms so they all have the same bottom number, called the **common denominator**. Then add the numerators, keeping the denominators the same.

All the original bottom numbers divide evenly into the common denominator. If it is the smallest number into which they all divide evenly, it is called the **least common denominator** (**LCD**). Addition is more efficient when the LCD is used than when any old common denominator is used.

Here are some tips for finding the LCD:

- See if the bottom numbers of all fractions to be added divide evenly into the largest bottom number.
- Check out the multiplication table of the largest bottom number until you find a number into which all the other bottom numbers divide evenly.

SAT TEST-TAKING TIP

The fastest way to find a common denominator is to multiply the two denominators together. Example: For $\frac{1}{4}$ and $\frac{3}{8}$ you can use $4 \times 8 = \mathbf{32}$ as your common denominator.

Example: $\frac{2}{3} + \frac{4}{5}$.

1. Find the LCD by multiplying the bottom numbers: $\quad 3 \times 5 = 15$

2. Raise each fraction to 15ths, the LCD: $\quad \frac{2}{3} + \frac{10}{15}$
   $\quad \frac{4}{5} = \frac{12}{15}$

3. Add as usual: $\quad \frac{22}{15}$

4. Reduce to lowest terms or write as an equivalent mixed number, if applicable: $\quad \frac{22}{15} = 1\frac{7}{15}$

Pictorially, we convert each pizza into one divided into the number of slices equal to the least common denominator. Then, we add as before.

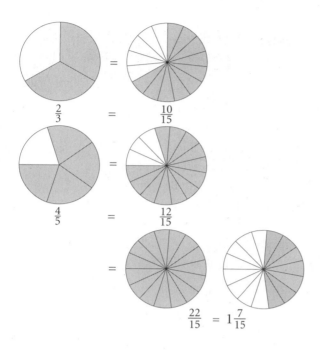

$$\frac{2}{3} = \frac{10}{15}$$

$$\frac{4}{5} = \frac{12}{15}$$

$$\frac{22}{15} = 1\frac{7}{15}$$

Adding Mixed Numbers

Mixed numbers, you remember, consist of a whole number and a proper fraction. To add mixed numbers:

1. Add the fractional parts of the mixed numbers. (If they have different bottom numbers, first raise them to higher terms so they all have the same bottom number.) If the sum is an improper fraction, change it to a mixed number.
2. Add the whole number parts of the original mixed numbers.
3. Add the results of steps 1 and 2.

Example: $2\frac{3}{5} + 1\frac{4}{5}$.

1. Add the fractional parts of the mixed numbers and change the improper fraction into a mixed number:

$$\frac{3}{5} + \frac{4}{5} = \frac{7}{5} = 1\frac{2}{5}$$

2. Add the whole number parts of the original mixed numbers:

$$2 + 1 = 3$$

3. Add the results of steps 1 and 2:

$$1\frac{2}{5} + 3 = 4\frac{2}{5}$$

Subtracting Fractions

As with addition, if the fractions you're subtracting have the same bottom numbers, just subtract the second top number from the first top number and write the difference over the bottom number.

Example: $\frac{4}{9} - \frac{3}{9} = \frac{4-3}{9} = \frac{1}{9}$.

Visually, start with a pizza with 4 of 9 slices shaded. Then, erase 3 of those shaded slices. The fraction left is the difference. Pictorially, we have

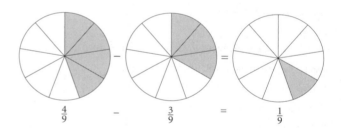

$$\frac{4}{9} \qquad - \qquad \frac{3}{9} \qquad = \qquad \frac{1}{9}$$

To subtract fractions with different bottom numbers, raise some or all of the fractions to higher terms so they all have the same bottom number, or **common denominator**, and then subtract as shown in the example. As with addition, subtraction is often more efficient if you use the LCD rather than a larger common denominator.

Example: $\frac{5}{6} - \frac{3}{4}$.

1. Find the LCD. The smallest number into which both bottom numbers divide evenly is 12. The easiest way to find the LCD is to check the multiplication

table for 6, the larger of the two bottom numbers.

2. Raise each fraction to 12ths, the LCD:

$$\frac{5}{6} = \frac{10}{12}$$

3. Subtract as usual:

$$\begin{aligned} &\frac{5}{6} = \frac{10}{12} \\ -&\frac{3}{4} = \frac{9}{12} \\ \hline & \qquad \frac{1}{12} \end{aligned}$$

Subtracting Mixed Numbers

To subtract mixed numbers:

1. If the second fraction is smaller than the first fraction, subtract it from the first fraction. Otherwise, you'll have to "borrow" (explained by example further on) before subtracting fractions.
2. Subtract the second whole number from the first whole number.
3. Add the results of steps 1 and 2.

Example: $4\frac{3}{5} - 1\frac{2}{5}$.

1. Subtract the fractions: $\frac{3}{5} - \frac{2}{5} = \frac{1}{5}$
2. Subtract the whole numbers: $4 - 1 = 3$
3. Add the results of steps 1 and 2: $\frac{1}{5} + 3 = 3\frac{1}{5}$

When the second fraction is bigger than the first fraction, you'll have to perform an extra "borrowing" step before subtracting the fractions, as illustrated in the following example.

Example: $7\frac{3}{5} - 2\frac{4}{5}$.

1. You can't subtract the fractions in the present form because $\frac{4}{5}$ is bigger than $\frac{3}{5}$. So you have to "borrow":

- Rewrite the 7 part of $7\frac{3}{5}$ as $6\frac{5}{5}$: $\qquad 7 = 6\frac{5}{5}$

  (Note: Fifths are used because 5 is the bottom number in $7\frac{3}{5}$; also, $6\frac{5}{5} = 6 + \frac{5}{5} = 7$.)

- Then add back the $\frac{3}{5}$ part of $7\frac{3}{5}$:

$$7\frac{3}{5} = 7 + \frac{3}{5} =$$
$$6\frac{5}{5} + \frac{3}{5} = 6\frac{8}{5}$$

2. Now you have a different, yet equivalent, version of the original problem:

$$6\frac{8}{5} - 2\frac{4}{5}$$

3. Subtract the fractional parts of the two mixed numbers:

$$\frac{8}{5} - \frac{4}{5} = \frac{4}{5}$$

4. Subtract the whole number parts of the two mixed numbers:

$$6 - 2 = 4$$

5. Add the results of the last 2 steps together:

$$4 + \frac{4}{5} = 4\frac{4}{5}$$

Multiplying Fractions

Multiplication by a proper fraction is the same as finding a part of something. For instance, suppose a personal-size pizza is cut into 4 slices. Each slice represents $\frac{1}{4}$ of the pizza. If you eat $\frac{1}{2}$ of a slice, then you've eaten $\frac{1}{2}$ of $\frac{1}{4}$ of a pizza, or $\frac{1}{2} \times \frac{1}{4}$ of the pizza (*of*, in this context, means *multiply*), which is the same as $\frac{1}{8}$ of the whole pizza.

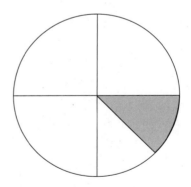

Multiplying Fractions by Fractions

To multiply fractions:

1. Multiply their top numbers together to get the top number of the answer.

2. Multiply their bottom numbers together to get the bottom number of the answer.

Example: $\frac{1}{2} \times \frac{1}{4}$.

1. Multiply the top numbers:
2. Multiply the bottom numbers: $\qquad \frac{1 \times 1}{2 \times 4} = \frac{1}{8}$

Example: $\frac{1}{3} \times \frac{3}{5} \times \frac{7}{4}$.

1. Multiply the top numbers:
2. Multiply the bottom numbers: $\qquad \frac{1 \times 3 \times 7}{3 \times 4 \times 5} = \frac{21}{60}$
3. Reduce: $\qquad \frac{21 \div 3}{60 \div 3} = \frac{7}{20}$

Now you try. Answers to sample questions are at the end of the lesson.

Cancellation Shortcut

Sometimes you can *cancel* common factors before multiplying. Canceling is a shortcut that speeds up multiplication because you will not have to reduce the fraction to the lowest terms in the end. Canceling is similar to reducing: If there is a number that divides evenly into a top number and a bottom number in any of the fractions being multiplied, do that division before multiplying.

Example: $\frac{5}{6} \times \frac{9}{20}$.

1. Cancel a 3 from both the 6 and the 9: $6 \div 3 = 2$ and $9 \div 3 = 3$. Cross out the 6 and the 9, as shown: $\qquad \frac{5}{\overset{}{\underset{2}{6}}} \times \frac{\overset{3}{9}}{20}$

2. Cancel a 5 from both the 5 and the 20: $5 \div 5 = 1$ and $20 \div 5 = 4$. Cross out the 5 and the 20, as shown: $\qquad \frac{\overset{1}{5}}{\underset{2}{6}} \times \frac{\overset{3}{9}}{\underset{4}{20}}$

3. Multiply across the new top numbers and the new bottom numbers: $\qquad \frac{1 \times 3}{2 \times 4} = \frac{3}{8}$

By the way, if you forget to cancel, don't worry. You'll still get the right answer, but you'll have to reduce it.

Multiplying Fractions by Whole Numbers

To multiply a fraction by a whole number:

1. Rewrite the whole number as a fraction with a bottom number of 1.
2. Multiply as usual.

Example: $5 \times \frac{2}{3}$.

1. Rewrite 5 as a fraction: $\qquad 5 = \frac{5}{1}$
2. Multiply the fractions: $\qquad \frac{5}{1} \times \frac{2}{3} = \frac{10}{3}$
3. Optional: Change the product $\frac{10}{3}$ to a mixed number. $\qquad \frac{10}{3} = 3\frac{1}{3}$

Have you noticed that multiplying any number by a proper fraction produces an answer that's smaller than that number? It's the opposite of the result you get from multiplying whole numbers. That's because multiplying by a proper fraction is the same as finding a *part* of something.

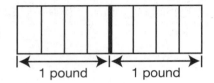

1 pound   1 pound

Multiplying with Mixed Numbers

To multiply with mixed numbers, change each mixed number to an improper fraction and multiply.

Example: $4\frac{2}{3} \times 5\frac{1}{2}$.

1. Change $4\frac{2}{3}$ to an improper fraction: $4\frac{2}{3} = \frac{4 \times 3 + 2}{3} = \frac{14}{3}$

2. Change $5\frac{1}{2}$ to an improper fraction: $5\frac{1}{2} = \frac{5 \times 2 + 1}{2} = \frac{11}{2}$

3. Multiply the fractions: Notice that you can cancel a 2 from both the 14 and the 2. $\frac{\overset{7}{14}}{3} \times \frac{11}{\underset{1}{2}}$

4. Optional: Change the improper fraction to a mixed number. $\frac{77}{3} = 25\frac{2}{3}$

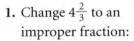

⚠ CAUTION

Do NOT simply multiply the whole numbers and the proper fractions when multiplying mixed numbers.

Dividing Fractions

Dividing means determining how many times one amount can be found in a second amount, whether you're working with fractions or not. For instance, to find out how many $\frac{1}{4}$-pound pieces a 2-pound chunk of cheese can be cut into, you must divide 2 by $\frac{1}{4}$. As you can see from the following picture, a 2-pound chunk of cheese can be cut into eight $\frac{1}{4}$-pound pieces. $(2 \div \frac{1}{4} = 8)$

Dividing Fractions by Fractions

To divide one fraction by a second fraction, invert the second fraction (that is, flip the top and bottom numbers) and then multiply.

Example: $\frac{1}{2} \div \frac{3}{5}$.

1. Invert the second fraction $(\frac{3}{5})$: $\frac{5}{3}$
2. Change ÷ to × and multiply the first fraction by the new second fraction: $\frac{1}{2} \times \frac{5}{3} = \frac{5}{6}$

Another Format for Division

Sometimes fraction division is written in a different format. For example, $\frac{1}{2} \div \frac{3}{5}$ can also be written as $\frac{\frac{1}{2}}{\frac{3}{5}}$. This means the same thing! Regardless of the format used, the process of division and end result are the same.

Reciprocal Fractions

Inverting a fraction, as we do for division, is the same as finding the fraction's *reciprocal*. For example, $\frac{3}{5}$ and $\frac{5}{3}$ are reciprocals. The product of a fraction and its *reciprocal* is 1. Thus, $\frac{3}{5} \times \frac{5}{3} = 1$.

Remember, when dividing a number by a positive fraction that is less than one, the answer is going to be larger than the original number. When dividing by an improper fraction (which has a value greater than one), your answer will be smaller than the original number. Use these facts to make sure your answers make sense.

Have you noticed that dividing a number by a proper fraction gives an answer that's *larger* than that number? It's the opposite of the result you get when dividing by a whole number.

⚠ CAUTION

When converting a division problem to a multiplication problem, remember to invert the fraction **after** the division sign, not before it.

Dividing Fractions by Whole Numbers or Vice Versa

To divide a fraction by a whole number or vice versa, change the whole number to a fraction by putting it over 1, and then divide as usual.

Example: $\frac{3}{5} \div 2$.

1. Change the whole number (2) into a fraction: $2 = \frac{2}{1}$
2. Invert the second fraction ($\frac{2}{1}$): $\frac{1}{2}$
3. Change $\div$ to $\times$ and multiply the two fractions: $\frac{3}{5} \times \frac{1}{2} = \frac{3}{10}$

Example: $2 \div \frac{3}{5}$.

1. Change the whole number (2) into a fraction: $2 = \frac{2}{1}$
2. Invert the second fraction ($\frac{3}{5}$): $\frac{5}{3}$
3. Change $\div$ to $\times$ and multiply the two fractions: $\frac{2}{1} \times \frac{5}{3} = \frac{10}{3}$
4. Optional: Change the improper fraction to a mixed number: $\frac{10}{3} = 3\frac{1}{3}$

Did you notice that the *order* of division makes a difference? $\frac{3}{5} \div 2$ is not the same as $2 \div \frac{3}{5}$. But then, the same is true of division with whole numbers; $4 \div 2$ is not the same as $2 \div 4$.

Dividing with Mixed Numbers

To divide with mixed numbers, change each mixed number to an improper fraction and then divide as usual.

Example: $2\frac{3}{4} \div \frac{1}{6}$.

1. Change $2\frac{3}{4}$ to an improper fraction: $2\frac{3}{4} = \frac{2 \times 4 + 3}{4} = \frac{11}{4}$
2. Rewrite the division problem: $\frac{11}{4} \div \frac{1}{6}$
3. Invert $\frac{1}{6}$ and multiply: $\frac{11}{\underset{2}{4}} \times \frac{\overset{3}{6}}{1} = \frac{11 \times 3}{2 \times 1} = \frac{33}{2}$
4. Optional: Change the improper fraction to a mixed number. $\frac{33}{2} = 16\frac{1}{2}$

Shortcuts with Fractions

Shortcut for Addition and Subtraction

Instead of wasting time looking for the least common denominator (LCD) when adding or subtracting, try this "cross multiplication" trick to quickly add or subtract two fractions:

Example: $\frac{5}{6} + \frac{3}{8} = ?$

1. Top number: "Cross multiply" 5×8 and 6×3; then add:
2. Bottom number: Multiply 6×8, the two bottom numbers:

$$\frac{5}{6} \bigtimes \frac{3}{8} = \frac{40 + 18}{48}$$

3. Reduce:

$$= \frac{58}{48} = \frac{29}{24}$$

When using the shortcut for subtraction, you must be careful about the order of subtraction: Begin the cross multiply step with the top number of the first fraction. (The "hook" to help you remember where to begin is to think about how you read. You begin at the top left—where you'll find the number that starts the process, the top number of the first fraction.)

Example: $\frac{5}{6} - \frac{3}{4} = ?$

1. Top number: Cross multiply 5×4 and subtract 3×6:
2. Bottom number: Multiply 6×4, the two bottom numbers:

$$\frac{5}{6} \bigtimes \frac{3}{4} = \frac{20 - 18}{24}$$

$$= \frac{2}{24}$$

3. Reduce:

$$= \frac{1}{12}$$

This works the same way for sums and differences involving whole numbers and improper fractions.

Example: $3 + \frac{11}{8} = \underline{\ ?\ }$

1. Write 3 as $\frac{3}{1}$: $3 + \frac{11}{8} = \frac{3}{1} + \frac{11}{8}$
2. Top number: Cross multiply 3×8 and add 1×11.
3. Bottom number: Multiply 8×1: $\frac{3}{1} + \frac{11}{8} =$
$$\frac{3 \times 8 + 1 \times 1}{8 \times 1} = \frac{24 + 11}{8} = \frac{35}{8}$$
4. Reduce and convert to a mixed number:
$$\frac{35}{8} = 4\frac{3}{8}$$

Shortcut for Division: Extremes over Means

Extremes over means is a fast way to divide fractions. This concept is best explained by example, say $\frac{5}{7} \div \frac{2}{3}$.

But first, let's rewrite the division problem as $\frac{\frac{5}{7}}{\frac{2}{3}}$ and provide two definitions:

Extremes:
The numbers that are *extremely* far apart

Means:
The numbers that are close together.

Here's how to do it:

1. Multiply the extremes to get the top number of the answer:
2. Multiply the means to get the bottom number of the answer:

$$\frac{5 \times 3}{7 \times 2} = \frac{15}{14}$$

You can even use *extremes* over *means* when one of the numbers is a whole number or a mixed number. First change the whole number or mixed number into a fraction, and then use the shortcut.

Example: $\frac{2}{\frac{3}{4}}$.

1. Change the 2 into a fraction and rewrite the division: $\frac{\frac{2}{1}}{\frac{3}{4}}$
2. Multiply the extremes to get the top number of the answer:
$$\frac{2 \times 4}{1 \times 3} = \frac{8}{3}$$
3. Multiply the means to get the bottom number of the answer:
4. Optional: Change the improper fraction to a mixed number:
$$\frac{8}{3} = 2\frac{2}{3}$$

Working with Decimals

A decimal is a type of fraction. You use decimals every day when you deal with measurements or money. For instance, $10.35 is a decimal that represents 10 dollars and 35 cents. The decimal point separates the dollars from the cents. Because there are 100 cents in one dollar, 1¢ is $\frac{1}{100}$ of a dollar, or $0.01; 10¢ is $\frac{10}{100}$ of a dollar, or $0.10; 25¢ is $\frac{25}{100}$ of a dollar, or $0.25; and so forth. In terms of measurements, a weather report might indicate that 2.7 inches of rain fell in 4 hours, you might drive 5.8 miles to the intersection of the highway, or the population of the United States might be estimated to grow to 374.3 million people by a certain year.

If there are digits on both sides of the decimal point, like 6.17, and the number to the left of the decimal point is not 0, the number is called a **mixed decimal**; its value is always greater than 1. In fact, the value of 6.17 is a bit more than 6. If there are nonzero digits only to the right of the decimal point, like 0.17, the number is called a **decimal**; its value is always less than 1. Sometimes, the 0 before the decimal point is left off and 0.17 is written more succinctly as .17. A whole number, like 6, is understood to have a decimal point at its right (6.).

Decimal Names

Each decimal digit to the right of the decimal point has a special name. Here are the first four:

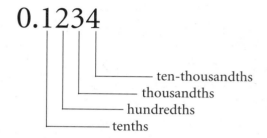

The digits have these names for a very special reason: The names reflect their fraction equivalents.

$$0.1 = 1 \text{ tenth} = \frac{1}{10}$$
$$0.02 = 2 \text{ hundredths} = \frac{2}{100}$$
$$0.003 = 3 \text{ thousandths} = \frac{3}{1,000}$$
$$0.0004 = 4 \text{ ten-thousandths} = \frac{4}{10,000}$$

As you can see, decimal names are ordered by multiples of 10: 10ths, 100ths, 1,000ths, 10,000ths, 100,000ths, 1,000,000ths, and so on. Be careful not to confuse decimal names with whole number names, which are very similar (tens, hundreds, thousands, etc.). The naming difference can be seen in the *ths*, which are used only for decimal digits.

Reading a Decimal

Here's how to read a mixed decimal, for example, 6.017:

1. The number to the left of the decimal point is a whole number. Just read that number as you normally would: 6
2. Say the word "and" for the decimal point: and

3. The number to the right of the decimal point is the decimal value. Just read it: 17

4. The number of places to the right of the decimal point tells you the decimal's name. In this case, there are three places: thousandths

Thus, 6.017 is read as *six and seventeen thousandths*, and its fraction equivalent is $6\frac{17}{1,000}$.

Here's how to read a decimal, for example, 0.28:

1. Read the number to the right of the decimal point: 28

2. The number of places to the right of the decimal point tells you the decimal's name. In this case, there are two places: hundredths

Thus, 0.28 (or .28) is read as *twenty-eight hundredths*, and its fraction equivalent is $\frac{28}{100}$.

Informally, you could also read 0.28 as *point two eight*, but it doesn't quite have the same intellectual impact as *28 hundredths!*

Adding Zeros

Adding zeros to the **end** of the decimal does NOT change its value. For example, 6.017 has the same value as each of these decimals:

6.0170
6.01700
6.017000
6.0170000
6.01700000, and so forth

Remembering that a whole number is assumed to have a decimal point at its right, the whole number 6 has the same value as each of these:

6.
6.0
6.00
6.000, and so forth

⚠ CAUTION

Adding zeros **before** the first decimal digit **does** change its value. That is, 6.17 is NOT the same as 6.017.

SAT TEST-TAKING TIP

Decimals are all around us! They are used in money, measurement, and time, so it's important to read this section carefully and make sure you feel comfortable with them. Using decimals is essential in mastering practical, real-world math skills.

Changing Decimals and Mixed Decimals to Fractions

To change a decimal to a fraction:

1. Write the digits of the decimal as the top number of a fraction.

2. Write the decimal's name as the bottom number of the fraction.

Example: Change 0.018 to a fraction.

1. Write 18 as the top of the fraction: $\frac{18}{}$

2. Since there are three places to the right of the decimal, it's thousandths.
3. Write 1,000 as the bottom number: $\frac{18}{1,000}$
4. Reduce by dividing 2 into the top and bottom numbers: $\frac{18 \div 2}{1,000 \div 2} = \frac{9}{500}$

Changing Fractions to Decimals

To change a fraction to a decimal:

1. Set up a long division problem to divide the bottom number (the *divisor*) into the top number (the *dividend*)—but don't divide yet!
2. Put a decimal point and a few zeros on the right of the dividend.
3. Bring the decimal point straight up into the area for the answer (the *quotient*).
4. Divide.

Example: Change $\frac{3}{4}$ to a decimal.

1. Set up the division problem: $4\overline{)3}$
2. Add a decimal point and 2 zeros to the dividend (3): $4\overline{)3.00}$
3. Bring the decimal point up into the answer: $4\overline{)3.00}$.
4. Divide:

$$
\begin{array}{r}
0.75 \\
4\overline{)3.00} \\
\underline{28} \\
20 \\
\underline{20} \\
0
\end{array}
$$

Thus, $\frac{3}{4} = 0.75$, or 75 hundredths.

The same approach works when converting mixed numbers and improper fractions to decimals. In the case of mixed numbers, hold off on the whole part and tack it onto the left side of the decimal point once

you have performed the division. For an improper fraction, the same approach works, but expect there to be nonzero digits *before* the decimal point.

Example: Change $\frac{26}{5}$ to a decimal.
1. Set up the division problem: $5\overline{)26}$
2. Add a decimal point and 2 zeros to the dividend: $5\overline{)26.00}$
3. Bring the decimal point up into the answer:

$$5\overline{)26.00}$$.

4. Divide:
$$
\begin{array}{r}
5.2 \\
5\overline{)26.00} \\
\underline{-25} \\
10 \\
\underline{-10} \\
0
\end{array}
$$

Repeating Decimals

Some fractions may require you to add more than two or three decimal zeros in order for the division to come out evenly. In fact, when you change a fraction like $\frac{2}{3}$ to a decimal, you'll keep adding decimal zeros until you're blue in the face because the division will never come out evenly! As you divide 3 into 2, you'll keep getting 6s:

$$
\begin{array}{r}
0.6666 \ etc. \\
3\overline{)2.0000} \ etc. \\
\underline{18} \\
20 \\
\underline{18} \\
20 \\
\underline{18} \\
20 \\
\underline{18} \\
20
\end{array}
$$

A fraction like $\frac{2}{3}$ becomes a *repeating decimal*. Its decimal value can be written as $0.\overline{6}$ or $0.6\frac{2}{3}$, or it can be approximated as 0.66, 0.666, 0.6666, and so forth. Its value can also be approximated by *rounding* it to 0.67 or 0.667 or 0.6667, and so forth. (Rounding is covered later.)

If you really have *fractionphobia* and panic when you have to do fraction arithmetic, it is fine to convert each fraction to a decimal and do the arithmetic in decimals. Warning: This should be a means of last resort—fractions are so much a part of daily living that it's important to be able to work with them.

Comparing Decimals

Decimals are easy to compare when they have the same number of digits after the decimal point. Tack zeros onto the ends of the shorter decimals—this doesn't change their value—and compare the numbers as if the decimal points weren't there.

Example: Compare 0.08 and 0.1.

⚠ CAUTION

Don't be tempted into thinking 0.08 is larger than 0.1 just because the whole number 8 is larger than the whole number 1.

1. Since 0.08 has two decimal digits, tack one zero onto the end of 0.1, making it 0.10.
2. To compare 0.10 to 0.08, just compare 10 to 8. Ten is larger than 8, so 0.1 is larger than 0.08.

Comparing repeating decimals is a little trickier, but relies on basically the same approach. Generally for these, it makes sense to write enough digits for all the decimals being compared so that you can choose a block of digits of the same length after the decimal point and compare them as you would compare whole numbers. Consider the following example.

Example: Put these decimals in order from least to greatest:
$$0.\overline{17}, 0.\overline{117}, 0.1\overline{7}$$

Observe that
$$0.\overline{17} = 0.171717\ldots$$
$$0.\overline{117} = 0.117117\ldots$$
$$0.1\overline{7} = 0.177777\ldots$$

How many digits after the decimal point do we need? Well, one is not enough because all three decimals have a 1 in the tenths slot. And, while two digits after the decimal point is better, it also is insufficient because two of the decimals have a 7 in the hundredths place. However, we can conclude that the one decimal with a 1 in the hundredths place must be the smallest of the three decimals. Finally, note that the digit in the thousandths place differs for the remaining two decimals, so we can stop here and conclude that the order of the decimals, from least to greatest, is: $0.\overline{117}, 0.\overline{17}, 0.1\overline{7}$.

Rounding Decimals

Rounding a decimal is a means of *estimating* its value using fewer digits. To find an answer more quickly, especially if you don't need an exact answer, you can round each decimal to the nearest whole number before doing the arithmetic. For example, you could use rounding to approximate the sum of 3.456789 and 16.738532:

$$\left.\begin{array}{l} 3.456789 \text{ is close to } 3 \\ 16.738532 \text{ is close to } 17 \end{array}\right\} \begin{array}{l} \text{Approximate their} \\ \text{sum: } 3 + 17 = 20 \end{array}$$

Since 3.456789 is closer to 3 than it is to 4, it can be **rounded down** to 3, the nearest whole number. Similarly, 16.738532 is closer to 17 than it is to 16, so it can be **rounded up** to 17, the nearest whole number.

Rounding may also be used to simplify a single figure, like the answer to an arithmetic operation. For example, if your investment yielded $14,837,812.98 (wishful thinking!), you could simplify it as *approxi-*

mately $15 million, rounding it to the nearest million dollars.

Rounding is a good way to do a *reasonableness* check on the answer to a decimal arithmetic problem: Estimate the answer to a decimal arithmetic problem and compare it to the actual answer to be sure it's in the ballpark.

Rounding to the Nearest Whole Number

To round a decimal to the nearest *whole number*, look at the decimal digit to the immediate right of the whole number, the tenths digit, and follow these guidelines:

- If the digit is less than 5, **round down** by dropping the decimal point and all the decimal digits. The whole number portion remains the same.
- If the digit is 5 or more, **round up** to the next larger whole number.

Examples of rounding to the nearest *whole number*:

- 25.3999 **rounds down** to 25 because 3 is less than 5.
- 23.5 **rounds up** to 24 because the tenths digit is 5.
- 2.613 **rounds up** to 3 because 6 is greater than 5.

Rounding to the Nearest Tenth

Decimals can be rounded to the nearest *tenth* in a similar fashion. Look at the digit to its immediate right, the hundredths digit, and follow these guidelines:

- If the digit is less than 5, **round down** by dropping that digit and all the decimal digits following it.
- If the digit is 5 or more, **round up** by making the tenths digit one greater and dropping all the digits to its right.

Examples of rounding to the nearest *tenth*:

- 45.32 **rounds down** to 45.3 because 2 is less than 5.
- 33.15 **rounds up** to 33.2 because the hundredths digit is 5.
- 2.96 **rounds up** to 3.0 because 6 is greater than 5. Notice that you cannot simply make the tenths digit, 9, one greater—that would make it 10. Therefore, the 9 becomes a zero and the whole number becomes one greater.

Similarly, a decimal can be rounded to the nearest hundredth, thousandth, and so forth by looking at the decimal digit to its immediate right and applying the following rule of thumb:

- If it's less than 5, **round down**.
- If it's 5 or more, **round up**.

SAT TEST-TAKING TIP

Remember, when rounding to the nearest *tenth*, you are actually looking at the *hundredth* place to see if you need to round down or up. It works the same way with other rounding: when rounding to the nearest *hundredth*, you must look at the *thousandth* place to determine the rounding. When rounding to the nearest *thousandth*, you must look at the ten-thousandth place.

Operations with Decimals

Adding Decimals

There is a crucial difference between adding decimals and adding whole numbers; the difference is the *decimal point*. The position of this point determines the accuracy of your final answer; a problem solver cannot simply ignore the point and add it in wherever it "looks" best. In order to add decimals correctly, follow these three simple rules:

1. Line the numbers up in a column so their decimal points are aligned.
2. Tack zeros onto the ends of shorter decimals to keep the digits lined up evenly.
3. Move the decimal point directly down into the answer area and add as usual.

SAT TEST-TAKING TIP

The number one pitfall in adding and subtracting decimals happens when the *numbers* are lined up, instead of the **decimals**. Before you start adding or subtracting with decimals, add zeros after the last digit to the right of the decimal point to all the numbers until they each have the same amount of digits to the right of the decimal point. For a whole number, just add a decimal point and then add zeros to the right of it. Example:

4.2	4.200
0.34	0.340
5.871	5.871
+ 18	18.000
	28.411

Example: 3.45 + 22.1 + 0.682.

1. Line up the numbers so their decimal points are aligned:

   3.45
   22.1
   0.682

2. Tack zeros onto the ends of the shorter decimals to fill in the "holes":

   3.450
   22.100
   + 0.682

3. Move the decimal point directly down into the answer area and add: 26.232

To check the *reasonableness* of your work, estimate the sum by using the rounding technique you learned in Lesson 6. Round each number you added to the nearest whole number, and then add the resulting whole numbers. If the sum is close to your answer, your answer is in the ballpark. Otherwise, you may have made a mistake in placing the decimal point or in the adding. Rounding 3.45, 22.1, and 0.682 gives you 3, 22, and 1, respectively. Their sum is 26, which is *reasonably* close to your actual answer of 26.232. Therefore, 26.232 is a *reasonable* answer.

Look at an example that adds decimals and whole numbers together. Remember: A whole number is understood to have a decimal point to its right.

Example: 0.6 + 35 + 0.0671 + 4.36.

1. Put a decimal point at the right of the whole number (35) and line up the numbers so their decimal points are aligned:

   0.6
   35.
   0.0671
   4.36

2. Tack zeros onto the ends of the shorter decimals to fill in the "holes":

   0.6000
   35.0000
   0.0671
   + 4.3600

3. Move the decimal point directly down into the answer area and add: 40.0271

Subtracting Decimals

When subtracting decimals, follow the same initial steps as in adding to ensure that you're subtracting the correct digits and that the decimal point ends up in the right place.

Example: $4.8731 - 1.7$.

1. Line up the numbers so their
   decimal points are aligned:

   $$\begin{array}{r} 4.8731 \\ 1.7 \end{array}$$

2. Tack zeros onto the end of the
   shorter decimal to fill in the "holes":

   $$\begin{array}{r} 4.8731 \\ -1.7000 \\ \hline \end{array}$$

3. Move the decimal point directly
   down into the answer and subtract: $\quad 3.1731$

Subtraction is easily checked by adding the number that was subtracted to the difference (the answer). If you get back the other number in the subtraction problem, then your answer is correct. For example, let's check our answer to the previous subtraction problem.

Here's the subtraction:

$$\begin{array}{r} 4.8731 \\ -1.7000 \\ \hline 3.1731 \end{array}$$

1. Add the number that was
   subtracted (1.7000) to the
   difference (3.1731): $\quad +1.7000$

2. The subtraction is correct because
   we got back the first number in
   the subtraction problem (4.8731): $\quad 4.8731$

You can check the *reasonableness* of your work by estimating: Round each number to the nearest whole number and subtract. Rounding 4.873 and 1.7 gives 5

and 2, respectively. Since their difference of 3 is close to your actual answer, 3.1731 is *reasonable*.

SAT TEST-TAKING TIP

When subtracting mixed decimals gets rid of any whole numbers, write a zero in the ones place. Example: $5.67 - 4.9 = \mathbf{0}.77$, and should not be written as .77.

Borrowing

Next, look at a subtraction example that requires borrowing. Notice that borrowing works exactly the same as it does when you're subtracting whole numbers.

Example: $2 - 0.456$.

1. Put a decimal point at the right of the
   whole number (2) and line up the
   numbers so their decimal points
   are aligned:

   $$\begin{array}{r} 2. \\ 0.456 \end{array}$$

2. Tack zeros onto the end of the shorter
   decimal to fill in the "holes":

   $$\begin{array}{r} 2.000 \\ 0.456 \end{array}$$

3. Move the decimal point directly
   down into the answer and subtract
   after borrowing:

   $$\begin{array}{r} {\scriptstyle 9\ 9} \\ {\scriptstyle 1\ \cancel{10}\ \cancel{10}\ 10} \\ 2.000 \\ -0.456 \\ \hline 1.544 \end{array}$$

4. Check the subtraction by addition:

   $$\begin{array}{r} 1.544 \\ +0.456 \\ \hline \end{array}$$

   Our answer is correct because we
   got back the first number in the
   subtraction problem: $\quad 2.000$

Combining Addition and Subtraction

The best way to solve problems that combine addition and subtraction is to "uncombine" them; separate the numbers to be added from the numbers to be subtracted by forming two columns. Add each of the columns and you're left with two figures; subtract one from the other and you have your answer.

Example: $0.7 + 4.33 - 2.46 + 0.0861 - 1.2$.

1. Line up the numbers to be *added* so their decimal points are aligned:

   0.7
   4.33
   0.0861

2. Tack zeros onto the ends of the shorter decimals to fill in the "holes":

   0.7000
   4.3300
   +0.0861

3. Move the decimal point directly down into the answer and add: 5.1161

4. Line up the numbers to be *subtracted* so their decimal points are aligned:

   2.46
   1.2

5. Tack zeros onto the end of the shorter decimal to fill in the "holes":

   2.46
   +1.20

6. Move the decimal point directly down into the answer area and add: 3.66

7. Subtract the step 6 answer from the step 3 answer, lining up the decimal points, filling in the "holes" with zeros, and moving the decimal point directly down into the answer area:

   5.1161
   −3.6600
   1.4561

Working with Decimals and Fractions Together

When a problem contains both decimals and fractions, you should change the numbers to the same type, either decimals or fractions, depending on which you're more comfortable working with.

Example: $\frac{3}{8} + 0.37$.

Fraction-to-decimal conversion:

1. Convert $\frac{3}{8}$ to its decimal equivalent:

$$\begin{array}{r} 0.375 \\ 8)\overline{3.000} \\ \underline{24} \\ 60 \\ \underline{56} \\ 40 \\ \underline{40} \\ 0 \end{array}$$

2. Add the decimals after lining up the decimal points and filling the "holes" with zeros:

   0.375
   + 0.370
   0.745

Decimal-to-fraction conversion:

1. Convert 0.37 to its fraction equivalent: $\frac{37}{100}$
2. Add the fractions after finding the least common denominator:

$$\frac{37}{100} = \frac{74}{200}$$
$$+\frac{3}{8} = \frac{75}{200}$$
$$\frac{149}{200}$$

Both answers, 0.745 and $\frac{149}{200}$, are correct. You can easily check this by converting the fraction to the decimal or the decimal to the fraction.

Multiplying Decimals

To multiply decimals:

1. Ignore the decimal points and multiply as you would whole numbers.
2. Count the number of decimal digits (the digits to the *right* of the decimal point) in both of the numbers you multiplied. Do NOT count zeros tacked onto the end as decimal digits.
3. Beginning at the right side of the product (the answer), count left that number of digits, and put the decimal point to the *left* of the last digit you counted.

Example: 1.57×2.4.

1. Multiply 157 times 24:

    $$\begin{array}{r} 157 \\ \times\ 24 \\ \hline 628 \\ 314\ \ \\ \hline 3768 \end{array}$$

2. Because there are a total of three decimal digits in 1.57 and 2.4, count off 3 places from the right in 3768 and place the decimal point to the left of the third digit you counted (7):   3.768

To check the *reasonableness* of your work, estimate the product by rounding. Round each number you multiplied to the nearest whole number, and then multiply the results. If the product is close to your answer, your answer is in the ballpark. Otherwise, you may have made a mistake in placing the decimal point or in multiplying. Rounding 1.57 and 2.4 to the nearest whole numbers gives you 2 and 2. Their

product is 4, which is close to your answer. Thus, your actual answer of 3.768 seems reasonable.

> ### ⚠ CAUTION
>
> The number of decimal digits in 3.768000 is *three*, NOT *six*.

In multiplying decimals, you may get a product that doesn't have enough digits for you to put in a decimal point. In that case, tack zeros onto the left of the product to give your answer enough digits; then add the decimal point.

Example: 0.03×0.006.

1. Multiply 3 times 6: $3 \times 6 = 18$
2. The answer requires 5 decimal digits because there are a total of 5 decimal digits in 0.03 and 0.006. Because there are only 2 digits in the answer (18), tack three zeros onto the left: 00018
3. Put the decimal point at the front of the number (which is 5 digits in from the right):   .00018

Multiplication Shortcut

To quickly multiply a number by 10, just move the decimal point **one digit to the right**. To multiply a number by 100, move the decimal point **two digits to the right**. To multiply a number by 1,000, move the decimal point **three digits to the right**. In general, just count the number of zeros, and move the decimal point that number of digits to the **right**. If you don't have enough digits, first tack zeros onto the right.

Example: $1,000 \times 3.82$.

1. Since there are three zeros in 1,000, move the decimal point in 3.82 three digits to the right.
2. Since 3.82 has only two decimal digits to the right of the decimal point, add one zero on the right before moving the decimal point: 3.82**0**

Thus, $1,000 \times 3.82 = 3,820$

SAT TEST-TAKING TIP

To multiply by any multiple of 10, you can ignore the last zero digits, and add them back on to your answer in the end. For example, with $22\underline{0} \times 3,\underline{000}$, think of it to start as $22 \times 3 = 66$. Then, add back the four zeros that were temporarily removed: $22\underline{0} \times 3,\underline{000} = 66\underline{0,000}$.

Dividing Decimals

Dividing Decimals by Whole Numbers

To divide a decimal by a whole number, bring the decimal point straight up into the answer (the *quotient*), and then divide as you would normally divide whole numbers.

Example: $4\overline{)0.512}$.

1. Move the decimal point straight up into the *quotient* area: $4\overline{)0.512}$

2. Divide:

$$\begin{array}{r} 0.128 \\ 4\overline{)0.512} \\ \underline{4} \\ 11 \\ \underline{8} \\ 32 \\ \underline{32} \\ 0 \end{array}$$

3. To check your division, multiply the quotient (0.128) by the *divisor* (4).

$$\begin{array}{r} 0.128 \\ \times\quad 4 \\ \hline \end{array}$$

If you get back the *dividend* (0.512), you know you divided correctly. 0.512

Dividing by Decimals

To divide any number by a decimal, first change the problem into one in which you're dividing by a whole number.

1. Move the decimal point to the right of the number by which you're dividing (the *divisor*).
2. Move the decimal point the same number of places to the right in the number you're dividing into (the *dividend*).
3. Bring the decimal point straight up into the answer (the *quotient*) and divide.

SAT TEST-TAKING TIP

Remember that dividing by a decimal that has a value less than 1 will give you a bigger number!

Example: $0.03\overline{)1.215}$.

1. Because there are two decimal digits in 0.03, move the decimal point two places to the right in both numbers: $0.03.\overline{)1.21.5}$

2. Move the decimal point straight up into the quotient:

$$3.\overline{)121\overset{\cdot}{1}5.}$$

3. Divide using the new numbers:

$$\begin{array}{r} 40.5 \\ 3\overline{)121.5} \\ \underline{12} \\ 01 \\ \underline{00} \\ 15 \\ \underline{15} \\ 0 \end{array}$$

3. Divide using the new numbers:

$$\begin{array}{r} 40. \\ 3\overline{)120.} \\ \underline{12} \\ 00 \\ \underline{00} \\ 0 \end{array}$$

Case 2

The answer doesn't come out evenly when you divide.

Under the following conditions, you'll have to tack zeros onto the right of the last decimal digit in the dividend, the number into which you're dividing:

Case 1. There aren't enough digits to move the decimal point to the right.

Case 2. The answer doesn't come out evenly when you divide.

Case 3. You're dividing a whole number by a decimal. In this case, you'll have to tack on the decimal point as well as some zeros.

Case 1

There aren't enough digits to move the decimal point to the right.

Example: $0.03\overline{)1.2.}$

1. Because there are two decimal digits in 0.03, the decimal point must be moved two places to the right in both numbers. Since there aren't enough decimal digits in 1.2, tack a zero onto the end of 1.2 before moving the decimal point:

$$0.03.\overline{)1.20.}$$

2. Move the decimal point straight up into the quotient:

$$3.\overline{)120\overset{\cdot}{1}}$$

Example: $0.5\overline{)1.2.}$

1. Because there is one decimal digit in 0.5, the decimal point must be moved one place to the right in both numbers:

$$0.5.\overline{)1.2.}$$

2. Move the decimal point straight up into the quotient:

$$5.\overline{)12\overset{\cdot}{1}}$$

3. Divide, but notice that the division doesn't come out evenly:

$$\begin{array}{r} 2. \\ 5\overline{)12.} \\ \underline{10} \\ 2 \end{array}$$

4. Add a zero to the end of the dividend (12.) and continue dividing:

$$\begin{array}{r} 2.4 \\ 5\overline{)12.0} \\ \underline{10} \\ 20 \\ \underline{20} \\ 0 \end{array}$$

Example: $0.3\overline{).10.}$

1. Because there is one decimal digit in 0.3, the decimal point must be moved one place to the right in both numbers:

$$0.3.\overline{).1.0}$$

2. Move the decimal point straight up into the quotient:

$$3.\overline{)1\overset{.}{1}0}$$

3. Divide, but notice that the division doesn't come out evenly:

$$\begin{array}{r} 0.3 \\ 3\overline{)1.0} \\ \underline{9} \\ 1 \end{array}$$

4. Add a zero to the end of the dividend (1.0) and continue dividing:

$$\begin{array}{r} 0.33 \\ 3\overline{)1.00} \\ \underline{9} \\ 10 \\ \underline{9} \\ 1 \end{array}$$

5. Since the division still did not come out evenly, add another zero to the end of the dividend (1.00) and continue dividing:

$$\begin{array}{r} 0.333 \\ 3\overline{)1.000} \\ \underline{9} \\ 10 \\ \underline{9} \\ 10 \\ \underline{9} \\ 1 \end{array}$$

6. By this point, you have probably noticed that the quotient is a repeating decimal. Thus, you can stop dividing and write the quotient like this:

$$0.\overline{3}$$

Case 3

When you're dividing a whole number by a decimal, you have to tack on the decimal point as well as some zeros.

Example: $0.02\overline{)19.}$

1. There are two decimals in 0.02, so we have to move the decimal point to the right two places in both numbers. Because 19 is a whole number, put its decimal point at the end (19.), add two zeros to the end (19.00), and then move the decimal point to the right twice (1900.):

$$0.0\underset{\smile}{2}.\overline{)19.0\underset{\smile}{0}.}$$

2. Move the decimal point straight up into the quotient:

$$2.\overline{)1900\overset{.}{\uparrow}}$$

3. Divide using the new numbers:

$$\begin{array}{r} 950 \\ 2\overline{)1900} \\ \underline{18} \\ 10 \\ \underline{10} \\ 00 \\ \underline{00} \\ 0 \end{array}$$

Division Shortcut

To divide a number by 10, just move the decimal point in the number **one digit to the left**. To divide a number by 100, move the decimal point **two digits to the left**. Just count the number of zeros and move the decimal point that number of digits to the **left**. If you don't have enough digits, tack zeros onto the left before moving the decimal point.

Example: Divide 12.345 by 1,000.

1. Since there are three zeros in 1,000, move the decimal point in 12.345 three digits to the left.

2. Since 12.345 only has two digits to the left of its decimal point, add one zero at the left, and then move the decimal point:

$$0.0\underset{\smile}{1}2.345$$

Thus, $12.345 \div 1{,}000 = 0.012345$

ADDITIONAL ONLINE PRACTICE

Using the codes below, you'll be able to log in and access additional online practice materials!

Your free online practice access codes are:
FVEOTIEAWB3FBPP6GSEH
FVER52UVMYC0BMSP6MMD

Follow these simple steps to redeem your codes:

- Go to **www.learningexpresshub.com/affiliate** and have your access codes handy.

If you're a new user:

- Click the **New user? Register here** button and complete the registration form to create your account and access your products.
- Be sure to enter your unique access code only once. If you have multiple access codes, you can enter them all—just use a comma to separate each code.
- The next time you visit, simply click the **Returning user? Sign in** button and enter your username and password.
- Do not re-enter previously redeemed access codes. Any products you previously accessed are saved in the **My Account** section on the site. Entering a previously redeemed access code will result in an error message.

If you're a returning user:

- Click the **Returning user? Sign in** button, enter your username and password, and click **Sign In**.
- You will automatically be brought to the **My Account** page to access your products.
- Do not re-enter previously redeemed access codes. Any products you previously accessed are saved in the **My Account** section on the site. Entering a previously redeemed access code will result in an error message.

If you're a returning user with a new access code:

- Click the **Returning user? Sign in** button, enter your username, password, and new access code, and click **Sign In**.
- If you have multiple access codes, you can enter them all—just use a comma to separate each code.
- Do not re-enter previously redeemed access codes. Any products you previously accessed are saved in the **My Account** section on the site. Entering a previously redeemed access code will result in an error message.

If you have any questions, please contact Customer Support at Support@ebsco.com. All inquiries will be responded to within a 24-hour period during our normal business hours: 9:00 A.M.–5:00 P.M. Eastern Time. Thank you!

NOTES

NOTES

NOTES

NOTES

NOTES

NOTES